ALA Fundamentals Series

Fundamentals of
Children's
Services

Michael Sullivan

AMERICAN LIBRARY ASSOCIATION
Chicago   2005

While extensive effort has gone into ensuring the reliability of information appearing in this book, the publisher makes no warranty, express or implied, on the accuracy or reliability of the information, and does not assume and hereby disclaims any liability to any person for any loss or damage caused by errors or omissions in this publication.

Design and composition by ALA Editions in Galliard and Optima using QuarkXPress 5.0 on a PC platform

Printed on 50-pound white offset, a pH-neutral stock, and bound in 10-point cover stock by McNaughton & Gunn

The paper used in this publication meets the minimum requirements of American National Standard for Information Sciences—Permanence of Paper for Printed Library Materials, ANSI Z39.48-1992. ∞

Library of Congress Cataloging-in-Publication Data

Sullivan, Michael, 1967 Aug. 30-
    Fundamentals of children's services / Michael Sullivan.
      p. cm. — (ALA fundamentals series)
    Includes bibliographical references and index.
    ISBN 0-8389-0907-8 (alk. paper)
    1. Children's libraries—United States. I. Title. II. Series.
    Z718.2.U6S85 2005
    027.62'5'0973—dc22   2005012335

Printed in the United States of America

09 08 07 06 05   5 4 3 2 1

This book is dedicated to Professor Margaret Bush,
whose dedication, knowledge, and commitment
to the good of children has inspired me
and a generation of children's librarians.
Thank you.

CONTENTS

ACKNOWLEDGMENTS

Once again, I must assert that this work would not have been possible without the skill, support, and dedication of my editor, Renée Vaillancourt McGrath. I appreciate as well the confidence shown by Patrick Hogan and all the staff at ALA Editions when entrusting to me this most important topic.

This work was born of necessity; it began with the development of an overview class on children's services for the New Hampshire State Library's continuing education modules. Much of the structure comes from the combined input of Tom Ladd, Ann Hoey, and Lesley Gaudreau. Their efforts are gratefully acknowledged.

The patience and flexibility of the staff and trustees at the Weeks Public Library in Greenland, New Hampshire, have been indispensable. These good folks understood how much I needed to write this work, and had the foresight to understand that I would be a better librarian thanks to the process.

And, of course, I owe gratitude to the colleagues I have worked with over so many years, who have helped me, taught me, challenged me, and inspired me. You are too many to mention without leaving out someone deserving, but suffice it to say, the people I have had the privilege of working with remain the greatest blessing in this profession.

PREFACE

The modern public library is a very different place than it was twenty, ten, even five years ago. To enter the field of children's librarianship today is to walk into a challenging and vibrant maelstrom, and excellent children's librarians who have been in the field for decades may suddenly find themselves lost in a rapidly evolving world. Technology, massive social change, competition from for-profit entities, and emerging issues of budgeting, management, and governance within our own libraries require us to be flexible, adaptable, and courageous in the face of new challenges. But always we must keep in focus the needs of children. This is our grounding; this is what makes all the rest worthwhile.

If we are to thrive, if we are to serve those who need us so much, we must almost consider ourselves newly minted librarians every day of our careers. This book is intended to be a guide for the new or future children's librarian; a very practical, hands-on manual to being a children's librarian in a public library. But I hope it will be so much more. This may be seen as a re-beginner's manual, a new and modern look at what we as children's specialists are all about, but this primer on children's services is not for children's librarians alone.

I have worked in public libraries for more than fifteen years, sometimes as an administrator, sometimes as a children's librarian, but always as someone deeply involved in children's work. I have had the privilege of seeing children's services from both sides of what sometimes seems to be a broad divide. As the director of the Nichols Memorial Library in Centre Harbor, New Hampshire, a one-person library, I did it all and never thought of children's services as separate from any other aspect of the library. As the head of children's services at the Parlin Library in Everett, Massachusetts, I stood between administration and children's services, with one foot in each camp. As the director of the Wiggin Memorial Library in Stratham, New Hampshire, the director of the Weeks Public Library in Greenland, New Hampshire, and the Putterham branch manager for the

Public Library of Brookline, Massachusetts, I both supervised and worked side by side with children's staff in their daily work.

I have come to believe that in order for public libraries to be most effective, they must find a way to bridge the divide between administration and children's services. Administrators must come to understand not just the workings of children's services but also the vital role children's services play in the success of the library. Children's librarians must understand the workings of the larger library, and specifically how they can help the administration to help them do their jobs well. I travel widely now, speaking on issues of children's services and teaching at Simmons College in Boston, Massachusetts, and Plymouth State College in Plymouth, New Hampshire. I have had the privilege of meeting thousands of librarians in all aspects of library work and have found that most of our colleagues share a genuine desire to do whatever it takes to see that our publics are well served. Too often, though, they are baffled by what their coworkers do and why they do it. This book is an attempt to change that.

The Who and Why of This Book

This book will explore what a public library children's librarian does all day, and why. This is important if you are, or are going to be, a children's librarian, but also if you have to hire or supervise a children's librarian, if you have to work effectively beside a children's specialist despite the fact that you have no background in children's work, or if you have to plan for effective library service. In short, children's librarians, children's services supervisors, adult services staff, directors, and trustees can all benefit from a careful look at the fundamentals of children's services. If, as I will argue in this book, children's services drive public libraries, then an appreciation of children's work by all those involved in the library is vital.

Though the focus is clearly on public librarians, much of this book will be useful or illuminating for school librarians as well. School librarians (or media specialists and generalists) face many of the same issues and have many of the same concerns as their public library counterparts. Both types of librarians share some of the same audience—children—though each has responsibilities to a distinct and broader clientele. Finally, public and school librarians must work together to be as effective as they can be, and a greater awareness of the other's roles can only further cooperation.

Introduction

In some ways, the idea of covering all of children's library service in a single volume is a daunting, even impossible task. The tasks and responsibilities that fall to children's librarians are almost endless. In another way, though, children's services are a simple matter. The focus must be on what is best for the child. If everything else flows from this simple premise, then the work may be complex and challenging, but it will not be beyond our abilities. In the early pages of this book on the fundamentals of children's services, it is worth putting forth some basic beliefs, the underpinnings of all that is to come.

Core Beliefs

Children's Services Drive Libraries

Thirty-seven percent of library users are under the age of twelve.[1] Our children's rooms are responsible for 36.5 percent of our circulation. Children account for more than 51 million in program attendance per year and ask more than half the reference questions that public libraries answer.[2] Thus children are a huge part of our audience. They bring with them parents, grandparents, and caregivers. Serving children is also an investment in the future. Turn children into library users and you can look forward to many decades of loyal patronage.

Children's Services Are Undervalued

Despite the obvious importance of children to public libraries, most libraries fail to dedicate a corresponding percentage of their resources to support children's work. Children's services seldom get the staff hours, book budget, program budget, or space that its impact would seem to justify. The reason for this is tied to the lack of understanding among library administrators and decision makers, many of whom have no background in children's work.

There Is More to Serving Children

Children's librarians may do what they do well, but they often fail either to consider what they do or to communicate it effectively. Children's specialists are among the most dedicated, even missionary, members of our profession. They do what they do, often with inadequate pay, support, or respect, because they love to work with children. What they fail to see is that they could leverage their efforts more effectively by looking beyond their day-to-day work and taking action to assure that children are well served, even if those activities have no direct or immediate effect on children.

Children's services people are seldom at the table when policies and procedures are being developed or when resources are being allocated. If they were, then libraries would be better designed for children. Because children's services are not as strong as they could be, libraries as a whole are not as strong as they could be. In our modern "bang for the buck" approach to government services, we need to recognize and communicate that children's libraries are a great investment. Indeed, children's services produce more results with less money than any other library services, but libraries fail to appreciate this efficiency. By focusing on children's services, a public library becomes more efficient and more effective—to the benefit of the whole library.

The Approach

This book will look at some activities that are specific to children's services. In these instances, the approach will be practical, detailed, and hands on. Some examples of these types of activities are story hours, homework help, and cooperation with schools. While not exhaustive, the treatment will be such that a new practitioner can use this book as a starting point to begin designing services.

The book will also deal with some areas that are not traditionally considered children's work, but are common to all parts of the library. Some will even be considered administrative functions and thus beyond the scope of children's services. In these sections, the focus will be on how these general or administrative functions affect children, and how they affect children and adults differently. No attempt will be made here to be comprehensive on these topics; they are better addressed in their own context. The book will touch on cataloging, public relations, statistics and budgeting, and many other topics. The theme that will resonate throughout this work is that children's specialists should concern themselves with any aspect of the library that affects children, whether or not it traditionally falls within their realm.

The Organization

This treatment is broken down into five parts. Part 1, "Children's Services and the Mission of the Library," will put children's services in perspective by exploring how children's services relate to the library and the community as a whole, why we do what we do, and whom we aim to serve. Part 2, "The Collection," will talk about how we select, organize, and maintain the various library materials we use. Part 3, "Services," looks at the reasons people come to our library, including after-school services, reference, readers' advisory, and the Internet. Part 4, "Programming," looks at the things we do to invite people into our library and to promote our services and collections. Part 5, "Management, Administration, and Leadership," is a catchall for the other things that children's services specialists must do in order to be effective.

Integration

The divisions used here are convenient for study and discussion, but in some ways they are arbitrary. All these parts of our job are connected, at least if we do it well. The collection should support programming, the services should rely on the collection, programming should promote the use of the collection, and the community should influence all of the choices we make.

In the same way, children's services should be integrated into the larger library. Public libraries serve the whole person, the whole family, and the whole community. Children graduate from children's services, pass through teen services, and make their way into adult services. When we serve children, we often must interact with parents, caregivers, and teachers as well. Children's services are affected by all administrative functions, and children's services are a cornerstone of public relations and community outreach. Adult services staff will invariably come into contact with children, and children's services staff must deal with adults. What one staff member does must impact everyone else in the organization.

Some aspects of library work will appear in nearly all sections of this book, whether or not they have a section of their own. Intellectual freedom is an issue in developing the collection, reference, and readers' advisory. The Internet affects collection development, homework help, and budgeting. Community outreach is a component of programming and curriculum support. There are, of course, countless other examples. And so, while division is necessary for clarity, we must remember that interconnectedness is the reality. Nothing that goes on in a library happens in a vacuum. This is a nuts-and-bolts truth that needs to be considered in even the most mundane tasks of library work. Children's services are important, they impact on every function of a public library, and they deserve close consideration—for the good of the child, the library, and the community.

NOTES

1. Virginia A. Walter, *Children and Libraries: Getting It Right* (Chicago: American Library Association, 2001), 17.

2. Adrienne Chute and others, *Public Libraries in the United States: Fiscal Year 2001* (Washington, DC: U.S. Department of Education National Center for Education Statistics, June 2003), 26; Walters, *Children and Libraries,* 29.

Children's Services and the Mission of the Library

A Historical View

The history of public libraries dates only to the first half of the nineteenth century, and children's services did not appear until nearly the twentieth century.[1] Even then, children's services emerged solely in big cities, making their way into rural areas much later. There is a modern parallel in teen services. Only recently have smaller and more rural libraries begun dedicating space, collections, and ultimately staff to young adults. In a historical sense, there really is not a tradition of children's services. The whole idea is still in its infancy, and so is in a state of flux. The one constant is the strong and focused orientation toward service that stands out in children's work.[2]

Early children's rooms focused more on atmosphere and surroundings than on collections. Why? Because there were few children's books to be had, so the collection was not much of an issue.[3] Indeed, children's services and children's publishing grew up together.[4] In the earliest days, children's services focused more on storytelling, activities, and the transmission of culture, and less on literature. Today, the collection has become the main focus of most children's departments, and promoting reading is the goal of most programming and services.

Early children's specialists had a nearly missionary zeal. They blazed new trails in service, fought established library practice, and too often went it alone in their organizations.[5] This tendency still reverberates today. Children's library services have a strong tradition of reaching out to the underserved and the underprivileged, and an association between children's services and social services still exists in the minds of both practitioners and the public.[6] And while this zeal may have ebbed somewhat, children's services remain the most idealistic of library services.

Today's Perspective

History is not to be ignored if we wish to understand the world in which we must live and work. Echoes of the past still shape present-day children's services. In many organizations, children's services have not yet been integrated into the larger library. Yet children's services staff remain more idealistic than their colleagues elsewhere in the library, and have stronger ties to the community than is true of other library employees. As a young and still evolving component of public library service, children's services are constantly redefining themselves—taking on new challenges and addressing new clienteles.

Chapter 1, "Where We Fit In," explores the place of children's services in the library, and in the community at large. Clarifying the position of children's services is a constant battle, but it is not an academic exercise. When children's services successfully align themselves with the greater mission of the library and clearly articulate to administrators and decision makers their contribution to the institution as a whole, the result is often increased resources. Demonstrating the role of children's services to the larger community, and then articulating their contribution to funding agencies and community-wide decision makers, can generate increased resources for the library as a whole.

There is also value in taking a look at who we are and whom we are trying to serve. Chapter 2, "Principles of Children's Librarianship," looks at what children's librarians believe and stand for. We must understand the reasons we do things before we can decide what we will do. Chapter 3, "Whom Do Children's Librarians Serve?" will focus us on what really matters—our customers. Public libraries must always address the community; we have a broader and more diverse audience than any other type of library. We seek to serve everyone in our community, even those who do not presently feel a need for us, and nowhere is this attitude more critical than in children's services, where our potential impact is greatest.

NOTES

1. Virginia A. Walter, *Children and Libraries: Getting It Right* (Chicago: American Library Association, 2001), 1–2.

2. Virginia H. Matthews, "Children Couldn't Wait Then Either, but Sometimes They Had To," *American Libraries*, June/July 2004, 76.

3. Walter, *Children and Libraries*, 2–3.

4. Ibid., 5.

5. Ibid., 4–6.

6. Matthews, "Children Couldn't Wait," 79.

1

Where We Fit In

Children's services do not happen in a vacuum. If we attempt to do our jobs and fail to make a point of interacting with the larger library or the community as a whole, we run the risk of neglecting significant needs, missing opportunities to leverage our efforts to their greatest effect, and existing beyond the notice of many of our potential customers. Unfortunately, that is exactly what happens to a greater or lesser degree in many public libraries. Before considering what to do about this problem, it is necessary to provide a context.

Children's Services and the Library

Children's services do a great deal to further the mission of most public libraries, but the ways in which they do this may not be immediately evident. Children's services, of course, serve children, and that is intrinsically a good thing. Sixty percent of library users are under eighteen years old.[1] Children's services also draw into the library a wide range of people who are associated in one way or another with children. Those adults then are exposed to the other services that the library offers.

Children who are served in the library bring with them parents and caregivers who are often too busy to seek out resources for their own use.

Public libraries that lose teenagers when they finish school often get them back when they return to sign up their own children for library cards. Teachers—at least those who see the value of libraries for their students— may contact their local public library to arrange for materials in support of their class work, but they may also find materials or services that interest them professionally or personally. Grandparents, coaches, and activity leaders may also follow children to the library.

Once in the library, these people can be an asset to the library in general, not just the children's room. People who work with or care for children tend to be community minded, active, and energetic. Indeed, the most effective spokespeople, valuable volunteers, and invaluable advocates for the library are generally individuals who are connected with children. In addition, children served by libraries today become the customers of the future. Ask a person who supports libraries when the attraction began, and his or her first memory will most likely date back to childhood. It is much easier to make someone a lifetime library user at age four than at age forty.

There are huge public relations benefits to children's services, even for those who are not directly connected to children. The quality of a com- munity—and that community's pride—are usually tied up in the quality of life for its children. Real estate agents emphasize quality schools and public safety, and health officers trumpet the positive activities available to chil- dren. People take pride in how well children are cared for in their commu- nities, and they appreciate a library that makes a significant contribution to the lives of young residents.

Providing excellent children's services also enables the library to fulfill one of its duties—to provide equal access to all customers. Serving children takes more work than satisfying your typical adult fiction reader, but the community as a whole supports the library, and expects the community as a whole to be well served. It is hard to justify not going the extra mile to serve children, a population that represents such a large and important segment of the community. For reasons that are both practical and theo- retical, and that address the current and future needs of the customers, chil- dren's services are a vital part of the modern public library.

LIBRARIAN SHORTAGE AND PAY EQUITY

Children's services may be a vital part of the modern public library, but what role will children's services play in future public libraries if there are no children's librarians left? A study based on the 1990 census showed that more than 80 percent of the librarians who held master's degrees at that time would be sixty-five or older and presumably retired or retiring by the year 2020. Some 60 percent would reach that magic age between 2005 and 2019.[2] This study brought to light the impending librarian shortage. All areas of librarianship need to be concerned about this finding, but the librarian shortage has a special significance for children's services.

The shortage came about because of the closing of a quarter of America's library and information science schools—fifteen closures in all—between 1978 and 1993.[3] When the post–World War II baby boom dried up, there were fewer graduate students, and library schools suffered. When the last of the baby boom librarians reach retirement age, they will leave a huge void behind them.

In an attempt to reverse the trend, library schools broadened their scope, merging with other departments and expanding beyond the library to information management and computer network administration.[4] Library schools began awarding more degrees, but that is not likely to produce more children's librarians. Because of the specialized training in information management and computers, the graduates are more likely to go into fields other than librarianship, to libraries other than publics, and to specializations other than children's work. In 1997, only 23 percent of library school graduates took jobs in public libraries.[5]

What really makes the librarian shortage devastating to children's services is the clear lack of respect—and respect's most outward sign, money—that is afforded children's librarians. In 1997, the average beginning salary for MLS graduates in the United States who went into youth services was $27,896, as opposed to $30,270 for MLS graduates going into public libraries as a whole.[6] There can be many arguments for why different librarians might earn more or less over time, such as how much continuing education each type of librarian typically pursues and the greater willingness of one type of library professional to change jobs in order to advance. Neither of these arguments applies here, and this one statistic about the salary differential seems fairly telling—and rather stark. Quite simply, children's librarians make less than other librarians because they are children's librarians.

The fact that children's librarians earn less than other librarians leads to other questions. For example, do children's librarians suffer because children's librarians are traditionally female? Or is children's work in all fields compensated poorly? If the pool of librarians is shrinking, a compensation disadvantage will continue to make it harder to recruit children's specialists. Those concerned with children and libraries must not only concern themselves with developing their own skills, but they must also look to the viability of children's librarianship as a profession. It is imperative that today's children's librarians, and all those who understand the importance of public library work in children's services, seek out the next generation of dedicated children's professionals. They must also advocate for equal pay and respect, so that prospective children's specialists will not be discouraged from joining the field.

Children's Services and the Community

It is often asked why people who have no young children should have to pay taxes to support public schools. Similarly, some taxpayers who do not use the public library object that a portion of their tax dollars is spent to support the library. Those people who do not have children and who do not use the library may be doubly offended that their taxes support both the schools and the public library children's services. Perhaps we can derive something positive from this conflict about the use of public funds. It forces us to articulate what place children's library services have in the greater community, and, for very practical reasons, every children's librarian should have an answer.

The answer to the question about supporting schools is akin to the one about subsidizing public libraries. One does not pay school taxes in order to have one's own children educated; one pays school taxes for the privilege of living in a society in which children are educated. Similarly, one does not pay taxes in order to gain access to the library, but so that the library is there for anyone to use.

An educated, literate citizenry is important in a democratic society, and we cannot begin offering lessons on citizenship when people reach the age of eighteen. Whereas school curricula and programs of study emphasize learning a uniform base of knowledge and skills, public libraries are places of open exploration; it is within the unstructured environment of the library that children learn to make their own decisions about what they will investigate and how they will think.

Public libraries also function as community focal points, and are becoming more so despite the trends toward isolation and noninvolvement that seem to plague our modern world.[7] Unlike most public schools, libraries serve both children and adults—and both adults with children and adults without children. In fact, there are really no other organizations that reach so many segments of a local community, and public libraries are present in nearly all the communities in this country. That breadth of impact is lost if children's services do not reach a significant segment of their audience.

Increasingly, public libraries are becoming a place for children to spend productive, or at least nondestructive, hours. The smallest of our communities are becoming dangerous places for children, and exposure to the media is becoming so pervasive, and marketing to children so aggressive, that even our homes are becoming places in which children cannot spend large amounts of unsupervised time. This is not an argument for libraries as babysitting or social services, but children's services can fill an important role in the community by providing a consistent, positive alternative to our society's most vulnerable members. Our communities as a whole benefit, and the effect is well worth the investment, even to someone without children.

NOTES

1. Virginia A. Walter, *Children and Libraries: Getting It Right* (Chicago: American Library Association, 2001), 17.

2. Mary Jo Lynch, "Reaching 65: Lots of Librarians Will Be There Soon," *American Libraries*, March 2002, 55.

3. Barbara B. Moran, "Practitioners vs. LIS Educators: Time to Reconnect," *Library Journal*, November 1, 2001, 52–53.

4. Ibid.

5. Walter, *Children and Libraries*, 41.

6. Ibid.

7. Everyone concerned about community and shared values should read Robert D. Putnam, *Bowling Alone: The Collapse and Revival of American Community* (New York: Simon and Schuster, 2000).

2

Principles of Children's Librarianship

There are a few principles that form a foundation for all of children's work; these are the convictions of children's librarians, and in many ways the library profession as a whole. They are so fundamental that they constitute the subtext of everything we will talk about. Later on, we will look at the *what* of children's librarians' duties; the principles of children's librarianship represent the *why*—and reveal why we open the library doors each and every day. They may seem theoretical or idealistic, but they translate into practice, at least when children's services are done well.

The Power of Reading

Children's librarians believe that reading is necessary for success, and for reaching one's human potential. Reading is both a practical skill and a door to enrichment. Children need reading because the skill is much easier to attain and develop at an early age than later in life, and because children are forming views of the world that they will carry with them forever. Reading is effective at transmitting information, transferring culture, and encouraging self-reflection. Reading is an antidote to media overexposure in a world where the media focuses increasingly on violence without consequences, portrays simplistic views of complex realities, and uses language badly. Children who do not read will become adults who are not as productive as they should be, and who will miss out on much of the richness of life.

The act of reading itself is fundamental to acquiring the skill, a truism championed by Stephen Krashen in his book *The Power of Reading: Insights from the Research*. By promoting reading with literature-rich environments, leaving unstructured time to allow for reading, modeling good reading habits, and allowing children to choose what they would like to read, adults increase the likelihood that children will read more. By reading, children develop better vocabularies and grammar skills, become better writers, and even better spellers.[1] Indeed, reading is the only proven effective way of developing these skills.[2] Reading of any sort—even reading low-level material—forms the base for these skills and leads directly to high-level reading.[3]

There is a negative side to nonreading as well, a toll we see often enough in employment and income figures, but which we do not often see identified as a cause of personal and social ills. According to Jim Trelease, standard-bearer for reading aloud to children, 60 percent of prison inmates in America are illiterate.[4] Evidence now demonstrates that the inability to read is a risk factor for depression; the *Journal of Abnormal Child Psychology* found this to be true among children, reporting "robust links between severe, persistent reading problems and increased risk for depressed mood" among boys ages seven to ten.[5] Reading is powerful; not reading is dangerous.

Equal Access

For the children's librarian, equal access can be reduced to what might be called the Horton Principle: "A person's a person, no matter how small."[6] (If you get that reference, you can probably thank a children's librarian.) Children deserve the same service, respect, and dedication as adults. The official library language comes from the *Library Bill of Rights*: "A person's right to use a library should not be denied or abridged because of origin, age, background, or views."[7] This principle is also embodied in the *Code of Ethics of the American Library Association*: "We provide the highest level of service to all library users through appropriate and usefully organized resources; equitable service policies; equitable access; and accurate, unbiased, and courteous responses to all requests."[8] For the tax-supported public library, this is a legal issue as well. Federal and state laws restrict publicly funded entities from discriminating on the basis of many factors, age included.

SERVICE TO BOYS

We need to assure that our libraries serve all people, including children, but we also need to assure that we are serving all children. Preschool boys are as visible in most public libraries as preschool girls, yet by the time children reach the teen years boys are nearly invisible. This hard fact belies our claim that libraries provide equal access to library services for all. Clearly, we fail to offer boys what they need. Of course, studies show that boys do not read as much or at as high a level as girls do, but that is not the entire explanation for the scarcity of boys in libraries. Our attitudes toward boys and boys' reading are to blame as well.

Boys' Reading Gets No Respect

If our collections are the first and most important service offered to the public, then it should be of little surprise that school-age boys do not flock to the library in the same number as girls. The types of reading that appeal most to boys do not appeal to children's librarians, the vast majority of whom are women. Boys' brains are wired differently than girls' brains, and those differences show up in the way boys read. Boys see the world as a place to be mastered, and the components of the world as tools to be understood and used in order to accomplish the greater goals.[9] Theirs is a point of view that emphasizes breaking things down into component pieces, learning the rules, and finding a place in the world. Girls perceive that the world is based on personal relationships. They seek to understand others and themselves, to learn how to interact in order to get things done, and to find their place in an interconnected web of people, rather than in a large and impersonal world.[10]

Obviously, girls' outlooks lend themselves to language skills, which helps to explain the superiority of their language skills from age three all the way through high school.[11] But it also explains the differences between what girls like to read and what boys like to read, and why girls' reading gets so much more respect than boys' reading. Boys enjoy reading fantasy because the basic structure, borrowed from mythology, traces the path of an individual in search of his place in the world. Action and adventure books do much the same, and these, like fantasy, contain active plot lines that speak to boys' active natures. Librarians, the vast majority of whom are female, tend to see these books as less worthy than the standard juvenile novel, which typically emphasizes an inward journey of self-discovery, rather than the external journey favored by young male readers. Although it is admirable to want children to find reflection and self-evaluation in their reading, we must understand that this is a particularly female approach.

Librarians also find that much fantasy and adventure literature contains so much action that it tends toward violence, which has become anathema, especially after incidents like Columbine. What we sometimes fail to see is that literature can be a positive vehicle for looking at and dealing with such issues, and certainly a safer venue than the image-rich environment of the media or video games. A similar discomfort keeps many librarians from respecting humor. Boys love humor, especially the edgier kinds that drive adults crazy. That, of course, is the point. Boys see the world comprised of rules and methods, dos and don'ts. They are inherently rule bound, so how can they tell where the lines are if they do not dance over them now and then? Boys also like to read nonfiction, both because it helps them to understand how the world around them works and because it ties reading to the more active types of pastimes that speak to their kinetic nature.

Most libraries collect some of the types of books that boys enjoy, but not nearly as much as they collect books of interest to girls, and the books we promote are at least as important as the books we collect. It is not just that the books that appeal to girls speak to us as librarians, but we also promote them more because we believe they are better than boy books. Do you booktalk series and nonfiction books? Do you see funny books on the Newbery Award list, or other lists for best books? These types of books are not inherently worse than the books of personal pain and triumph, or the books about a family pet dying, so why do they not show up when we librarians are talking about the best of the best? It is simply because our point of view is primarily a female one, so we honor the books that speak to us. This does a great disservice to boys.

Going beyond the Books

The unwillingness to promote boys' reading is indicative of our approach toward boys in general. We design our spaces and our rules for quiet, solitary work and sustained reading, but boys are active learners. Their brains tend to work on one side or the other, whereas girls use both halves of the brain more regularly. Boys need added stimuli to engage both halves of their brains, stimuli that include sound, color, and motion, stimuli that are all but forbidden in too many public libraries.[12] We develop our programs the same way, as sedentary, quiet activities that, if they have any physical component at all, emphasize fine motor skills.

We have eliminated competition from many of our libraries—outlawing board games, taking incentives out of summer reading programs, and holding contests where everyone wins—despite the fact that competition motivates and interests boys. We have all but conceded that the fun, camaraderie, and excitement of healthy competition have no place in the intellectual world.

We can reverse this trend easily enough, and without making wholesale changes to our libraries. We can take solitary, sedentary activities like drawing and painting and increase their scale. Instead of having children draw a picture, for example, we might enlist a group of children to paint a wall or a mural. Instead of talking about a story in a book discussion, we might encourage the children stand up and act it out. We might also invite chess and other board games back into the library as family events. The library might even occasionally offer a prize.

Most of all, we need to invite men—themselves a rare sight in too many public libraries—into our children's rooms and into our programs. Boys are desperate for role models, and they have so very few when it comes to reading. Make men feel welcome, and they will show boys that books, libraries, and males go together.

Intellectual Freedom

Free inquiry and free thought are cornerstones of democracy. Libraries are places where people can decide for themselves what they will think, and children deserve this right as well. Libraries are not places where particular beliefs and points of view are presented to the exclusion of others. Parents certainly have the right and responsibility to guide their children's reading, but one parent does not have the right to restrict what ideas another parent's child is exposed to. For this reason, children's libraries present a diverse collection of materials that reflects a heterogeneous society. The *Library Bill of Rights* maintains that

> Books and other library resources should be provided for the interest, information, and enlightenment of all people of the community the library serves. Materials should not be excluded because of the origin, background, or views of those contributing to their creation. . . . Libraries should provide materials and information presenting all points of view on current and historical issues. Materials should not be proscribed or removed because of partisan or doctrinal disapproval.[13]

CHILDREN AND PRIVACY

Passage of the USA PATRIOT Act brought the issue of privacy and library records into national focus, but that debate centered on the rights of adults who might be investigated for matters of national security. Perhaps even more troublesome is the question of the privacy of children's library records. When we talk about children's records, the inquirer is usually not some faceless government agent, but most often the parent of the child in question.

In the *Library Bill of Rights,* the American Library Association states that a person's right to use a library should not be denied or abridged because of his or her age.[14] The law, on the other hand, does not always agree. There is no federal law protecting children's rights to privacy in their library records, so individual state laws hold sway.[15] Many states have laws that specifically allow parents access to their children's library records.[16] But the issue of children's privacy is much more complicated for public libraries than solid statements of ethics or law. We want involved parents who take an interest in their child's reading. We tell parents that they are responsible for their child's reading as the basis of our intellectual freedom arguments. Then we tell these parents that they must be responsible for what their children read without knowing what it is that they are reading.

Of course, this is a somewhat skewed version of the exchange. We intend to tell parents that they should be involved in choosing books with their children, reading the same books that their children read, and being present and involved when their children are online. We do not mean that parents should periodically drop in and expect us to bring them up to speed on the reading and viewing habits of their children. But we should be aware that parents—often interested, well-meaning parents—could easily see this situation differently. We should say what we mean, and realize that parents probably will not always make sense of "library speak." We should understand the difficulty of the relation-ship for those parents who see themselves as trying to do exactly what we told them to do, only to find us setting up roadblocks.

In the context of a parent's involvement in a child's reading, it makes little sense to lump all those under the age of eighteen under the label "children." A parent of a five-year-old who wants to know what her child has checked out means something altogether different than a parent of a sixteen-year-old who inquires about a child's reading habits. Unfortunately, laws and policies, especially those that apply a strict philosophical stand in favor of privacy, often make no such distinction. And the case that seems to attract the most public attention is the one in which a library sends a parent a bill for a child's overdue books but then refuses to tell the parent the titles so that he or she can locate them.[17] Can we make parents financially responsible for books without affording them the authority to ensure their return? The majority of the discussion that seems to take place in library circles on this topic centers on the extreme cases, such as children taking out books on divorce, child abuse, incest, and the like. While these cases are certainly of great concern, they do not reflect the vast majority of actual library experience.

The primary goal is to protect the free use of library materials by children, who should feel confident that their use will not be turned against them later on. We do not want children to opt out of knowledge because they are afraid of the consequences of inquiry. The secondary aim must be to prevent disproportionate reactions to privacy questions from undercutting our level of service. The prime example of this occurs when a library chooses to raise the minimum age for having a library card. Such policies do sidestep the possibility of violating a child's privacy, but they only achieve this end by denying service to a child who cannot or does not wish to rely on parents to check out the items he or she wishes to borrow. The delicate balance we must strike is how to provide the best possible service while still protecting privacy rights.

Some possible strategies for addressing privacy for children in the real world are worth considering. Some libraries have created policies that protect the confidentiality of children to the extent that a parent will not be informed of the titles that children have checked out, or even held on reserve, without the child's permission. This leads to the somewhat comical scenario in which a parent must bring in a note from a child in order to pick up a reserve. This permission, though, can be granted on a continuing basis and appended to the child's circulation record.

Some libraries offer a family card as an either/or option to parents who might be uncomfortable with the privacy implications of allowing their children to have their own cards. A family card allows everyone under its umbrella to use a single account, specifically excluding any pretense of privacy among any of the individuals using the card. If any family member does check something out on the card, then theoretically he or she should know that anyone else on the card has access to the information. How to ensure that the individuals involved understand how the card works and the implications of borrowing materials on such an account is a matter for further consideration.

It is most important to know the status of state laws, who is protected, whether the laws apply to school or public libraries or both, and what types of records or transactions are covered. We must know the policies of the libraries we serve, and we must verify that the policy and the law are not in conflict. It is important to know the accepted ethics of our profession, but to understand that both law and policy may trump these. To the extent possible, children's librarians should make their own beliefs known when libraries or library organizations are setting policy and ethical standards, and all librarians should be vocal when the law is stepping into the arena of libraries and their professional interaction with the public.

Library professionals certainly need to understand these privacy rules, but it is equally important for customers to know their rights. Our twelve-year-olds may have an expectation of privacy that is unrealistic under state law. Their parents may have an expectation of access to their children's records that our policies do not support. It is our job to inform both of these audiences about their rights before a conflict arises. However, harping on extreme cases can make librarians sound alarmist and our libraries seem bureaucratic and out of touch. The best option is to provide new customers with a matter-of-fact statement explaining who will have access to their accounts. That way a parent can understand the implications of allowing a child to have his or her own library card.

It is important to remember that the law, even laws designed to protect privacy, may classify various library records as public records, and in doing so require the library to maintain those records for specified amounts of time. The oft-cited strategy of destroying records—either by shredding paper copies or setting computers to dump records as soon as a transaction is complete—may in fact be in violation of the law. It is a great embarrassment to call to our defense the protection of the law, only to have it publicly announced that we are in violation of the law.[18]

FURTHER READING

Michael Gurian and Patricia Henley, with Terry Trueman, *Boys and Girls Learn Differently! A Guide for Teachers and Parents* (San Francisco: Jossey-Bass, 2001).

Stephen Krashen, *The Power of Reading: Insights from the Research* (Englewood, CO: Libraries Unlimited, 1993).

Thomas Newkirk, *Misreading Masculinity: Boys, Literacy, and Popular Culture* (Portsmouth, NH: Heinemann, 2002).

Michael Sullivan, *Connecting Boys with Books: What Libraries Can Do* (Chicago: American Library Association, 2003).

NOTES

1. Stephen Krashen, *The Power of Reading: Insights from the Research* (Englewood, CO: Libraries Unlimited, 2004), 3.

2. Ibid., 37.

3. Ibid., 116.

4. David M. Schwartz, "Ready, Set, Read—20 Minutes Is All You'll Need," *Smithsonian*, February 1995, 82.

5. Barbara Maughan and others, "Reading Problems and Depressed Mood," *Journal of Abnormal Child Psychology*, April 2003, 219.

6. Theodor Seuss Geisel, *Horton Hears a Who!* (New York: Random House, 1954).

7. American Library Association, *Library Bill of Rights* (adopted June 18, 1948; amended February 2, 1961, and January 23, 1980; inclusion of "age" reaffirmed January 23, 1996, by the ALA Council), http://www.ala.org/ala/oif/statementspols/statementsif/librarybillrights.htm.

8. American Library Association, *Code of Ethics of the American Library Association* (adopted June 28, 1995, by the ALA Council), http://www.ala.org/ala/oif/statementspols/codeofethics/codeethics.htm.

9. Deborah Langerman, "Books and Boys: Gender Preferences and Book Selection," *School Library Journal* 36 (March 1990): 132–34.

10. John Gray, *Men Are from Mars, Women Are from Venus: A Practical Guide for Improving Communication and Getting What You Want in Your Relationships* (New York: HarperCollins, 1992), 16–18.

11. S. Vogel, "Gender Differences in Intelligence, Language, Visual-Motor Abilities, and Academic Achievement in Students with Learning Disabilities: A Review of the Literature," *Journal of Learning Disabilities* 23, no. 1 (1990): 44–52.

12. Michael Gurian and Patricia Henley, with Terry Trueman, *Boys and Girls Learn Differently! A Guide for Teachers and Parents* (San Francisco: Jossey-Bass, 2001), 46–47.

13. American Library Association, *Library Bill of Rights*.

14. Ibid.

15. Helen R. Adams, "Privacy and Confidentiality: Now More Than Ever, Youngsters Need to Keep Their Library Use under Wraps," *American Libraries* (November 2002): 46.

16. Walter Minkel, "AK to Nix Kids' Privacy Rights," *School Library Journal*, April 2004, 22.

17. George M. Eberhart, "Two State Bills Affect Minors' Reading Privacy," *American Libraries*, December 2003, 21.

18. Adams, "Privacy and Confidentiality," 45.

3

Whom Do Children's Librarians Serve?

The question of whom children's librarians serve is not as simple as it might seem. Children, yes, but that is a very broad term, and there are so many more people to serve as well. We must focus not just on serving children but also on serving the needs and best interests of children, and that means serving all those who share that goal as well. In addition, our skills and resources, designed to fit the needs of children, can sometimes be turned to the benefit of other audiences because of their special circumstances.

Children

Children are our primary audience. While all the services of a public library should be available to customers of all ages, we recognize that children have special developmental needs. We offer many of the same services that adult staff members offer, but we, and our libraries, know that children are not just little adults. Additionally, *children* encompasses a wide range of developmental stages. One of the reasons to have children's specialists is because identifying the distinct needs of a three-, a six-, and a twenty-year-old is far more difficult and important than differentiating between the needs of a thirty-, a forty-, and a fifty-year-old.

Babies

The age range addressed in children's libraries is small compared to the range serviced in adult libraries. That range, though, is much greater than it was even a generation ago. Children's specialists now serve children from birth. Babies, roughly from birth to age one and a half, are forming structures of the mind. They are learning to react to various stimuli such as sound, rhythm, color, and touch. Children's librarians now develop collections and programs that introduce and reinforce these concepts, though these services are far from universal. The "baby lap-sit" program is still a relatively new and inventive concept. Board books, with their sturdy cardboard pages designed to withstand hard use by children too young to appreciate a book as something other than a physical object, are becoming standard. Tactile books, which integrate different textures into the pages, are becoming more than a novelty.

Toddlers

Toddlers, roughly one and a half years to three years old, are developing an appreciation for story, learning to interact with others outside their immediate family, and exploring the world around them. Children's librarians serve these needs in a language-rich environment, and begin to develop in these children an appreciation of the role that books and reading can play in doing so. No longer are these children addressed only as the younger siblings of the children in our regular programs; toddler story hours are becoming common, and some libraries set aside social play times when children can interact with others of similar ages and parents can meet and socialize as well. Concept books, read-to-me-level nonfiction, and picture book treatments of nursery rhymes and songs help to make the connection between books and experience.

Preschoolers

Preschoolers, roughly three- to five-year-olds, are an audience with whom most children's libraries are familiar and comfortable these days. They are preparing to enter school and to learn to read. They are developing a sense of structure, an awareness of rules and routine. Programs now become almost ritualized play; in fact parents and children alike may begin to refer to programs as "library school." This is a time when children begin to imitate their elders and see this as acting grown up. Our established picture book collections are well suited to this age, and fairy tale and folklore collections appeal to the need of preschool children for structured story. Preschool story hour is the most basic and recognizable of our programs.

Early Elementary

Children in preschools and kindergartens may well continue to use the library as they always have, but once they enter early elementary school, from roughly ages six to eight years old, that relationship changes dramatically. Most important for the library, this is the age when children move from passive accepters of language to independent readers. Books are no longer valuable for this age group only because of the language contained in them, but, rather, represent a skill to master. Children's librarians no

The author with preschoolers in Everett, Massachusetts

longer act as readers and nurturers, but have become teachers and guides. This is the period that fulfills the old adage that if you give a man a fish he will eat for a day; if you teach a man to fish he will eat for life.

After the richness and complexity of the picture books and folklore, children in this group need to take a step back because they have begun to practice reading on their own. They will be using "Step Readers" or "I Can Read" books that have very simple text, few words per page, and straightforward story lines. They will be looking for very low-level nonfiction to fulfill early school projects. The public library needs to remind these children—and their parents—that reading is a joy; for the first time for these young people, reading has become work. Programs and displays should highlight high-interest reading. This is a good time to promote joke books, alphabet books, and other books that break down the text into small chunks that can be read independently.

As these children progress through first and into second grade, they will be ready for easier chapter books that form a bridge between the first readers and the more traditional juvenile novels. This particular type of literature is far more common and well developed than it was even a decade ago. Many characters and series from picture books and the preschool media, such as *Arthur*, *The Berenstain Bears*, and *Pokemon*, now have early chapter book versions. Whole new series have been developed for this age, such as Paula Danzinger's *Amber Brown* series and the wildly popular *Magic Tree House* series by Mary Pope Osborne. There is no longer any significant gap in popular literature as children progress from nonreaders to independent readers. Children's specialists just need to make sure their collection reflects this.

Tweenagers

Until very recently, we made little distinction between the early elementary years and the later elementary years, from about age eight to twelve. The new awareness of the special needs of this group is best shown in the emergence of the term *tweenagers*, signifying that these children are not kids in the sense that they were a few years ago, nor are they ready to be treated as teenagers. They are between ages, hence tweenagers or tweens. It may be a sign that children are growing up faster, or a result of more specialized and aggressive marketing and media focus, but children of this age do not want to be associated with their early elementary counterparts. Tweens are developing a keener sense of curiosity about the world, and about themselves. They are sophisticated in the sense that they are less accepting of what others say and more inclined to investigate on their own.

At the same time, they still crave adult attention and interaction. They are desperate for role models among adults or teenagers, and they are aware of this need, as opposed to younger children who will simply identify with adults on a less conscious level. The more sophisticated modern juvenile novels appeal to this age. This is also the time when children truly discover genre fiction, both because genres introduce experiential elements in a structured, predictable way, and because tweenagers are developing a sense of their own preferences and comfort levels. Bruce Hale's *Chet Gecko* mysteries, Jon Scieszka's *Time Warp Trio* humor/science fiction books, and the fantasy series *Secrets of Droon* by Tony Abbott have clearly defined this age group and their reading tastes. Programming for this age largely involves connecting books and literature to the wider world, and to the types of activities in which tweens are involved.

Teenagers/Young Adults

Twelve- to eighteen-year-olds are not truly children and not truly adults. It is a time of growing independence in thought, action, and belief. They are establishing their own relationships—with peers, with books, with the world in general. While this is a period of experimentation and new experiences, it is also a frightening and unsettling time, often sparking regression to counter feelings of insecurity. This age group is beyond the scope of this book, but children's librarians should be aware that this age group will often require their attention. Some teens will seek the comfortable, familiar setting of the children's library where they have happy memories. Others will need the children's collection if their reading skills are lagging. Many libraries do not have a separate department, staff, or even collection to serve teens, so the teens will have to choose whether to make do with the children's department or to make the leap to the adult department.

Parents

In decades past, children's librarians have had an ambivalent relationship with parents. We wanted them to be interested in their children's reading and eager to bring their children to the library, but then we asked them to wait outside the room during story hour. We told parents to be responsible for returning the books their children borrowed, but too often we preferred to be the ones choosing books with their children. A great deal has changed in recent years, and parents have become an increasingly important part of the mission of the children's librarian.

The family literacy approach suggests that we best serve the needs of children by focusing our efforts on teaching parents about fostering literacy. The reason is simple: parents spend a great deal more time with children than we do. Teaching parents to do what we do is leveraging our efforts to the greatest effect. The trend now is to include parents in programming whenever possible in order to model good literacy. We also focus on talking with parents about literature for children and encourage them to continue reading with and to their children even after the children become independent readers. Many children's libraries include a parenting section, materials for parents that focus on child rearing and development that are housed in the children's room so that parents can spend time with their children and find reading materials at the same time. Parenting sections are also a great place to keep local information on child services, child care opportunities, schools, and the like.

Homeschool Families

In 1999 an estimated 850,000 children in grades K–12, 1.7 percent of the school-age population, were being educated at home. Their demographics did not differ greatly from those of the general student population as far as family income or urban vs. suburban vs. rural locations.[1] In short, homeschoolers are everywhere. Still, they are so seldom seen in libraries, and when they are they so seldom express any unusual needs. Consequently, public library staff members often do not know there are any homeschoolers in their communities.

Homeschool families are largely invisible in most communities, sometimes by their own design. They often feel that local schools resent their choice, and they are often justified. Sometimes schools are open and welcoming with their resources and facilities, sometimes they are not, and even when they are, the homeschool parents may not feel comfortable using those facilities. If they chose not to put their children in public schools because of the poor learning environment, as a quarter of them do, then they may not want to expose their child to that environment even for a library visit.[2] Their reasoning is not important to the public library; what is important is homeschool families' needs for our collections and our services.

Public librarians, though, have not always been welcoming to home-schoolers. Homeschool families do not always use the library the way librarians expect it to be used. For example, they may seek to borrow large numbers of books in a single subject area, and run afoul of circulation limits. The rules, established to keep one or two students from monopolizing books needed for a class project, make little to no sense when there is only one child, or one family of children, studying a topic. Librarians do not always react as well to the exception as they do to the rule. It is not unknown for a children's staff member to notice a homeschooler in the library on a school day, and, seeing the child apparently healthy and of school age, to call the truancy officer.

Teachers and School Librarians

Teachers, like parents, spend a great deal more time with children than many of us could ever wish for. As is true of parents, we can be most effective by working with and through teachers rather than by counting on our own direct influence on children. Teachers can bring children to the library, so serving their needs may increase our exposure to children. Teachers also have continuing education needs that sometimes require our special knowledge, experience, and resources. Teachers who hope to keep up with developmental issues, or just to stay familiar with children's literature, are more likely to be in the children's room than the adult room.

Teachers today also include the school librarians, known now as school media specialists or school media generalists, and known colloquially as teacher librarians. Increasingly, these colleagues are on teacher contracts, work teacher schedules, and teach regularly scheduled classes. If there was usually less than perfect communication between school and public library children's specialists, now that gap may be pushed wider because of the school staff's broader duties. The importance of bridging that gap is greater as well; school library staff have more contact with children than public library staff could ever dream of. If we want to take our services continuously to the greatest number of children, then we need to make sure this relationship is strong.

Nonnative Speakers of English

Story hour in an urban library can be both shocking and revealing. In greeting the participants, both children and adults, it may quickly become apparent that no one in the room besides the librarian speaks any English at all. Furthermore, there may be more adults than children; each family represented by one or more children, one or both parents, and often an aunt or uncle and a grandparent. Story hour may be interrupted almost immediately by a child walking up to the book, pointing to a picture, and speaking a word in a language other than English. The child will then look up expectantly for you to say the name of the object he is pointing to, and when you do, he or she then repeats the word in English and his native language to the adults who accompanied the child to the program. This not too uncommon occurrence is enough to convince anyone that the story hour has become a beginning English class for immigrant families.

Our children's collections and services are designed to introduce language, specifically the English language, to those who need to learn it, and that will benefit adults who do not speak English as well as children who are developing language skills in general. We may refer these people to English as a Second Language programs either in the library or elsewhere in the community, but many of them will feel more comfortable learning under the cover of educating their children.

Adults with Low Literacy Skills

Similar to nonnative English speakers, adults with low literacy skills may seek out the children's library because that is where language skills are acquired. They may also come under the guise of bringing in their children, though not always. I mentioned in an earlier chapter the principle of equal access, in the context of library services needing to be open to children and adults alike. In serving low-literacy adults, we need to remember that this principle works both ways. If children's services have offerings that will benefit adults, they deserve access as much as children do, and we should provide it in a dignified, nonjudgmental way.

Being welcoming to adults is not always simple for children's librarians, however, whose focus is naturally on children. An adult may enter the children's room with a child, and the natural assumption is that he or she is there on the child's behalf. Similarly, a staff member may assume that an adult who enters the children's room alone is looking for something for an absent child. Worse, an unattended adult may cause unease or distrust on the part of children's staff. While we must always be vigilant against possible abusers, there is no justification for giving less service or being unwelcoming to a customer based solely on his or her age, an argument we are fond of making in a different context. The best response to the lone adult in the children's services department, from both a safety and a customer service standpoint, is to engage the person quickly with friendly, open offers of assistance. Ignoring or misreading the intention of a potentially dangerous person is likely to make the situation more volatile, and doing so to a potential customer who is uneasy about approaching you is likely to squander a golden chance to impress.

This is especially important in the case of an adult who is learning to read or improving lacking reading skills because such an adult may feel embarrassed by having to choose reading material that is designed for children. The payoff, though, is great. Like helping a child learn how to read, helping these adults creates customers for the future, and they will be grateful if the library is able to help them with a problem that has plagued them for many years.

FURTHER READING

Jane Marino, "B Is for Baby, B Is for Books," *School Library Journal*, March 1997, 110–11.

NOTES

1. Stacey Bielick, Kathryn Chandler, and Stephen Broughman, *Homeschooling in the United States: 1999*, NCES Technical Report, 2001–03 (Washington, DC: U.S. Department of Education, National Center for Education Statistics, 2001), 3–7.

2. Ibid, 10.

PART II

The Collection

The children's collection is the most important offering we have to give to young people. Children need a vast amount of reading material, and the types of materials they need change rapidly. An adult of thirty may use the same materials at age forty, but a child of two will certainly not be using the same materials at age twelve. Few people can satisfy the reading needs of children in their own homes, and fewer would like to try. By the same token, a children's library contains various small collections to address the needs of children at many developmental levels. Choosing, acquiring, organizing, and accessing these many collections are a challenge, and these activities take up the majority of most children's librarians' time.

The Collection Development Policy

The management of any library collection begins with its collection development policy. This document should lay out the general goals of the collection and the criteria on which choices will be made—what the priorities are, who is being served, and for what purposes. A collection development policy may also contain specifics about what formats will be chosen, which authors or publishers the library will collect, and other more procedural issues, though such specifics should be kept to a minimum to allow the staff to best fulfill the general goals under changing conditions.

Throughout this section, we will explore each of these aspects of the collection. The choices each library makes are recorded in its collection development policy. But the best answers for the needs of children may not be the best answers for the needs of adults. It is important to recall these different needs, and to advocate for the acknowledgment of the needs of children when this policy is being developed or reviewed.

It is vital to keep in mind the collection development policy when selecting materials because that is the standard against which you may rightly be judged, either in a performance review or when a question arises about the appropriateness of a particular material selected for the children's library. When the collection development policy is out of date or unsuitable for the needs of children's services, the children's staff needs to be proactive in suggesting changes and pushing for revision.

Included in the following are excerpts from actual collection development policies that deal with children's materials. These are real documents, from real libraries, and their inclusion is not to be construed as an endorsement for all libraries everywhere; neither are they meant to be an exhaustive list of components that every collection development policy should have. They are included in order to show some of the basic components of a collection development policy and how the interests of children's services may be represented within such a document.

Mission and Vision Statements

Vision statements speak to the grander design, to what the world would be like if the library collection were absolutely effective. Mission statements speak to what, in the broadest sense, the collection is meant to do or be. It is most important that children's services are mentioned here because these statements are the most visible part of any policy. If one part of the collection policy is seen or quoted, it will most likely be a mission or vision statement.

> The mission of the Tempe Public Library is to provide materials and services to help community residents of all ages obtain information meeting their educational, professional, and recreational needs. Special emphasis is placed on supporting students at all academic levels and on stimulating children's interests and appreciation for reading and learning. The Library serves as an information and educational resource for the community.
>
> In order to meet this mission, the Tempe Public Library's collection must provide a wide range of materials for users of all ages, all educational levels, and all socio-economic backgrounds. The purpose of this document is to further public understanding of the purpose and nature of the library's collection and to provide guidance and direction to the library staff for the development and maintenance of the Library's collection. (Tempe [AZ] Public Library)[1]

The Beebe Library provides people with information for managing their lives. The Library responds to the independent learning and information needs of all ages, and supports educational endeavors from kindergarten through high school. The Beebe Library provides people with recreational reading for enriching their lives, with special emphasis on nurturing a love of reading in young children. (Beebe Memorial Library [Wakefield, MA])[2]

Community Analysis

Community analysis should describe not just the people the library serves but also their needs and circumstances, in order then to lay out explicitly why the library will be important to the community. It is not enough to simply list the ages of the children in the community; rather, the statement should provide details pertaining to education, socioeconomic issues, and the presence or lack of other community resources that might affect what services the library should provide.

> Preschool and elementary age children form an extremely important part of the library's clientele. Fifteen percent of Tempe's population is under the age of twelve. Fostering a love of books and reading is crucial to building an educated and responsible population. Materials for the Youth Services section have an important role in the collection.
>
> The Tempe Public Library's hours of operation are considerably longer than those of school libraries. Since the public library is open in the evening and on weekends, high school, middle school, and elementary students frequently use its facilities and collections for research and study purposes. For that reason, materials are selected specifically with their study needs in mind. Students require access to a broad range of general interest periodicals and newspapers, as well as an accurate and efficient indexing system to locate the information contained within them. The reference collection must include a variety of encyclopedias, dictionaries, collections of literary criticism and other reference tools geared to their age level and subject interests. (Tempe [AZ] Public Library)[3]

Service Roles

Service roles set priorities, helping to focus the library on key concerns and activities. The different service roles involving children's services that the library may choose are discussed in chapter 4, "Purposes and Components." It is vital that children's services be involved in selecting these roles so that children's needs not be pushed aside for other issues deemed more pressing.

Preschool Door to Learning: The library encourages an interest in literacy development and early learning in young children through services to them, their families and caregivers. The Picture Book collection receives primary resource and attention from staff knowledgeable about early childhood development and materials for young children. The Parent Center is a vibrant collection of resources for parents, teachers and caregivers on parenting issues, child development, childcare, preschool learning, home schooling and other relevant topics. This collection also includes special format resources especially for childcare providers, including activity boxes and toys. (Neill Public Library [Pullman, WA])[4]

Responsibility for Selection

Responsibility for selection lays out not just who has ultimate authority, but usually who does the day-to-day work of choosing materials. It is important that the people entrusted with such decisions about the children's collection possess knowledge and experience in children's services and children's literature.

> Final responsibility for the selection of materials rests with the Library Director who acts in accordance with accepted professional practice and those policies established by the Village Board of Trustees and the Library Advisory Committee. The Library Director may delegate materials selection duties to members of the library staff who possess training and experience in the principles and practices of materials selection. The Children's Librarian is primarily responsible for determining the collection needs and ordering materials within the juvenile and young adult areas of the collection. The Library Director gives final approval to all orders. Titles and formats suggested by library staff members and by the general public are given thoughtful consideration and are generally purchased if they conform to the principles of selection outlined in this policy. (Forsyth [IL] Public Library)[5]

Selection Criteria

Selection criteria form the basis for making decisions about what will be added to the collection. Though some criteria may apply to the whole collection, some differentiation has to be made. In the case of children's collections, reading level is the most obvious. Selection criteria are at issue most often when a question arises about the appropriateness of a work for children, or for children of a particular age.

The same selection criteria apply for children as for adults. The subject, vocabulary and format must be suitable to the age and abilities of the children for whom the material is intended. A book of high quality may be approved, however, even though it contains some words and ideas not normally appropriate for children, if they are necessary to portray a period, environment, character, or incident with accuracy and authenticity. (New City [NY] Public Library)[6]

Collections

Many collection development policies break down the collection into more or less specific sections and address the content and purpose of each subsection. These descriptions might address the intended audience, the intended use, or the intended effect of each subsection. Because the children's collection is usually more fragmented than the adult collection, this is one part of the policy where the needs of children take center stage. Collections beyond the traditional print collections—such as audiovisual materials, games, toys, and manipulatives—need special attention here. These collections are often considered to be luxuries—even superfluous— and are therefore the first targets for budget cuts. Their purpose must be defined clearly so that the library staff understands and can articulate what benefits they bring to the community.

> The children's collection serves children through grade five. The children's collection focuses on highly recommended picture books for preschoolers and on popular reading for children of school age. The young adult's collection serves young people from sixth through ninth grade. Beebe Library cooperates with the public school libraries so that these services may complement each other. An effort is made to assemble nonfiction materials that complement the curriculum and homework needs of students through elementary, junior and senior high school.
>
> The collection for children is carefully chosen with the emphasis on materials which entertain, stimulate the imagination, develop reading ability and enable children to learn about the world around them. Materials are purchased in print and nonprint formats including, but not limited to books, periodicals, videocassettes, and computer software. (Beebe Memorial Library [Wakefield, MA])[7]

PICTURE BOOKS

Generally designed for the preschool or primary grade child, picture books may be either fiction or nonfiction. They are distinguished by the art work which may be integrated with, or take precedence over, the text. The quality of illustration and format are of equal importance to the literary merit. (New City Public Library)[8]

BEGINNING READERS

Beginning Readers are intended for kindergarten through early third-grade readers. They are characterized by a controlled vocabulary, large print, heavy use of illustrations, and a limited number of pages. (Tempe Public Library)[9]

JUVENILE FICTION

This collection serves students from late third-grade through sixth-grade. The books feature age-appropriate vocabulary and subject matter, a limited number of pages and very few illustrations. (Tempe Public Library)[10]

JUVENILE NONFICTION

The Juvenile non-fiction collection includes materials to serve the information needs of preschoolers, elementary-age, and middle school students. The subject matter, vocabulary, organization and scope must be age-appropriate. (Tempe Public Library)[11]

REFERENCE

Reference material for children should satisfy their personal interests, their scholastic requirements, and their cognitive abilities. The children's reference collection may also house what is normally circulating material in order to assure that appropriate information is always available. (New City Public Library)[12]

VIDEO COLLECTION

This collection includes films in video or digital video disc (DVD) formats. It is intended to serve the educational and recreational needs of children, ranging from infants through middle school students. The collection includes both fiction and non-fiction selections. (Tempe Public Library)[13]

AUDIOBOOKS

This collection contains recorded books in audio-cassette and compact disc formats. It is intended to serve preschoolers through middle school students. Emphasis is placed on beginning reader materials, however, age appropriate fiction and non-fiction titles are also selected for older children. (Tempe Public Library)[14]

RECORDED MUSIC

This collection includes popular music, educational songs, and games recorded in compact disc format. It is intended to serve infants through elementary school children. (Tempe Public Library)[15]

PARENT COLLECTION

The Parent Collection provides practical advice on child rearing. It is intended for parents, teachers and other interested adults who work with children. Books in the collection deal with areas of physical, emotional, social, and educational development of children from birth through teens. In addition to books, the collection may house newsletters, pamphlets, newspaper and magazine articles. (New City Public Library)[16]

INTERNET

Selection policies which serve to govern the library's purchase of materials are not applicable to material accessed electronically; however, electronic resources are not exempt from routine Collection Maintenance. The library does not endorse the viewpoints or vouch for the accuracy of information provided, including information obtained through the internet.

As with all library materials, it remains the responsibility of the patron (or the parent or guardian) to determine what electronic material is appropriate. (Marshall Public Library [Pocatello, ID])[17]

TOYS

A collection of educational toys, intended for use by pre-schoolers, is available at the Central library and each of the branches. It provides this age group with a way of learning about their world through play and builds a foundation for reading through the development of motor and cognitive skills. The collection consists of items such as puppets, puzzles, and blocks. Each toy is accompanied by an educational card for the parents, detailing ways to use the toy to further enhance skill development. The foundation for reading is also strengthened by attendance at preschool storytimes. To encourage this attendance, the toys are only available for check-out by parents one-half hour before and after storytime. (Pasadena [CA] Public Library)[18]

Intellectual Freedom

Most collection development policies include a statement about Intellectual Freedom and how it relates to the collection. Much of this statement will be relevant to the entire collection, but some mention should be made of the rights of children, since the majority of challenges to the principles of intellectual freedom involve children and the materials they use. Most notably, the library should state clearly and forcefully that it will not be responsible for restricting the materials available to minors.

> The Library does not act in loco parentis by restricting a minor's access to the library, its services, or its collections. The responsibility for monitoring reading, listening, and viewing choices made by children and adolescents belongs to parents. (Polk County [NC] Public Library)[19]

NOTES

1. Tempe Public Library, "Tempe Public Library Collection Development Policy" (approved by the Library Advisory Board April 3, 2003), http://www.tempe.gov/library/admin/colldev.htm.

2. Beebe Memorial Library, "Collection Development Policy" (adopted by the Board of Library Trustees 1997), http://www.wakefieldlibrary.org/acolldev.htm.

3. Tempe Public Library, "Collection Development Policy."

4. Neill Public Library, "Collection Development Policy, Neill Public Library, Pullman, WA" (adopted by the NPL Board July 9, 1997, revised February 2002), http://www.neill-lib.org/colldev.htm#service.

5. Forsyth Public Library, "Collection Development Policy of the Forsyth Public Library: Responsibility for Selection," http://www.forsythlibrary.lib.il.us/policy/3.htm.

6. New City Public Library, "Collection Management Policy" (adopted by the New City Library Board of Trustees March 20, 2003), http://www.newcitylibrary.org/coll-policy-2003.html#children.

7. Beebe Memorial Library, "Collection Development Policy."

8. New City Public Library, "Collection Management Policy."

9. Tempe Public Library, "Collection Development Policy."

10. Ibid.

11. Ibid.

12. New City Public Library, "Collection Management Policy."

13. Tempe Public Library, "Collection Development Policy."

14. Ibid.

15. Ibid.

16. New City Public Library, "Collection Management Policy."

17. Marshall Public Library, "Collection Development Policy" (revised January 18, 2000), http://www.lili.org/marshall/gen_collect.html#VI).

18. Pasadena Public Library, "Collection Development Policy," http://www .ci.pasadena.ca.us/library/collection.asp#Mission%20Statement.

19. Polk County [NC] Public Library, "Library Policies: Collection Development" (approved by the Board of Trustees April 14, 1994), http://www.publib.polknc .org/about/collectiondevelopment.htm.

4

Purposes and Components

Public libraries began at a time when reading materials were expensive and in short supply. Part of the reason for their existence was the desire to bring together what was available to create a critical mass of text. This approach is being relived today in poorer nations around the world, desperate for something—anything—to read. But those days are gone for all but the most needy of public libraries in America. By and large we address not a lack, but an overwhelming flood of text and information. We must choose what we will collect and why, or we will offer no service to the great mass of our customers who are suffering from information overload.

By the same token, public libraries today face the specter of mission creep, the ever expanding scope of our work that threatens to eat away at our ability to do anything well. Nowhere is this more apparent than in our collections, through which we try to inform, enrich, amuse, acculturate, inspire, and uplift our audience, all with limited dollars, space, and staff. The diversity of the community we serve adds a whole other dimension to the challenge of collection development. Before we do anything, we must step back and think. We must decide what we will provide and why.

Roles/Service Responses

Before you decide what materials you will add to the children's collection and how you will use them, you must decide why you are building the collection in the first place. No library has unlimited space and money, so it is important to maintain focus. Not all libraries build their collections to fulfill the same roles, so not all libraries will include the same components. Nor do all libraries address the same roles in their children's collections as they do in their adult collections. Deciding which roles the library will serve is part of the planning process, as laid out in the Public Library Association (PLA) planning documents *Planning for Results: A Public Library Transformation Process* and *Planning and Role Setting for Public Libraries: A Manual of Options and Procedures.*[1] These chosen roles should be codified in the collection development policy, but remember that role selection affects much more than just collection development. There will be more discussion of how to go about making those decisions in chapter 19, "Planning." First, let us take a look at some of the roles (or service responses, depending on which planning method your library uses) and how they might affect collection development in the children's room.

Preschoolers' Door to Learning/Basic Literacy

Even before children read on their own, our role begins as children's doorway to literacy. It is vital that children get an early start on literacy because those children who score low in reading in the early years tend to fall farther behind with time.[2] Literacy requires children to understand the role of language, the use of books, and the structure of story, and to possess the more obvious decoding skills. All of these necessities are provided in our concept and phonics books, our picture books that use visual clues to help fill in the gaps for those who do not yet read, and our early step readers that help children practice newly acquired skills.

Popular Materials Library/Current Topics and Titles

The desire to foster productive use of leisure time was one of the primary incentives for the establishment of public libraries. This objective has a special meaning in the children's room, where we are not only providing materials for recreation but also encouraging the habit of using leisure time productively. In order to fulfill this role, we need to maintain a fiction collection that is up to date, accessible, and interesting to a broad range of readers. Even so, nonfiction is becoming pleasure reading, and this trend is driven in part by publishers who have responded by offering more biographies and high-interest nonfiction at a low reading level.

Reference Library/General Information

A children's library collection can provide the means for children and those who serve them to expand their minds and satisfy their curiosity. To accomplish this, it is necessary to commit time, space, and resources in order to develop a broad and balanced nonfiction collection, including high-interest titles that can be read for pleasure, and also reference-type materials designed to answer questions on a variety of subjects.

Formal Education Support Center/Formal Learning Support

In order for a library to claim that it can offer curriculum support, the collection must include materials that students will use to fulfill the requirements of local schools. This is very different from building a broad and balanced collection to provide information. Curriculum support requires a library to identify which schools' curricula will be supported, by obtaining and reviewing those curricula and then building strong collections in areas of specific concentration within the curricula. Such an effort may actually make building a broad and balanced collection more difficult because space and resources will be dedicated to a narrow range of subjects. Curriculum support also requires a library to collect the materials that educators will need in order to prepare lessons and teach the curriculum.

These efforts are not to be taken lightly; they are expensive, they impact other parts of collection development, and they place the library at the whim of the schools, who may choose not to consult the library about curriculum changes that can require the library to revamp its entire collection. Many public libraries decide not to undertake this task, especially if the local schools have strong media centers whose purpose is more focused. If you do choose to take on this task, make sure you can get copies of the curriculum to keep on hand. Collection development is a continuous process, and the curriculum will be helpful in day-to-day selection, for weeding, and for evaluating the collection. It is also important to keep abreast of changes in the curriculum, so it is worth finding out about the mechanism the schools use to update the documents.

Cultural Awareness

Preservation and transmission of culture are a cornerstone of many libraries' missions. It involves collecting and storing the best of the best from the past, along with the highest-quality materials of the present. It also means collecting representative materials from our own and other cultures—to build awareness and to form a basis for comparison. It is an expensive and space-intensive prospect. Because popularity is not a necessary attribute for this section of the collection, many of these materials will not be used heavily. On the other hand, the use of these materials will likely be slow but constant, whereas popular materials may be used heavily for a while but fall quickly out of favor.

Formats

Little more than a decade ago, the big argument in public libraries was whether paperbacks were appropriate in children's collections, and it was far from universally accepted that they were. Children's collections meant hardcover books. Children's librarians today have to deal with a dizzyingly diverse set of materials. Just the physical format of materials in the collection can cause organizational problems, and every format adds to the pressure on both space within the building and the budget for materials.

Print Materials

Hardcover books are still the basis for most public library children's collections, though their dominance is eroding quickly. Hardcovers stand up to the types of heavy use we expect library books to experience, and are the clear choice for materials we expect to be used often and over a long period of time.

Paperback books have the advantage of being cheap, and therefore easier to replace or collect in multiple copies. They have the disadvantage of not wearing well, and either falling apart or looking ragged after a few uses. For materials whose usefulness or popularity will be short lived, paperbacks are a good choice. They also have the advantage of being preferred by many young readers who equate paperbacks with accessibility. Children's librarians often note that, to a child, a book is acceptable reading only if it fits in a back pocket.

Sales figures for juvenile paperbacks bear out this perception. In 2002, Americans spent $1.6 billion on juvenile paperbacks, up 60 percent from 1998 and nearly matching the amount spent on hardcover juvenile titles, whose sales stayed nearly flat during the same period. Publishers now produce many more juvenile paperbacks (228 million copies in 2002) than juvenile hardcovers (153 million copies in 2002), a reversal of the situation in 1998, when publishers produced 32 million more juvenile books in hardcover than they did in paperback.[3] Paperbacks may look ragged quickly, but even a ragged-looking paperback looks newer and fresher to many young readers than a pristine hardcover, and paperbacks are cheap enough to allow for replacements when they do start looking worn.

Board books are printed on heavy cardboard stock, making them virtually indestructible. They are usually designed for use by babies and toddlers, so they are resistant to tears, saliva, and banging from users who have not quite figured out the real purpose of a book.

Magazines are an ever-growing issue in children's libraries; advertisers have reached for younger and younger audiences and so have supported more and more magazines aimed at children. These publications are a cheap and simple way to bring current, high-interest reading material into the children's section on a regular basis. Like paperbacks, their strength is their currency and accessibility, and when they are no longer current and shiny, it is time to get rid of them and replace them with the next new and interesting thing.

Comic books have made a comeback in recent years, due in part to the nostalgia of the baby boomers and in part to Hollywood's reintroduction of the cartoon character in high-profile movies. Comic books are a cross between a fiction series and a limited-run magazine, so they cannot be treated exactly like a book or a magazine. They are definitely high appeal, and should be featured when they are new, but unlike magazines they have a story line that makes them useful even after the next edition arrives. They are pure pleasure reading, and really fit none of the other roles that libraries may adopt, but what they do, they do well. Many readers with different learning and reading styles are attracted to comic books even if they may not like any other kind of reading. It is not unusual to find adults who say that comic books were the only thing they read voluntarily as children.

Graphic novels are book-length works in comic book format, with text interspersed among the illustrations that dominate the layout. Most are being produced for the young adult/teen market, but some are being produced for, and marketed to, younger readers. One advantage of the format is that children will identify these works with the material that teenagers are reading, and this will make them feel grown up. One potential disadvantage is that parents may make the same connection, and either fear that the younger graphic novels are as violent and risqué as the older ones are believed to be, or fear that a move into graphic novels will lead their children too quickly to the older versions. Librarians must also contend with the difficulty of choosing age-appropriate graphic novels from the limited information in reviews. We need to overcome these fears about this genre because its format appeals to comic book readers and helps them transition into longer stretches of text and more complex story lines.

Nonprint Materials

Not long ago, an audiovisual collection might have consisted of videocassettes, phonograph albums, and a few music cassettes. Audiovisual materials now come in many other formats, and they are taking up more and more space and collection dollars. Because formats are changing so rapidly, these new materials also add complexity to both the development and the organization of collections.

Audio collections may contain both music and the spoken word in both cassette and compact disc formats. Furthermore, compact discs can be in either standard or MP3 format. Spoken word items (books on tape or books on CD) can be either abridged or unabridged, and unabridged works can come either with or without an accompanying book.

Video collections may come in videocassette (VHS) or digital video disc (DVD) format. Although VHS is rapidly being displaced, it will hold on longer in children's movies because many parents will not want to give up collections of old favorites. One could also make distinctions between video for entertainment and video for information or instruction (documentaries).

Digital and interactive media are certainly the most rapidly changing formats the library must confront. The days of computer disks in varying sizes and compatibilities are largely past; most portable digital media is now available on compact disc read-only memory (CD-ROM). The alternative now is CD-ROM versus online access over the Internet. Libraries may choose to buy access to computer files that can then be updated daily by the companies that produce them, and of course much of what is available on the Internet is free. The downside of access over ownership is the lack of control over the information. If the library purchases a game on CD-ROM, for example, the library may use the material whenever it wants and for as long as it wants. The same game, resident on a web page, is no longer available when the web page is down or if the company that maintains the website decides to take the game off the page.

Libraries use different types of digital resources for a number of purposes. The basic example is informational databases for accessing information. More and more, publishers are producing their databases as online resources because Internet access is so prevalent and because updating resources online is so quick; this eliminates the delivery and storage problems that plagued CD-ROM-based databases,. A great example of how these online databases help children's services is Novelist K–8, a fee-based service that finds fiction series, reviews, reading levels, and other information connected with books for children (http://www.epnet.com/school/novelist.asp). Internet access and readers' advisory are both services the library provides (see part 3, "Services"), but the ability to select, purchase, and offer access to databases through the Web makes those databases a collection issue that should be addressed in a collection development policy.

Other digital resources the library may collect include games, usually on CD-ROM, and digital texts, or e-books. E-books are less common in children's rooms than adult rooms, but children's librarians should be aware of them. Every generation is becoming increasingly comfortable with emerging technologies, so these technologies will undoubtedly impact children's services before long. The two problems with electronic texts continue to be reading devices and formats. One needs a device to read an electronic text, even if that device is a personal computer; because full-sized computers are not mobile, the need to use one to gain access to an e-book detracts from the appeal of this new technology. Laptops can also be used, as well as personal digital assistants (such as Palm handhelds) or reading devices designed for this purpose (such as the Rocket e-book reader). Since many people do not own such devices, and so could not use an electronic text collection, some libraries have begun lending out devices as well as texts. Of course the electronic text needs to be compatible with the reader in order for these loans to be useful.

There are numerous problems associated with the licensing and administration of electronic libraries, and much market shakedown may be required before standards emerge that will make these libraries more feasible. Electronic texts have another drawback that is keeping them out of most children's rooms: the inability to present high-quality illustrations. Add to that the fact that children are even less likely to own a device that would enable them to view an electronic text, and it seems likely that children's collections will continue to lag behind adult collections in e-text holdings. Still, children's librarians should keep an eye on digital formats to see which will next invade their children's rooms.

The future may be on display in the International Children's Digital Library (http://www.icdlbooks.org), a free online resource from the University of Maryland and the Internet Archive. It solves the reader problem by making texts available at any Internet workstation, and it solves the illustration problem by using scanned images of the entire book. The downside, of course, is that it lacks the portability of other digital text systems, but the future may find some combination of these approaches in a viable electronic book option.

Many libraries collect and circulate toys, games, puppets, and other objects that enhance the experience of language. These are generally categorized as *manipulatives*. A toy, a puppet, an art tool, or some other item may spark young readers at home just as these objects spark young readers in story hour. Their existence in the collection serves the library's goal of not only providing recreational reading but also promoting reading for recreation. Keeping these items clean and in good repair, ensuring their safety and suitability for different ages, and storing and maintaining the collection are all issues to be considered when beginning a manipulatives collection.

Mixed Media (Kits)

Some libraries collect different media into a unit to produce a multi-format kit that can then be taken into a home or used in a childcare facility as the basis for a program. Usually organized thematically, a kit may include books, audiovisual materials, a manipulative or two such as puppets, games, or a felt storyboard, and art supplies or reproducible items. It is also worthwhile to add materials about the library, its programs, and services for the purpose of cross-promotion. (See chapter 21, "Public Relations, Promotion, and Marketing.")

Kits add a special level of complexity for library staff because the different components must be checked whenever the kit is borrowed or returned: the circulation staff needs to verify that all the contents are there, the children's staff must refill the consumables and check items for currency (art supplies, reproducible items, and promotional materials), and catalogers may find these materials tricky as well. You want people to know what is available in the kits, but customers need to understand that a book included in a kit is only available as part of the kit. Kits also tend to be bulky and hard to store if your library is short on space. Even with the problems and complexities of offering kits, they can be an effective outreach tool, leveraging what the library does through programming by allowing others to re-create the experience at home or in a daycare center. Kits highlight the role of the library as preschoolers' door to learning by emphasizing that it is not just about books but also about the entire language experience.

Reading Levels

Picture Books

Picture book collections are often designated with an *E* for *easy* or *easy reader*, a designation that made more sense before the advent of step readers, which are written at a significantly lower level. Still, the *E* designation is enshrined in Library of Congress cataloging and classification practice, so it is likely to remain a standard for a long time. Picture books are designed to be read to a pre-reading child or by a child reading at an early elementary level. The illustrations tend to be more than decoration; they offer visual clues that reinforce the words, and make the story more rich and more clear than it would be with just the text.

Ellen Tirone, a school media specialist employed at the Greenland Central School in Greenland, New Hampshire, did not like the moniker *easy reader* for picture books. She knew that some children struggled to read these complex stories often designed for adults to read to children, and she believed that calling them *easy* implied that anyone who could not read them was slow or stupid. Still, the collection was marked with an *E*, and everyone in the school was used to connecting that *E* with the picture book collection. So she changed the meaning of *E* to *everybody reads*, embracing the idea that picture books are to be read by a child or to a child.

First Readers

First readers, often called *step readers*, are designed for children just beginning to read; they have large type, few words on a page, and a layout dominated by pictures. First readers are published in a format that looks more like a juvenile novel than a picture book, in order to highlight the fact that children are becoming independent readers. First readers actually take a large step backward in vocabulary and complexity from the picture book collection because picture books are generally designed for adults to read to children.

Juvenile

In most libraries, the juvenile collection constitutes the bulk of the children's collection, ranging from first chapter books up to the young adult/teen collection. That top end varies widely, and how to define the classification is a constant question on electronic discussion lists and in discussion groups; the target age generally ranges from about twelve to fourteen, depending on the strength of the young adult services in the individual library. This means that the juvenile collection may include everything from a forty-page *Magic Tree House* book to an eight-hundred-page volume of *Harry Potter*. For this reason, juvenile collections may be divided in any number of ways or marked with stickers indicating age levels.

The juvenile collection can also be divided by the emergence of genre fiction at this age level. Children throughout these ages are becoming independent, not just in their outlook but also in their tastes. Many libraries choose to create separate shelving areas for science fiction, historical fiction, fantasy, mystery, horror, and humor. In schools that assign genre reading for book reports, the library can create easy-to-find separate collections that are convenient for both students and staff.

Series fiction is also popular at this age because children are still developing as readers and may struggle to get involved in longer books and sustained reading. Reading in series provides familiar settings, characters, and language, helps children continue from one book to the next, and gives them confidence in their skills. Many libraries separate out series fiction so that children, parents, and staff can easily find the next book in a series, or the next series itself. All of these divisions offer some guidance to the library user, but they can also make the juvenile collection a confusing place to be. (See chapter 6, "Organization and Cataloging.")

This is the age range where nonfiction for information first becomes an issue, since this is when children become students needing to do research for school. There will be nonfiction books at the picture book and first reader levels, but at those ages children are reading just for the sake of reading. Most libraries either shelve fiction and nonfiction together at these levels, making no distinctions, or shelve all the nonfiction in the children's room together regardless of the level. The first option has the advantage of putting nonfiction forward as pleasure reading for those children, often boys, who naturally want to read for understanding. The second has the advantage of grouping together books on the same subject on many levels, giving the option of reading level to the one who might need information but not have strong reading skills.

Young Adult/Teen

A young adult or teen collection may be housed in some libraries in the children's room, especially if there is not a dedicated young adult staff and the children's staff is expected to serve this population, but this is not an ideal situation. Young adults generally prefer to be separated from children's services because they feel separate from children, and also because at that developmental level they just want their own space. They also have very distinct needs, which show up in the content of the young adult collection. Books on emerging sexuality, social pressures and problems, rebellion and consequences, even college and career information are beyond the experience of most children and really should be separated from the children's room.

FURTHER READING

Donna Celano and Susan B. Neuman, *The Role of Public Libraries in Children's Literacy Development* (Harrisburg: Pennsylvania Library Association, 2001).

Michael A. Rettig, "Guidelines for Beginning and Maintaining a Toy Lending Library," *Early Childhood Education Journal* 25, no. 4 (1998).

NOTES

1. Ethel Himmel and William James Wilson, *Planning for Results: A Public Library Transformation Process* (Chicago: American Library Association, 1998); Charles R. McClure and others, *Planning and Role Setting for Public Libraries: A Manual of Options and Procedures* (Chicago: American Library Association, 1987).

2. Donna Celano and Susan B. Neuman, *The Role of Public Libraries in Children's Literacy Development* (Harrisburg: Pennsylvania Library Association, 2001), 9.

3. U.S. Bureau of the Census, *Statistical Abstract of the United States* (Washington, DC: Government Printing Office, 2003), 724.

5
Selection and Acquisition

election and acquisition are the process of bringing materials into the library for use by the public. Selection is choosing what materials will be added to the collection, and acquisition means securing those items and paying for them. If the collection is the greatest resource children's services offer to our customers, then selection and acquisition are the most vital activities we do.

Selection

Selecting materials for the collection requires identifying possible items, evaluating them, and then making decisions about what will be added and what will not. Why is the process so important? Because no library can hope to add every available item, or even every item that it deems useful or worthy. The collection development policy is a vital guide, but inevitably the library must choose between items that all fit the criteria as written. In addition, selection and acquisition take resources, most notably the time of librarians who could be performing public service. And if time is money, then every dollar spent paying staff to do selection is a dollar that cannot be spent on something else, like the collection itself.

There is always the concern that choosing between what goes in and what stays out will slip into censorship. This occurs when the decision is based not on the qualities of the item chosen, but on qualities of the item excluded that have nothing to do with the item's usefulness in the collection. Before selection begins, two vital building blocks must be in place— a strongly written collection development policy that outlines the priorities and positive reasons for building a collection, and a clear policy on intellectual freedom. (See chapter 20, "Policy and Procedures.")

Selection Tools

The collection development policy may specify the types and uses of selection tools. For example, librarians might only be authorized to choose juvenile fiction based on a positive review from *Library Journal, Horn Book*, or *Booklist*. The more specific the policy is, however, the less flexibility the staff has to attain the general goals. Under the restrictive rules mentioned above, can the children's staff order the latest in the hot new series about a wizards' school, three woeful orphans, or three time-traveling buddies early enough to have the books available on a much-publicized release date?

Selection tools like those mentioned above are critical or evaluative; they use independent reviewers to judge the quality, scope, and usefulness of a work. These reviews are helpful for selecting books based on quality in so much as you trust the review source. They are not always helpful in determining what will be popular. They are limited in the number of items they can review, and often in the speed with which they publish reviews. Often, the release of popular works will be preceded by large publicity blitzes, and your customers may be convinced they want the book long before you or a reviewer have made up your mind. Critical or evaluative selection tools include *Library Journal, School Library Journal, Booklist, Book Links*, and the *Children's Library Catalog*, specifically the regular updates that list newer works judged worthy of inclusion in a core collection. If you are charged with buying for the young adult/teen section, you might check *Voice of Youth Advocates* (*VOYA*), *KLIATT*, and the Young Adult Library Services Association's annual "Best Books for Young Adults."

Noncritical or nonevaluative sources offer either no review, or reviews that are intended to sell, and as such are suspect in their completeness and honesty. On the other hand, these sources often mention prepublished titles months before they appear in the more critical review sources. Some, such as *Publishers Weekly*, give valuable commercial information about printing size, marketing efforts, and author activities that may affect demand for a particular title. These sources have more relevance for popular or timely materials than the critical review sources. Noncritical or nonevaluative sources include *Publishers Weekly, Forthcoming Books,* individual publishers' catalogs and websites, which often announce new releases long before other sources, and catalogs produced by the major book jobbers, the companies that distribute publishers' works to bookstores and libraries, such as Baker and Taylor or Brodart.

Centralized Selection

In larger library systems, selection may be centralized, which means that one person or a committee chooses which items will go in all of the branches. The advantage of this approach is to streamline the process and not take frontline service staff away from their primary duties. It works because there is probably little variation between the wants and needs of different neighborhoods in the same community. The disadvantage of this system of selection is that it may not address localized differences, and failure to take these into account may mean that some customers are not well served. Being on the selection committee is one way to make sure those needs are met, and to gain some valuable professional experience (see chapter 22, "Professional Development"). Even if you are not part of centralized selection, you must devote some of your time to making suggestions to the selector(s). After all, if you are the one working with your local customers, you know better than anyone what they are reading.

In smaller libraries, centralized selection may just mean that one person chooses materials for all age levels. Efficient, yes, but to make this kind of selection work the people working closest with the customers must be willing to make suggestions regularly, and the selector has to be aware that personal relationships are a surer way of choosing materials to satisfy people's needs than any review source could ever be.

Automated Selection

There are any number of ways to streamline the process of selecting materials, many based on the effective use of technology and allowing specialized vendors to use economies of scale to do much of the grunt work more efficiently. Like centralized selection, these methods seek to save resources that would have gone into selection (staff time mainly) for more service-oriented work. Each of these methods promises to do just that, but at a cost of some control. In each case, a vendor is offering a value-added service: we will do some part of the acquisitions task if you buy our materials. You should weigh the time saved against the loss of control in order to decide if automated selection is worthwhile.

Standing orders are the simplest and most innocuous of these automated selection approaches, and even the smallest of libraries are likely to have some standing orders. A standing order is for forthcoming installments in a series. Once the next book is published, you tell your supplier, just ship it. This saves time if you have already gone through the selection process for the series and know that it is something you want to keep current. Often review sources will not review later installments in a series if they have already reviewed an earlier one, so relying on reviews for the selection process of these titles would actually be impossible.

The downside is that you do not get to pick and choose which books from the series meet your needs. If you place a standing order on a series of books about countries around the world, you may have little need for an entire book on a small principality in Europe, but if that is the next book in the series it will come to you nonetheless. Some standing-order plans allow you to return individual titles; make sure you know the rules on returns before entering into an agreement.

Blanket orders are broader, saving more time but also proving more problematic. A blanket order is an instruction to a supplier to ship anything it carries by a certain author, on a certain topic, or from a certain publisher. (The supplier and the publisher may be one and the same.) For libraries with a strong and specific mission, such as a seminary library that will surely buy everything produced by several small religious publishers, this not only saves time, but it also ensures the completeness of their collections. For a public library, however, it is more likely that a blanket order on a popular author or from a small publisher focused on local issues would make sense. The loss of control here is even greater than with a standing order, and even if returns are allowed, if the library spends more time sorting through materials it doesn't want than it saves on the front end, then the whole process may be counterproductive.

Approval plans are more common in public libraries and especially in children's services. With an approval plan, the library fills out a profile of the type of items it might be interested in purchasing, and the supplier ships selections that fit the criteria on a regular basis. The staff of the library then reviews each item and decides which it will buy. The process of selection still goes on, but the supplier streamlines some of its components. It collects new publication information and weeds out items in areas in which the library does not collect. Often the supplier will include reviews with the items for consideration, and this can save the staff considerable legwork. For children's items especially, the ability to hold the item, examine illustrations, glossaries, indexes, and the like is a great improvement over buying from a printed review. The downside is that selection must be done on a regular basis. There is a contract to fulfill, and the staff must meet the schedule the library has agreed to.

Gifts

Libraries add donated books and other materials as a way of filling out a collection for no more than the cost of processing the items. Especially valuable are those gifts that come from avid readers who must have the latest and hottest book, and cannot wait even a few days to get their hands on it. Once they have read the book, they may hand it over to the library; these extra copies of the latest and hottest books shorten reserve lists for everyone else. But gift books are a two-edged sword, especially when the library is inundated with books that would not be of any benefit to the collection, donated by people who are sure they would be.

On one hand, it is outrageous to think that a book that was not fitting for a personal collection would be usable in a public collection. On the other hand, it is sometimes hard to justify to a well-intentioned donor that you need to spend tax money buying books when you will not accept a perfectly good book for free. Of course there are other issues. Gifts of books may well reflect a very personal point of view, may in fact be polemics or even falsehoods, and while adult collections often include a fair amount of this type of material, most children's collections try to avoid it. Books get hard use in public libraries, children's books harder than most, at least if they are any good. A book that has been used a few times by a child at home may have little shelf life left in it.

The time-tested way of handling gift books is to put them through the same selection process as any book being considered for purchase. If your collection development policy addresses gift books, as it should, then it probably says something similar. If the issue is not addressed in the collection development policy, children's librarians especially need to see that it is. Feelings always run hotter around children, and you do not want to be in a position of justifying why you did or did not accept a gift book into the collection without some basis to fall back on.

Acquisition

Once you have selected items, you then have to procure them. This is the process of acquisition, and children's librarians may not have much to do with it in many libraries. Some type of order form or suggestion form is filled out and handed off to the acquisitions department, and the book simply appears at a later date. Children's librarians should be aware, however, of what goes into what might be seen as a simple process, because they may someday be in a library small enough that the children's librarian must order his or her own materials. Even when there is an acquisitions department, knowledge of the process will help a children's librarian understand how to make the process work efficiently, and what will make it grind to a halt.

Ordering

The trend these days is clearly toward electronic ordering of materials. If done well, this saves a huge amount of time that can then be plowed back into some more productive activity. If not done well, electronic ordering just adds one level of complexity to an old and unproductive system. Find out exactly what information is needed to place an order. If you are not actually ordering materials yourself, watch someone else go through the process. What does the acquisitions librarian need to identify the item you want? What are the most likely mix-ups?

Specifying a board book on your request form might ensure the proper format, unless the online ordering package that is being used does not display format prominently. In that case, listing the International Standard Book Number (ISBN) might be more effective, unless the supplier uses its own proprietary ordering number. You can fill out voluminous order forms with title, edition, page numbers, Library of Congress Control Number, format, publisher, city of publication, and a thousand other details, but if the ordering system allows the librarian to simply enter a string of ISBNs then you have wasted a huge amount of time that might have been better spent serving children.

Find out what purchasing contracts and consortium-buying agreements the library is involved in. These may affect when orders need to be placed, which materials are available in which format, and how requests have to be made. They may also affect the cost of materials because some agreements will give better discounts than others. Find out, too, if the library takes requests from customers, and if so, how seriously. Does the library automatically buy what customers request, or does it simply consider them? This will affect how popular materials are ordered. Understanding in advance how the library handles these aspects of ordering will save you much time and aggravation.

Record Keeping and Budgeting

Depending on your level of autonomy in ordering materials, you may also need to keep track of how much you spend in order to budget your money over the year. Good record keeping is essential and well worth the time investment. You have to keep track not only of what has been delivered and paid for but also of what the library has ordered. Applying the cost of items to your accounts when they are ordered is called encumbering, which means setting money aside against a future expense. When you are encumbering money, remember to factor in discounts, shipping charges, and surcharges. Find out when orders to any given vendor expire, so you can disencumber the funds and either reorder the materials or order something different.

Budget your money out over the course of the budget cycle, which usually spans a year. That does not mean to divide all the accounts by twelve and spend the same amount each month. Neither children's publishing nor your schedule fit so easily into such a regular rhythm. Most children's trade books are published in spring and fall, and the large majority are released in spring. The children's book market is tight and competitive; if a book does not do well it may go out of print with amazing speed and be dropped into the remainder market, where it may become difficult and expensive to procure. If you want to purchase trade titles when they are new and fresh, you will need to pay close attention to their release times.

Mass-market publication is more constant. Series books come out every month or six months; big releases are spread out to cut down on competition. Marketing to a younger and younger audience is becoming commonplace, so children's titles are becoming demand sensitive the way adult mass-market titles have been for decades. Budgeting for these materials can be more regular, but you can also expect to pour extra resources into building a popular collection before the beginning of summer, so that you have more new titles on the shelves when demand for this type of reading materials is highest. By the same token, you should plan to spend more money on nonfiction in the fall, especially if you have a productive relationship with local teachers who let you know about upcoming projects while you still have time to order materials to fill in gaps.

THE POPULAR MATERIALS DEBATE

Few issues in children's librarianship are as heated, or as relevant to the lives of our customers, as the debate over the place of truly popular materials in our children's libraries. While it is now fairly standard for adult fiction collections to include, and even to be dominated by, transient, high-interest, low-literary-value materials, often purchased through demand-based acquisition, such is not the case in most public children's libraries. The reasoning is clear and honorable enough; we need to be more careful and protective of children who may lack the sophistication to make their own choices. The effect, though, is not so clear.

There are many librarians out there who believe that children's libraries should not contain paperbacks, or that paperback collections should not be cataloged or shelved with hardcover collections. On the other side are the librarians who see popular literature for children as a way to encourage reading for pleasure, and especially a way to reach out to reluctant readers. Books that appeal to boys seem to get a disproportionate amount of scorn, a point not unconnected to the fact that boys tend to read less than girls. *The CREW Method*, a manual for collection evaluation and weeding, states that books "featuring cartoon characters such as Strawberry Shortcake, the Care Bears, and the Teenage Mutant Ninja Turtles are not suitable for library use . . . are trite commercial publications intended only to sell a product." But many librarians see books with media tie-ins as an excellent outreach tool.

Some of the disconnect will be bridged by time and the evolution of children's publishing. The old belief that any book truly worth reading is worth publishing in hard cover is a relic of the past; quality children's books are now regularly republished in paperback or even originally published in paperback. Librarians have largely accepted that many children prefer to read paperbacks, either because of their portability or because they look cooler. The quality of many series books, even the monthly pulp series, is rising dramatically, and well-established children's writers such as Gary Paulsen have published in this periodic format. The push for free or undirected reading in schools is changing the patterns of demand in public libraries. Media tie-ins today are just as likely to be to developmentally conscious programming like *Bob the Builder*, *Blue's Clues*, or *Bear in the Big Blue House*, as they are to be to simple corporate shills.

These purely practical circumstances will change the popularity versus quality debate, but there is also a philosophical aspect to the issue, and it involves the principle of equal access (the "Horton Principle" from chapter 2, "Principles of Children's Librarianship"). If public libraries routinely serve the desire of adults to read for pure, escapist pleasure, then why do we not afford the same service to children? Go back to your collection development policy and see if Popular Materials Library is one of your chosen roles, or if Current Topics and Titles are high on your list of service responses. Does the policy state that only one set of customers is deserving of this consideration? If not, then you have a real basis for building popular materials into your children's collection. If the policy does distinguish between who is deserving of popular materials and who is not, then you have a reason to sit down with the policy makers in your library and discuss the library's commitment to equal access.

6

Organization and Cataloging

Having the right materials in your collection is meaningless if you cannot present it in a way that people find useful. The organization of library materials is a skill that librarians take great pride in, and rightly so. The great libraries manage to put incredible volumes of information in a logical arrangement—a place for every book, and every book in its place. Unfortunately, much of the cataloging and organization of materials is done with an eye toward the expert, either the subject expert or the librarian. As a reference instructor once joked, a cataloger's job is to hide books so the reference librarian can go find them.

Cataloging has not always made a smooth transition from the research or university library to the public library. Even less well suited is this academic model to the children's library. We have to understand that the model we might see in the great libraries, or even learn in library schools, fits the needs of its environment. We need to copy its spirit, not necessarily its form. When done right, the organization of library materials in the public library children's room is the first step toward user-friendly customer service.

Organization

Multiply the number of components in your children's collection by the number of formats, and then by the number of reading levels, and you have some idea of how a children's library is organized. You could easily have separate collections for board books, picture books, easy readers, first readers, first chapter books, juvenile fiction, juvenile nonfiction, juvenile reference, juvenile mysteries, juvenile science fiction, juvenile fantasy, juvenile historical fiction, juvenile series books, fairy tales, award-winning books, new books, easy reader books and cassettes, easy reader books and compact discs, juvenile audio cassettes, juvenile compact discs, juvenile videos, juvenile DVDs, parenting books, circulating puppets, and story hour kits.

That right there are twenty-five separate collections, not counting any purely local distinctions you might make for school reading lists, local interests, and the like. Each collection needs its own call numbers, and possibly its own material type or designation on the computer cataloging system. This confusing cataloging also creates the potential for a shelving nightmare that might make your collection exceedingly difficult for your customers or other staff members to navigate.

Choosing how many separate collections to have and what they will be also decides how accessible the collection will be. Even if the children's staff does not catalog its own materials, the staff members should be responsible for determining how the children's collection is organized. Too little division, and the collection will not be accessible to browsers. Too much division, and maintenance and order will be difficult to maintain, and those looking for specific items will find it hard to locate them. There was one very small library in New Hampshire that made no division, by age, format, or any other criteria. Every item in the library was assigned a Dewey number and shelved in one long continuous sequence, with fiction distributed through the 800s. Another library, not thirty miles away, had to resort to a chart showing more than sixty call number patterns, colored dots, and genre stickers dividing just the children's book collection; audio and video materials were separate.

Cataloging

In some libraries, especially small and rural ones, the children's librarian may be assigned to catalog the children's collection. There is no way to detail how to catalog in this book. Some fine and useful books about cataloging are available, but a cataloging class is best for the nuts and bolts. What is covered here are those parts of cataloging that most directly affect children and children's services, and those areas where children's material cataloging differs from adult material cataloging. Even if you never do any cataloging in your library, it is important to know how cataloging is done if you are going to use the library's catalog. The children's librarian should also represent the interests of children and parents in determining local cataloging protocol—and yes, there are local differences in cataloging.

How does children's cataloging differ from adult cataloging? The users of the catalog are often children who lack some of the sophistication of adult users. They are more likely to type *bunny* instead of *rabbit*, less likely to know the difference between a subject and a keyword, or to be looking for a specific author or title, and more likely to be browsing. Parents, too, will be using the catalog differently than if they were searching for adult material; they might be looking for subject access to fiction or for reading-level assistance, for example, both of which are routinely left out of local library cataloging protocols.

Children's specialists should always represent the needs of children and those who care for them. Sometimes that will mean developing local policy or deciding between two recognized practices. Children's librarians must always remember, though, that the catalog serves all the library's customers, and the library's cataloging may be part of a much larger union catalog. Catalogers may be sympathetic to children's needs, but limited in what they can do to alter cataloging by agreements set up at the consortium level to ensure a unified and understandable catalog.

Descriptive Cataloging Elements

While cataloging rules apply to all materials, some elements of a Machine-Readable Cataloging (MARC) record (or old-fashioned catalog card) are more helpful when cataloging children's materials, either because of the nature of the item, or more often, because of the needs of the intended audience. Remember, too, when using these elements that library staff, both children's and non-children's, will be using these records for reference and readers' advisory.

Notes in general give flexibility to address specific needs. The summary note (MARC record field 520) describes the important elements of the book in simple, nonjudgmental terms. It is useful to expect keyword searching when writing this note. Synonyms of difficult or ambiguous terms in the title are helpful, as well as words that may come to mind more naturally than those used in the subject terms. A target audience note

(MARC 521) can be used to highlight either reading level or interest level, which are not always the same.

The awards note (MARC 586) is the place for noting Newbery, Caldecott, *Horn Book*, Coretta Scott King, and local or state awards.[1] These awards are much more likely to come in handy for readers' advisory than the various awards for adult writing, so catalogers who handle mostly adult materials might not think to add them. Even if your library receives cataloging from an outside source, the local and state awards are probably not included. Also, these awards can be announced well after the library has purchased a copy of the book, so it is up to children's specialists to note the awards and ask catalogers to add them to the records.

Subject Headings

Standard Library of Congress (LC) subject headings often do not serve children well, and so the Library of Congress provides Annotated Card (AC) headings, which can be substituted for the standard headings. AC headings are designed for catalogs that only contain children's materials, or for Online Public Access Catalogs (OPACs) that can be set to access only children's materials. They drop such distinctions as juvenile, children's, juvenile fiction, and juvenile literature. AC headings include form designations such as stories in rhyme, which would not be included in standard LC subject headings. They also substitute common names of animals, plants, and the like for the scientific names that are used in regular LC headings.[2]

AC headings apply both a general and a specific subject heading if an item contains information that could be used by someone looking for information at either level, a circumstance that is much more likely for children's material than for adult material. A third-grade student doing a report on bears is likely to find something useful in a book on polar bears, and the same student doing a report on polar bears is likely to be helped by a general book on bears.

When printed on paper catalog cards or in Cataloging-in-Publication (CIP) data, AC headings appear in brackets, allowing the cataloger to choose which headings to use. When records are downloaded into online cataloging systems, both sets of headings appear with the only difference being AC subject headings have a numeral *one* in the second indicator in the 6*xx* field, making both subjects look equal to the user. It is common practice to leave both subject headings in the record.[3]

The major alternative to LC subject headings is the *Sears List of Subject Headings*. Sears is a system designed particularly for use in small public libraries. It is significantly shorter, one small volume to four enormous volumes of LC headings. It is more flexible, offering guidelines and examples, then explicitly allowing the cataloger to use the example to create new headings for specific subjects. Sears tends to use simpler terms and less academic language.[4] While the two sets of headings are very similar in many ways, Sears tends to simplify matters in ways that benefit smaller collections and less sophisticated users, and so it is very attractive for children's collections. Its major drawback is that LC headings come standard on most cataloging records. Vendors may be able to supply Sears headings as part of the library's cataloging profile, but Sears headings may also mean more work for catalogers over the long haul.

Libraries need to make a decision about which headings to use and be consistent about the choice, especially if more than one person in the library does cataloging and all the more so if one of those people is a children's specialist. Using LC headings in one case and Sears headings for a different item on the same subject makes it hard for library users to find all the material that might be useful to them. While it is permissible to use either standard or AC Library of Congress subject headings for the same subject when the items are at different levels (children's and adults), it is by no means necessary to do so. AC cataloging rules allow both scientific and common names to be used for the same item, allowing access via the common name for children and consistency with adult items at the same time. It is important to remember that the catalog is a tool used by all, and the goal is for everyone's needs to be met. The catalog can serve children, and the children's collection can serve adults; equal access is a two-way street.

Classification

Classification involves the assigning of call numbers to items. This cannot be done effectively until decisions are made about the organization of the collection as a whole and the item itself has gone through descriptive cataloging and subject analysis. Of course, cataloging records from the Library of Congress or a cataloging vendor will likely have classification included. Classification, though, is much more of a local issue than any other part of cataloging. Chances are, your library has locally developed classification rules. Make sure you know what they are and how they apply to children's materials. While standardization is a major goal of cataloging and classification, there are elements of classification especially that must be modified to make them work in the children's libraries. If catalogers are working under one single set of classification rules, children will not be well served.

Library of Congress cataloging rules assign fiction classifications of *E* when the item's intended audience is preschool through second grade. For third-grade through ninth-grade audiences, fiction is assigned a heading of *Fic.* Some larger public libraries use Library of Congress classification to assign call numbers to nonfiction items, but most assign Dewey Decimal. In either case, nonfiction classification is done at least at the *J* level from grades three to nine. What to do with clearly nonfiction titles written below that level is a purely local decision. Your library may simply assign these books an *E* designation and interfile them with the picture books, may assign them a *J* and a Dewey number and interfile them with juvenile nonfiction, or may have a separate *E* nonfiction section, though this is relatively rare.

Depending on the size of your library, the Dewey numbers may be assigned using the full *Dewey Decimal Classification and Relative Index*, the *Abridged Dewey Decimal Classification and Relative Index*, or some combination of the two. The abridged version is generally considered a better fit for children's collections, where nuances of approach and gradients of subject matter are not very useful. If the library has a single cataloging policy, it may assign children's numbers exactly the same way it assigns adult numbers, and that might mean unabridged Dewey numbers. Abridged Dewey numbers are not just shorter, and in fact that is not the primary distinction. Abridged Dewey numbers have fewer divisions, grouping larger numbers of subtopics under a single classification. It will chunk up a collection more with broader connections between books. For children still exploring broad topics, this is usually a better fit than the full Dewey numbers, which help a more sophisticated user find exactly what he or she wants.

Local cataloging policy might also stipulate the preferred length of a Dewey number. Dewey numbers listed on cataloging records from the Library of Congress or cataloging vendors are often broken up by slashes or apostrophes, showing places where a number can be logically divided in order to make a number more or less general. While it might make sense to separate cookbook numbers by nationality (641.5951 for Chinese cooking) for an adult audience, it could make more sense to use a more general number (641.5 for cooking) in the children's room.

Juvenile biographies can be assigned Dewey Decimal numbers consistent with what the person was known for, such as sports, medicine, or entertainment, or they can be assigned a *B* or *92* classification and shelved separately as biographies, filed alphabetically by the subject's last name. While sports fans are likely to appreciate finding all the books about baseball in one place, including biographies of famous baseball players, the value of shelving all biographies together usually outweighs any inconvenience it can create. Biography collections are helpful when there is a school biography assignment, and some young readers enjoy reading biographies for pleasure reading. You can use the subject analysis in your catalog to direct readers looking for specific topics to books that relate to those topics.

Folklore and fairy tales are a much larger part of most children's collections than most adult collections, so they deserve special attention. They may also represent a separate collection. If that is the case, local policy will dictate what qualifies for the folklore collection, and children's staff should of course be primary in making those distinctions. If folklore is retained in the classification sequence, then classification rules apply. Folklore comes from unwritten traditions of oral and visual transmission, and does not include modern works in imitation of older works. Faithful retelling of originally oral material qualifies as folklore, but drastic alterations of even traditional stories are considered fiction. Religious mythology and written scriptures are classed with religion.[5]

A CATALOGER'S VIEW

Linda Kepner, assistant director of the Peterborough, New Hampshire, Town Library is something of a cataloging guru, regularly giving classes, workshops, and conference presentations on the subject. Her priority for children's cataloging and classification: location.

1. The call number and spine tag should clearly mark the location of the book. If a book belongs in a special section, make sure that location is reflected in the call number so that the book appears in its proper place in the shelflist (computer-generated or otherwise).

2. Do not put reading level or genre designations on the spine if they do not relate to where the item is shelved. "I have had shelvers try to find the Science Fiction section for hours because there was a Sci-Fi sticker above the spine label, not knowing we don't have a special section."

3. Communicate with catalogers and other staff members. They do not use your collection every day. If you change your collections, let people know. "We've had the Overdues Librarian charge for missing books that neither she nor I nor the parent could find on the shelf, not knowing the children's librarian had 'created a new section' that only she knew about."

FURTHER READING

Melvil Dewey, *Abridged Dewey Decimal Classification and Relative Index*, 14th ed. (Albany, NY: Forest Press, 2004).

Carolyn W. Lima, *A to Zoo: Subject Access to Children's Picture Books*, 6th ed. (Westport, CT: Bowker-Greenwood, 2001).

Minnie Earl Sears, *Sears List of Subject Headings*, 18th ed. (New York: H. W. Wilson, 2004).

Sharon Zuiderveld, ed., *Cataloging Correctly for Kids: An Introduction to the Tools*, 3rd ed. (Chicago: American Library Association, 1998).

NOTES

1. Sharon Zuiderveld., ed., *Cataloging Correctly for Kids* (Chicago: American Library Association, 1991), 9–10.

2. Lois Mai Chan, *Cataloging and Classification: An Introduction*, 2nd ed. (New York: McGraw-Hill, 1994), 208–10.

3. Zuiderveld, *Cataloging Correctly for Kids*, 12–13.

4. Ibid., 67–70.

5. Ibid., 14.

7

Evaluation and Deselection/ Weeding

he director of a medium-sized Massachusetts library was holding the floor at one of those stand-around-and-make-small-talk types of gatherings, when he posed an interesting question. His library had just undergone a yearlong renovation, and for that time it had moved into a temporary space and had been forced to put 95 percent of the collection in storage. When he did his statistics for the year, the director was shocked to find that circulation had dropped only 3 percent. Now how should he react to this?

Two points here should be instructive to anyone managing a collection. The first is that this library was clearly carrying a great deal of material that was not of use to the community. Somehow the process of evaluating the collection had failed. The second point would be that when his staff prepared for moving to a smaller space, they did a masterful job of, in effect, weeding out 95 percent of the collection and keeping what really mattered. The best advice to the director may have been to forget where he put the 95 percent of his collection and to start his new library with the 5 percent that was working for him.

Choosing books in order to repair, remove, reclassify, or otherwise change their status is called collection maintenance. Collection maintenance is a job that few of us enjoy, and one that in fact too many of us avoid altogether, but it is vital to the effectiveness of our selection and acquisition activities. We need to move items out of the collection to make room for new items. The presence of superseded or dated items makes it hard to find relevant materials. In addition, when customers encounter ragged, unpleasant-looking, or unpleasant-*smelling* items in the library, this experience makes them not want to rummage through our collections, or to trust the content of the materials.

Before you begin to look at your collection as it is, look at the collection as it should be—by carefully reviewing the collection development policy. You need to do this for two reasons. First, you have to know what the policy says you should be doing to the collection. Check the roles or service responses to know where the emphasis of the collection is supposed to be. Check for rules that affect purely local issues, such as local authors, history, or genealogy. Find out if there are specific rules for weeding already in place, or specific programs to be followed.

Also, check to see who has the authority to weed. If that authority rests with an administrator, see what part of the process may be delegated and to whom. Never weed a collection without the knowledge and approval of the person or persons with final weeding authority. It is likely that your role will be only to pull items you think should be weeded and to set them aside for final approval by someone else.

The next step is to see if there are aspects of the policy that do not make sense and that need to be changed. It is not a good idea to simply disregard the policy as written and to go ahead with evaluation and weeding on your own terms. Weeding materials in a public library involves disposing of public property, which is a touchy subject both from a legal and public relations point of view. Your work will be judged in relation to the policy, and in the event of questions or problems down the road, you want a policy to back you up. (See chapter 20, "Policy and Procedures," for more on this.) Check the policy and bring specific suggestions for changes to your administrator, along with the reasons you believe the policy should be changed. Whatever the decision of the administration or governing body, you should proceed in accordance with it.

Evaluation

Before looking for individual items to weed, it is worthwhile to take a look first at the collection as a whole. What is the turnover rate (circulation divided by number of items) for all children's material? What is the turnover rate for all children's books? What is the average age of the collection? How much does the library spend on children's materials per year, and how many new items does that buy? These questions will give you a general baseline to look at when evaluating subsections of the collection. It will help you decide which parts of the collection are underused, outdated, or overdue for an overhaul.

Once a picture has been made of the whole collection, then look at discrete sections of the collection. That section may be as large as juvenile fiction, or as small as a few Dewey Decimal numbers. It may be divided by subject, format, or reading level. The important thing is to identify a group of materials that serve some similar purpose, and to see how those items are used. Modern circulation systems can give you vast amounts of information if you know how to ask for it. Find out the number of items in the section you have selected, the total circulation and average age, the individual age and circulation of each item, and when each item last circulated.

Laid out visually, this information may tell you valuable things about the usefulness and size of the section. If the average use of the items is low, and a few newer items have moderately better use than the rest, then the section is probably too large and would benefit from some stern weeding. If the average use is high despite the fact that the average age is high, then the section is too small and should be expanded through acquisition. If some newer items receive heavy use and older ones receive little to none, then you have a section that needs sprucing up by weeding and replacing the discarded titles with newer ones.

If a section contains newer materials but still does not receive consistent use, then you must make some decisions about why. Is it possible that this section doesn't meet any need that exists within the community? Is it not addressed in the school curricula, or at least not at this particular reading level? Is it a topic that was once popular, but now is not? Finally, do you have a classification problem? Books about holidays in different countries can be shelved together, but it might make more sense to break them up and put them with the countries they represent, especially if holidays are studied as part of a geography unit in the local schools and students are looking for many types of information on a single country.

Deselection/Weeding

Now you are ready to make decisions about individual items. It is important to remember that you are evaluating the collection, not just weeding.

Items that are not being used effectively may be weeded, but they may also be repaired if falling pages make an otherwise useful book too hard to handle, replaced if the physical condition of an item is too far gone for it to be useful, rebound if it is in bad shape but out of print, or moved to another part of the collection if it is just not classified where it will be of the most use. For each of these decisions, the cost of the action must be weighed against the general usefulness of the item. Newer items tend to be used more than older ones, so if the cost of saving or repurchasing an item is equal or greater than the cost of replacing it with a different title, then saving the item may not be worthwhile.

Deciding when to remove an item from the collection, sometimes called deselection, should be done based on clear criteria that also leave room for judgment. One basic approach, often enshrined in the collection development policy, is that deselection uses the same criteria as selection, or more simply, if the item would not be added to the collection today, then it should be weeded. Simplicity is this approach's great strength. A single set of criteria is used throughout the collection development process. This approach has one weakness: if the book is filling some need for which the library has no better substitute, it could be preferable to retain the less-than-ideal item than to create a hole. In areas such as medicine or law, of course, this argument holds no water. Outdated information in some areas is downright dangerous.

If a distinct set of criteria is to be adopted for deselection, the library may choose a predetermined methodology, such as the Continuous Review Evaluation and Weeding (CREW) method. This method systematizes the major factors to be considered when deselecting and puts them into a logical framework. Judgment and good common sense are always the final determinants. The manual for the CREW method lists these weeding factors for all materials as "date, author, publisher, physical condition, additional copies, other books on the same subject in the collection, expense of replacement, shelf time (i.e., time spent on the shelf without circulating), relevance of the subject to the community," and then adds the following factors for juvenile and young adult materials: "format, reading level, current interest in the subject matter, jacket art (contemporary vs. outmoded)."[1]

The CREW Manual and the subsequent revision entitled *The CREW Method* go on to chart these factors against specific portions of the collection, establishing clear guidelines for how old and how unused an item should be before it is weeded, and listing the factors that might automatically make an item a candidate for weeding. Those factors are embodied in the acronym MUSTIE: Misleading, Ugly, Superseded, Trivial, Irrelevant, or available Elsewhere through interlibrary loan.[2]

One of the real weaknesses of CREW is that it makes no clear distinction between children's and adults' materials, a shortcoming only partly addressed in the newer version. If CREW is adopted as a policy for all weeding in a library, children's staff should look to make clear exceptions at the procedural level where factors such as the local curriculum should affect weeding. If no preestablished method for weeding is articulated in the collection development policy, then a method for making deselection decisions must be developed. As *The CREW Method* points out, there are many factors to consider. These factors can be grouped under four basic headings: content, condition, currency, and accessibility.

Content

The content, or the information contained in an item, must be such that it is useful to library customers. The information, if it is a nonfiction item, must above all be accurate. This is more important to a children's collection than to an adult collection because children are less likely to have the skills needed to evaluate a work, to recognize an author or publisher, or to check the facts they read against other sources. The content must also be relevant in some way to what library customers are looking for. This is where evaluation of an entire section is most valuable. If the library has thirteen books on pet rocks, with a total annual circulation of two checkouts, then the content of this section dictates that most of those titles must go.

To judge the quality of content, check items against standard and best lists, such as Wilson's *Children's Catalog* and *Middle and Junior High Catalog*. For recent titles see *Booklist* magazine's annual Editor's Choice lists, published in the January 1 and January 15 editions each year. Of course there are any number of awards that can be used to mark works that are likely to have lasting value, such as the Caldecott, Newbery, *Horn Book*, and Coretta Scott King awards. If an item appears in these places, it is likely that the content is of high quality, and this should affect your decision. If the item does not appear in these places, it does not mean that its content is bad, but all other factors being equal, it is a more likely candidate for weeding than those items that are so mentioned.

Condition

The best book in the world is of no use (and therefore has no place in a public library children's room) if its condition is such that no one wants to use it or trusts that it is useful. No, you can't judge a book by its cover, but everybody does. In addition, the presence of tattered items makes the entire collection look old and unreliable. No one will trust a collection if it appears uncared for. Items suffering from mildew or disintegrating into dust can actually harm other materials shelved near them. Some negative physical conditions, such as illegible print or cumbersome bindings or rebindings, are products of how the item was made.

Other physical shortcomings come from age and use, such as worn pages, broken bindings, and superseded formats. Multipart items such as audiobooks, kits, and language sets can be missing valuable pieces, including tapes or compact discs, liner notes, and instruction books. Alterations by customers can include the innocent crayon markings of a two-year-old, or the purposeful censoring of an upset adult. Audiovisual materials can fade or deteriorate in picture or sound quality. Electronic media can become demagnetized.

If your collection is well built, then it will be well used. Books that are in bad shape because of heavy use may be good candidates for replacement, if it can reasonably be expected that the heavy use will continue. Otherwise, old, tired-looking items can often be replaced by newer titles that will serve the same purpose and hopefully become grizzled veterans themselves someday. While librarians often shudder at the thought of weeding, deselecting these particular items should make the librarian proud. They were appropriate choices that were well promoted and did what they were purchased to do.

Currency

Currency is especially important for items like popular fiction whose main draw is its freshness. Libraries should always have materials that are new and exciting, but if that material turns out to have little lasting value, then it should be removed when its popularity wanes in order to make way for the new and exciting material of the day. The currency of nonfiction materials, like content, is more important to a children's collection than to an adult collection. Children may not be as circumspect, and may have neither the background to pick up hints that information is woefully outdated nor the knowledge to check a copyright date.[3]

Even classics can be made current by replacing old, tired, and academic-looking versions with newer, brighter editions, perhaps in paperback, with modern-looking cover art or restored illustrations. When a classic children's story is made into a movie, there is likely to be a movie tie-in edition, one that uses scenes from the movie on the cover, and might include extras such as the cast's reflections on the book.

Currency for audiovisual materials may be as basic as format. As VHS faded, DVD rose, and well-built video collections suddenly became old news. Computerized circulation systems can usually tell you the turnover rate for each format. As an older format fades, you should consider replacing titles you want to keep in the new format, and substituting purely popular titles in the old format with newer titles in the new format.

Accessibility

If the content of an item is accessible to library customers in some other way, then deselecting an item is much easier. The most basic example of this is second copies. If one copy remains on the shelf, the other copy or copies may be expendable. An item is also expendable if there are other newer, more accurate, or better-written works in the library. Remember, though, that items are not accessible to people whose reading level is significantly below the level of the writing.

In the electronic age, computerized resources—either subscription information services or websites—may supersede some items. Indeed, in subjects that change rapidly, websites may be eminently more useful than printed resources. Counting on these resources is complicated, though. Websites must be identified and links maintained. The information on websites is also beyond the control of the library. The information may change or disappear. A website that offers excellent information one day can become useless the next; the information may be manipulated by the site operator, it may grow out of date because it is not updated, or it may become inaccessible because the site operator starts charging for access. Still, the availability of information on the Internet needs to be a factor when making decisions about what stays in a crowded, financially strained public library.

Check any union catalog from which the library may borrow items on interlibrary loan. If you learn that the material is readily available elsewhere, then this information could make it easier to weed an item from your library.[4] Conversely, if you discover that the material is not available within the system anywhere else, then the decision is much harder, both because it will then be unavailable to your customers and because it will be unavailable on interlibrary loan for the other libraries in your system. If your system has a last-copy rule, it may even be against your interlibrary loan agreement to get rid of the item. If your system has a last-copy depository, then the item may be weeded and sent there.

FURTHER READING

Anne Price and Juliette Yaakov, eds., *Children's Catalog*, 18th ed. (Fort Atkinson, WI: H. W. Wilson, 2001).

Anne Price and Juliette Yaakov, eds., *Middle and Junior High Catalog*, 8th ed. (Fort Atkinson, WI: H. W. Wilson, 2000).

Joseph P. Segal, *The CREW Manual: A Unified System of Weeding, Inventory, and Collection-Building for Small and Medium-Sized Public Libraries* (Austin: Texas State Library, 1976).

Joseph P. Segal, *The CREW Method: Expanded Guidelines for Collection Evaluation and Weeding for Small and Medium-Sized Public Libraries*, revised and updated by Belinda Boon (Austin: Texas State Library, 1995).

NOTES

1. Joseph P. Segal, *The CREW Method: Expanded Guidelines for Collection Evaluation and Weeding for Small and Medium-Sized Public Libraries*, revised and updated by Belinda Boon (Austin: Texas State Library, 1995), 9.

2. Ibid., 31.

3. Ibid., 19.

4. Ibid., 7.

Services

Services are what the library provides on demand to individual users. They include ways that we provide information and ways that we promote reading. Many public librarians chose the field specifically to help people, and children's librarians more so than most. If the collection is the *what* that we offer, then services are the *how*. There are three components to providing excellent service, none of which can be ignored—the skills to do the work, a positive attitude toward adults and children alike, and the personae to deal effectively with the public. Children's services specialists should constantly look for every opportunity for customer service training because it is often not the intent that causes customer service problems, but a lack of understanding of how actions will be perceived.

The key service time for children's librarians, at least for nine months out of the year, is after-school hours. This particular need deserves its own treatment, and is dealt with in chapter 8, "After-School Services." If, as experience tells us, addressing the motivation behind the request is vital to performing excellent service, then the after-school hours present a special challenge in that children are motivated by factors that often have little or nothing to do with the library. They are at the library because their parents are not at home, because it is cold, because their teachers told them they could find what they needed here, because their friends are here, because they are bored, and on, and on, and on.

The other services we provide—reference (see chapter 9) and readers' advisory (see chapter 10)—address the specific needs of children for information. In each case, the need to communicate effectively greatly outweighs the need to produce an answer. In each case, knowing the question is more than half the battle. Most librarians are trained in these skills, but it is important to look at the specific needs of children, and the ways in which we may need to address them differently in order to provide the best service.

In chapter 11, "The Internet," we look at this unique tool that is changing the way we address the needs of our customers. Everything about the Internet seems to be a double-edged sword. For all its great promise and advantages, it offers challenges unprecedented in library history. While children's librarians may be tempted to keep their heads down and let the battles over the Internet be fought at the administrative level, it is vital to remember that we not only serve children but also must represent them when policies are being written and services designed, since children are seldom part of such weighty deliberations.

8

After-School Services

I t's 2:09 p.m., and the children from the elementary school next door come pouring into the children's room. The last straggler drops his bag in the middle of the walkway in front of the children's desk, as he does every single day, and shuffles off to the restroom. As if this is some kind of cue, the middle school students from up the street literally hit the doors—because they are rushing to grab the last free computer—at 2:17 p.m. The arrival of the parochial school students can be counted on at 2:19 p.m. The afternoon would not be complete if the late bus from the elementary school across town did not disgorge an extra twenty students at 2:37 p.m., precipitating a flood of requests for books on reptiles, the last of which you checked out at 2:36 p.m. Welcome to after school in the children's room.

If you work in a large, inner-city library, the scene just described may seem tame. If you work in a small rural library, you might be wondering what it means to have more than one school in your town. Every children's librarian, though, has his or her own proportional version of this scenario. The short period after school and before dinnertime is when children's librarians have the greatest amount of contact with their audience, their most significant impact, and their greatest frustrations. What does one do with all those kids?

Latchkey Children

Mae Benne, author of *Principles of Children's Services in Public Libraries,* defined latchkey children as "those children between the ages of five and thirteen who care for themselves after the school day until their parents or guardians come home." Her estimates, published in 1991, were that there were between half a million and 2.5 million latchkey children in America.[1] A U.S. Bureau of the Census report in 2000 estimated that 6.9 million children ages five to fourteen regularly spent their afternoons without adult supervision, or one in five children in the age group.[2]

What Libraries Can Do

There are a number of ways that children's librarians can address the needs of these children, even outside the realm of direct service. Librarians can gather information about services and activities open to children in the after-school hours and make them available to children and parents through handouts, bulletin boards, or websites. We can even spearhead efforts to bring such providers together for cooperative planning sessions, helping to assure that these programs complement rather than compete with one another. The library can also offer its resources, collections, expertise, and programming skills to those providers, thus extending the library's cooperative efforts and helping to make those other programs more effective.[3]

Of course, the library may also choose to offer direct service to children and their parents. After all, the library is open to all members of the community, and making a judgment about why a certain customer requires our service is against the spirit of the public library. Still, when planning services for after-school populations, it is important to consider what, in the end, is best for the child. The library cannot put itself in the position of childcare provider, because this is a role to which the library is ill suited, and if it attempts to provide this service then children will not be well cared for.

The library must continue to remind children and parents that the staff cannot supervise children, and that libraries are public places that have their own inherent dangers. Also, library services only reach so far, and if children are expected to spend three, four, or even more hours per day at the library, those services will be inadequate for the active and exploring mind of a child. In the end, the child will wander off, become bored, or act out in inappropriate ways, no matter how energetic and engaging the library staff may be. Libraries should try in earnest to make their systems work for the good of children, but it is a disservice to those children to take on the responsibility of caretaker for long periods of time when we have no authority over them, and we lack the resources to adequately discharge such a responsibility.

The first step to ensuring the safety of children and the security of the library itself is to establish a policy on unattended children. First, you must determine an age at which children cannot be left unattended in the library. Second, you must strictly define what *unattended* means. Must the parent be within sight of the child? In the children's room? Anywhere in the library? Must the parent be actively supervising the child? Must it be a parent or guardian, or can an older sibling be in charge of the child? How old must the older sibling be to qualify? What will be the library's reaction to the violation of these rules? Will library staff members accompany the child until a parent or guardian is found? Will repeated offenses result in denying library privileges? At what point will the police or other authorities be called to ensure the safety of the child? Each of these questions requires a locally sensitive answer.

The next necessary component is a policy for dealing with problematic behavior by older children. This is often a more uncomfortable situation because it is not so black and white. A three-year-old should not be left at the library while a parent or babysitter goes shopping for half an hour; that is simple and clear. However, behavioral issues often deal in gray areas and develop over time. Time is, in fact, an important component. A child who comes to the library after school may spend an hour doing homework, another half hour in a craft program, even a half hour curled up with a book, but what then? Librarians who see this will find it hard to blame the child, who may have exhibited more self-control than could reasonably be expected. Blaming the parents may or may not be justified, depending on economic and community factors. The truth is, sometimes blame is not effective and all that counts is the reaction.

A policy on acceptable behavior must spell out what actions cannot be tolerated because of their effect on other library users. Such a policy should be nonjudgmental, meaning that it does not discriminate between different customers for arbitrary reasons. An example would be a noise rule that applies to fourth graders gossiping loudly at a table in the children's room, but not to adults debating politics at the circulation desk. It should be directly tied to the rights and comforts of others, and not punish children for doing things that do not affect anyone else. For example, playing board games should not be against the rules, but any sort of play that makes it difficult for others to use library resources because of excessive noise or space requirements should not be allowed. The policy should be clear and visible, posted prominently, and expounded regularly by library staff so there is no question of arbitrary enforcement.

These policies will help the library deal with the most dangerous or unstable situations, while freeing staff members to address less serious issues in a positive manner. They should be as loose and forgiving as possible because the library is a public place where different ideas and viewpoints can mix. Public library use remains a privilege, and those who clearly abuse that privilege should not be allowed to infringe on the rights of others.

Except for the most egregious abusers of the library, there are a number of ways that libraries can, within their stated missions, help children make the most of their after-school hours through direct service and programming. Programming for this time period would likely not be too heavily literature based, as the children have been in school all day and are likely to want a break. For programming tips, see chapter 15, "Entertainment and Enrichment Programs." A formal homework help program may enable children to use their after-school time well. Indeed, many children may already be coming to the library looking for such help.

Homework Help

While some public libraries expressly refuse to offer homework help, others make it a specialty. Some school libraries stay open late to help with homework, even starting homework clubs, but most do not, and students have nowhere else to go but the public library. Much of the support for homework typically falls under the guise of reference because of the immediate nature of the request. Still, the children's library can improve homework support by creating a homework help center, offered at a set time in a set place by staff or others dedicated for that time to this task. In many ways, it is like a very regular, ongoing program, except that those who benefit from the program initiate the service.

This is a far cry from the 1960s when many libraries refused to help children with homework or even answer reference questions from children. It was even argued that public libraries offering homework help would undercut funding for school libraries.[4] There are still those who argue that it is the school media specialist who supports the curriculum, and that public libraries should stay out of the business. If a child wants to access the same reference services that everyone else does, then he or she deserves the same information service, no more, no less. Many libraries have found, though, that children require a good deal more service than adults to make use of the available resources.

Homework centers are often staffed by volunteers and paid for with grant money. That does not make them free. Library staff members still need to write the grants, recruit the volunteers, set policies, and evaluate the initiative.

Informal Homework Help

Even without a formal homework center, there are ways of helping children with homework beyond the basic reference service that the library offers to everyone. Again, it is preplanning that makes a difference, and first and foremost that means getting assignment information before the children do. Some projects come up at the same basic time in the same grade every year. You can figure these out by keeping track of assignments on a calendar, by saving assignment sheets in a file (as will be discussed more fully later), or by going through the school's curriculum, which often has specific requirements for certain projects. This will only prepare you for a fraction of the projects assigned in a year. To be truly effective, you must contact the teachers for more details.

Getting homework assignments ahead of the students has been a goal and source of frustration for children's librarians for a long time, and probably for as long as there have been public library children's services. Public librarians constantly lament that the teachers never let them know about assignments ahead of time, and how simple it would be for them to do so. Teachers, it is charged, are hurting themselves and their students because they refuse to do the simplest forward thinking. The truth, of course, is not so simple, as any classroom teacher can tell you. Teachers' time is strictly regulated and tightly scheduled. School-day preparation time is by no means a universal privilege. Even an assignment anticipated months ahead of time may not be finalized in its details until days, or even hours, before it is assigned. Assignment sheets are written last minute, if at all. While teachers might be glad to have you well prepared to help their students, this is not their highest priority, and if the children have to take a few extra steps in their research this may not be an entirely bad thing. In short, teachers do not absolutely need the public library, so if their time is short they most likely will not seek you out.

There have been any number of methods used by public library children's staffs, and by school media personnel as well, to initiate the communication with teachers that will lead to advance notice of school assignments and projects. The most common, the homework alert, is a form that the teacher can fill out with all the pertinent information and return to the public library directly or through the school library. Legions of these forms have been designed; none has proved overly effective, for all the reasons mentioned above. Still, it is a useful tool to create and use as an introduction to teachers. It shows the teacher what the library needs to be the most effective in helping students, and it might initiate conversations about what the library can do to help. Some more modern versions of this project-alert form have been posted on library web pages, where teachers can fill out an online form, press a button, and the information is e-mailed to the library automatically.

The more effective, but vastly more time-intensive method of getting advance notice of homework projects is to engage teachers continually, asking what is coming and suggesting ways to help. Teachers may not think

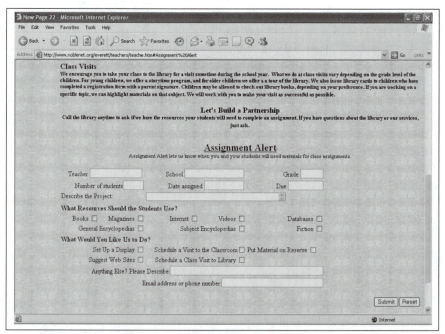

A simple fill-in form for teachers to submit assignment information over the Web (from the Parlin Library, Everett, Massachusetts)

to write even a short note, or to seek out a web page to enter an assignment alert, but they may respond to the simple question, "What are you studying next month?" While the children's staff of a public library may never have the time to contact every teacher in their service area every month, some progress may be made with regular contacts. For schools practicing team, or *pod*-style teaching, getting yourself invited to group planning meetings is a great leap forward. No matter what steps you take, though, recognize that you are not likely to be a high priority in the bell-driven world of elementary education.

Collect homework assignments that teachers send in ahead of time, or photocopy them from students when the first one asks for help. Having these documents on hand allows other staff members to prepare themselves for questions that will surely come, and makes it easier for the child or parent who comes in looking for resources but almost inevitably forgets to bring in the assignment sheet. You can also hold onto these for collection development purposes, and to try to predict the next year's projects. Make sure each assignment has a date, or if there is not one, put the date on the sheet before filing it in a folder or three-ring binder. That way, you can review the previous year's assignments for each month in an effort to be prepared.

If a student does not have a homework assignment, either because he or she failed to bring it or because no such assignment exists, the librarian can still garner some of the necessary information. Natalie Reif Ziarnnik, author of *School and Public Libraries: Developing the Natural Alliance*, suggests asking for the following: school, grade, teacher, due date, what types of resources the teacher has suggested, and whether any other classes are doing the same assignment.[5] Write everything down, and then add to it as more students arrive with more information, or call the teacher for clarification. This is a good time to remind the teacher how much you appreciate advance notice.

A homework resource collection can also be valuable. If space allows, you can put together some basic reference materials such as a dictionary, an almanac, a thesaurus, citation guides, books on how to write research papers, and the like. Add to these, copies of the current assignment sheets for those students who forget or lose theirs. A ruler, a protractor, a compass, a calculator, a magnifying glass, and other tools would be a welcome addition, as would some simple supplies such as paper, pencils, and pens. Centralizing this will give students a designated place to congregate when doing homework, even if the library does not offer a formal homework help program, thus allowing children's staff to keep track of which assignments are active.

Homework Web Directories

Librarians may choose to create directories on their web pages that include the links they find useful when offering reference service (see chapter 9, "Reference"). These can easily be adapted to homework help by creating homework directories. Add a page to the library's website specifically for homework help, and include the topic of each new assignment along with links to the pages that the librarians have found effective. If the library receives forewarning on the assignment, then this can be done in advance, during down time, in order to save a great deal of time in the busy after-school hours. If the first hint of the project is a student with assignment in hand, then frontline staff can make a simple note of what they found in answering the question, and the homework help directory can be updated at the first opportunity.

Speed, of course, is an issue, and the children's staff must have some hope of speedy updating of the web page in order to make such a directory work. If the children's staff writes the children's section of the web page, then this is far more likely. (See the section on Web writing in chapter 21, "Public Relations, Promotion, and Marketing," for more on this.) After the assignment is over, for the current year at least, the topic and suggested sites can be integrated into a general directory. If the assignment comes up again, the children's staff need only review the sites for currency, and they are ready to go.

The advantage of such a homegrown directory over the many good directories already out there is that this one is specific to the community, and to the assignments that children are actually doing. Any good general directory can give you information on colonial life, but if the assignment is on craftsmen's tools in the colonial period, then the sites offered may not fill the need, or the ones that do may be buried in other, more general sites. The children could use search engines to try to find useful sites, and if that is part of the assignment that is fine, but librarians can assess the quality of sites, organize the information, and present it in a rational way.

Interlibrary Loan

Interlibrary loan can be used to build a backup collection if the library can get the assignment early enough from teachers. Once received, interlibrary loan books can be checked out like any other book, or can be used as a backup collection allowing the library's own books to circulate, rather than being held for library use only. Of course, asking other libraries for Native American resources in October and November will not help because every library is facing the same report around Columbus Day and Thanksgiving. But libraries build broad collections to cover a great number of topics, and most of those collections sit idle for most of the year, waiting for the one moment when they will be of use. For most of the year, five books on seashells may be five books too many. Then for one week, a hundred books on seashells would not be enough. Sharing resources can even out the supply and demand ups and downs.

Check the interlibrary loan agreements that your library has made. See if there are any restrictions regarding this type of borrowing. If possible, make special agreements with other libraries offering your unused collections in exchange for similar considerations. If enough libraries are involved, then borrowing one book from each library may be enough to create a strong backup collection. Many adult libraries, and some children's libraries too, use this same approach to create reading group collections, rather than buying multiple copies that may never be needed again. In the case of a big project, a single library probably could not buy enough non-fiction to meet demand, and rather than turn to more and more restrictive reserve rules, libraries can use interlibrary loan to balloon the size of their collections in a specific area for a short period of time.

FURTHER READING

Cindy Mediavilla, *Creating the Full-Service Homework Center in Your Library* (Chicago: American Library Association, 2001).

NOTES

1. Mae Benne, *Principles of Children's Services in Public Libraries* (Chicago: American Library Association, 1991), 20.

2. Laurent Beslie, "Ranks of Latchkey Kids Approach 7 Million," *Christian Science Monitor*, October 31, 2000, 3.

3. Benne, *Principles of Children's Services*, 21–22.

4. Cindy Mediavilla, "Why Library Homework Centers Extend Society's Safety Net," *American Libraries*, December 2001, 40.

5. Natalie Reif Ziarnnik, *School and Public Libraries: Developing the Natural Alliance* (Chicago: American Library Association, 2003), 47.

9

Reference

Reference work is most often associated with adult services. Reference librarians usually have their desks in the adult portion of the library. In larger libraries and library systems, reference departments are often under the umbrella of adult services. And yet, children ask more reference questions per capita than adults do.[1] In children's services, reference is usually not a separate function, but part of what everybody does.

Reference work is basically a very simple concept. People ask us questions and we answer them. The process is not, of course, anywhere near that simple, especially when the customer is a child. Put yourself in the shoes of a public library reference librarian for the following scenario. A forty-year-old man walks up to you and asks, "What is the capital of Bolivia?" What would you do? You would almost certainly look up the answer and tell him. The man then opens up his portfolio, clicks a pen, and says, "By the way, what is thirty-seven times four?" Again, you would give him the answer without hesitation.

Now imagine you are at a children's room desk and an eight-year-old boy walks up to you and asks, "What is the capital of Bolivia?" What would you do then? While you are pondering your next move, he opens up his backpack, takes out a piece of white paper, clicks a pen, and says, "By the way, what is thirty-seven times four?" It is worth remembering that the goal is not simply to answer questions but also to serve needs. The best reference librarians will tell you that finding answers is the easy part; the real challenge is understanding what the real question is. The two people in the above scenarios may have asked the same questions, but their needs were very different. The forty-year-old would have no need of instruction on how to find and use an atlas. The eight-year-old would not be well served by being handed the answers to his questions.

The Reference Interview

The reference interview is the time when the librarian gets information from the customer in order to, in turn, give information back. A reference transaction is seldom as simple as someone walking up, asking a question, and receiving an answer. This is especially true when dealing with children who may be less skilled at formulating a question than adults are. It is the goal of the reference interview not just to discover what is the true nature of the question but also to understand what is required to provide an acceptable answer. This process is complicated when the motivation behind the question comes from something other than the child's interest, most frequently a school assignment. The child may not know him or herself exactly what the expected outcome is, or his or her interests may be in conflict with the assignment, causing contradictory answers to simple questions such as "Is this enough information?"

First, you will need to determine the question. A child is likely to ask not for what he or she wants, but for what he or she has determined will most likely produce the information needed. Of course, the child may not have determined the most effective search strategy. For example, a child asks if the library has any sports books. Of course the library does, but pointing out twenty shelves of books is not likely to serve the child well. The effective librarian must determine what information is actually needed, to what purpose, and what form the answer must take to fit the child's needs.

Finding out what information is actually needed requires getting the child to talk, and children are likely not to volunteer enough information on their own.[2] To counteract this tendency, librarians need to ask open-ended questions, ones that allow the customer to elaborate rather than forcing him or her to choose between narrow choices. This is often hard when a child's first responses are single words, nods, or shrugs. It is tempting to revert to multiple-choice questions featuring the options the librarian thinks most likely. In the above example, it does little good to ask if the child is interested in baseball, basketball, football, or some other sport. If the answer is "other," then you are off on another list. If the question instead is whether the child is interested in some specific sport, then the answer might be instructive. If the answer is "no," then you know to change tactics. Broaden your questions and let the child describe what he or she wants, and you are more likely to get to the real question.

One way to determine the true question is to discover the purpose to which the information will be put. Children are more likely to be willing, even eager, to tell you why they need information than an adult will be, but only if you ask them.[3] While librarians are often hesitant to ask someone's motivation, with children it is often necessary to know this in order to provide the service that is required. Remember, the motivation may come from someone other than the child him or herself—a teacher, a coach, or a parent. This is sometimes referred to as an *imposed query*. Knowing where the question comes from may help in deciphering exactly what is needed.

With the sports question cited above, it would be useful to ask what the child wants the sports book for. The child may simply like to read about baseball players, in which case there is a flaw in the child's predetermined search strategy. He or she needs to be looking in the biographies instead, or possibly even in fiction. What you have is a readers' advisory situation (see chapter 10, "Readers' Advisory"). If the purpose is a school report, then the librarian may ask if the child has an assignment sheet. If the purpose is to find practice drills before peewee football season starts, the true nature of the question becomes clearer.

Even if you determine what information the child wants and for what purpose, you still need to make sure that the information is acceptable in form, format, and usability.[4] The child needs to do a report on the history of swimming competition in the Olympics. You find a book, but can the child read it? You find the definitive book, but the child needs three sources. You find a book, an article, and a video, but the teacher will not accept audio-visual materials as sources. The teacher requires a book report on a book of a certain length, and the book you found is four pages short of the minimum. You place an interlibrary loan request for the ideal book, but the assignment is due tomorrow. These are all common situations in which finding the right answer to the right question is not enough. When you think you have found the answer, go back and ask the child if this will serve him or her well.

A good reference interview is vital to reference service. All the skills at information retrieval, the entire well-built reference collection, and all the analytical cataloging in the world is of no use if you do not know what you are looking for. Children do not always formulate questions well, so part of reference service for children is helping them determine exactly what it is they want. Ask open-ended questions, ones that do not guide the child toward an answer but ask them to point the way. Bring in questions of motivation and context, and let the child tell you what he or she wants as an end result. Finally, go back and see if what you find in the end actually fits the needs that underlie the motivation, and that nothing hinders the child from using the information you have provided.

Reference Resources

Traditionally, the first resource for answering reference questions was the reference collection, a carefully built selection of specialized information resources that were exempt from circulation and carefully watched over by trained reference librarians. Modern reference collections are not what they once were, and reference work today is more about process and less about collections than it ever was. For children especially, the use of specialized print resources is diminishing in importance. The advent of whole language curricula means that children are expected to read more and search out isolated facts less.

Changes in lifestyle have also changed the environment in which we build reference collections. Parents and children alike are busier and more scheduled, making the trip to the library for a few hours of research less practical. As Mae Benne expressed more than a decade ago, "Contemporary lifestyles are not conducive to long, uninterrupted periods at the library."[5] Libraries these days are opting to reduce the size of their reference collections, especially their dedicated children's reference collections, or allowing their reference materials to circulate, making them reference in name only. Most libraries do reserve some basic materials for the specific use of the staff when offering reference service—a dictionary, an almanac, one set of encyclopedias (even these commonly circulate these days), and some local information that might not be easily attainable. Even these tools for quick reference—or ready reference—are being supplanted by electronic resources, further shrinking the traditional reference collection.

More and more, the process of offering reference service leads to the resources in the general collection. Juvenile nonfiction collections are being built with an eye toward their usefulness in the modern curriculum, meaning a greater emphasis on books designed to be read through, rather than those designed to be referenced for specific information. Whole language curricula meld reference work with readers' advisory, the process of helping a customer select a book to read. (See chapter 10, "Readers' Advisory.")

Effective reference work for children requires sophisticated use of electronic resources. The printed *Readers' Guide to Periodical Literature*, once a staple of print reference collections, has been superseded by online periodical indexes, many of which offer access to full-text, and even full-image, articles. Much of what children once found, with our help, in print resources, they now find on the Internet, or at least hope to find there. Our function is quickly shifting from the collectors and organizers of information to the identifiers and evaluators of information.

Reference work often boils down to one-on-one instruction on using the Internet for informational purposes. We point customers toward the databases we offer, if any, through our web pages, and we can offer our own resources, in the form of collected web links and finding aids on our web pages as well.

Librarians have long known that the websites they find and use when answering a reference question may be useful for similar questions later on, so they have organized such sites into web directories. This is how the Librarians' Index to the Internet (http://www.lii.org) was born.[6] Local libraries can use this model to reduce repetitive reference searches and better serve their student customers. Whenever a website has proved useful, write down the address of the page, a subject or two, and a brief annotation. Write a web page that lists all this information and contains a direct link to the resource.

Online Periodical Databases

EBSCOhost
    http://www.ejournals.ebsco.com
Info Trac
    http://www.galegroup.com/libraries/index.htm
Readers' Guide
    http://www.hwwilson.com/databases/readersg.htm

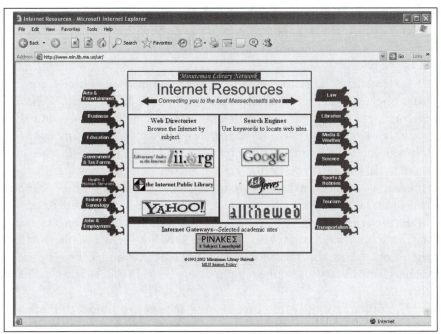

A directional web page for finding resources on the Internet (from the Minuteman Library Network, Massachusetts)

Shared Resources and Interlibrary Loan

As needs for information broaden, the ability of any one library—public or school—to own, house, organize, and access the requisite materials to satisfy those needs becomes more and more of a pipe dream. Children's resource needs are expanding faster than those of adults, thanks to more sophisticated classrooms and curricula. Increasingly, librarians must look outside the library for resources.

In public libraries, interlibrary loan, like reference, is a function usually associated with adult services, but the need is also there for children and those who serve children—teachers and school media personnel. The occasional request by a child for a specific book on interlibrary loan may very well be handled by adult services staff, possibly with the mediation of a children's librarian. The most effective use for interlibrary loan in children's reference, though, is the securing of backup materials when a school project threatens to overwhelm the capacity of the library. For this, the children's staff must be intimately involved. For more on this, see chapter 8, "After-School Services."

For teachers and school librarians, the most obvious source for information beyond internal holdings is the local public library. Some teachers may prefer to request materials directly from the public library, and they should be welcomed to do so. Indeed, in many communities any cooperation between schools and public libraries is to be nurtured. Still, the ideal situation is usually to have the school media personnel act as the go-between. If teachers make their requests first through the school library, then the school librarian can ensure that there are not relevant resources within the school media center that the teachers missed or were unaware of. The school media staff also then has early knowledge of the subjects being covered in the classrooms; this level of communication between teachers and library personnel might seem basic but is lacking in many schools.

The other reason for resource-sharing requests to funnel through the school library is to help the school media staff effectively and efficiently build the collection. If a resource is being borrowed repeatedly from the public library, then it makes sense for the school library to make that resource available and easily accessible in-house. If the material is asked for only occasionally, and the school media staff knows a copy is available at the public library, then they can forgo purchasing it.[7] This ability to shift buying based on resource-sharing requests leads directly to the greatest benefit of school and public library cooperation—coordinated buying.

The more public and school library personnel communicate what is needed and in what quantities, the more they can make informed decisions, even formal agreements, about who should purchase what. Nowhere is this truer than in the acquisition of reference materials, which are often expensive and specialized. Simply put, reference materials are more appropriately owned where they will be used most. If one library knows it does not have to purchase a particular item because it is readily available nearby, then the institution can use the resources—both money and space—to purchase a different item that in turn can be used by the other institution. This type of sharing actually creates a positive feedback loop. As the two libraries share resources, they also share information; this knowledge helps both libraries manage resources better, which in turn creates more sharing.

NOTES

1. Virginia A. Walter, *Children and Libraries: Getting It Right* (Chicago: American Library Association, 2001), 29.

2. Natalie Reif Ziarnnik, *School and Public Libraries: Developing the Natural Alliance* (Chicago: American Library Association, 2003), 47.

3. Mae Benne, *Principles of Children's Services in Public Libraries* (Chicago: American Library Association, 1991), 81.

4. Ibid., 82.

5. Ibid., 78.

6. "About Librarians' Index to the Internet (LII)," http://lii.org/search/file/about.

7. Ziarnnik, *School and Public Libraries*, 42.

10
Readers' Advisory

Readers' advisory is the process of helping someone find something to read. It is the most basic form of promotion librarians do. Our collections are physical products we have to offer; readers' advisory is our chance to make the best use of those collections.

Forms of Readers' Advisory

The usual form of readers' advisory is the personal interview. An individual, in our case a child, comes to the library looking for something to read, and we guide him or her through our collections, determine what his or her needs and desires are, and suggest titles that might be of interest. This process is complicated somewhat by the mediation of another person, such as a parent or grandparent, who may come alone to the library in order to choose a book for the child, or with the child in order to help the child make a selection.

Offering readers' advisory to a group is known as booktalking, and is covered under programming (see chapter 14, "Booktalking"). It differs from one-on-one readers' advisory in that the intended audience has a range of characteristics. No single book will be appropriate for everyone. Instead, a well-designed booktalking program will offer a range of titles to match the range of people in the audience. Also, in a booktalking program the communication is largely one way; the librarian presents information to the audience. As we will see later on, one-on-one readers' advisory allows for—indeed depends on—two-way communication.

Readers' advisory can also be done without direct communication at all. Instead, the librarian prepares hints, suggestions, and lists and puts them into a format that people can access on their own. Examples of this are bibliographies, finding aids, newsletter articles, web pages, and any other form of static communication.

The Readers' Advisory Interview

In many ways, the conversation that takes place during readers' advisory is similar to the reference interview (see chapter 9, "Reference"). It is most important to get the customer talking about what he or she wants, what needs might be filled, and what is acceptable as a final answer. It is useful to determine what the child has enjoyed reading in the past, and a favorite question among many librarians is, "What books have you read and enjoyed recently?" This question is helpful if not taken as the beginning and end of the conversation. If the librarian responds to the child's answer by pulling out similar titles without probing further, a great deal may be missed. What about the book did the child like? Were there things that the child did not like about the book? Is there something different the child would like to read about?

Ask specifically if the request is for a homework assignment.[1] If it is, then all the factors of the reference interview come into play. You must determine exactly what is being asked. Was a specific title assigned? A specific author, or an author with some particular trait, such as nationality or gender? Was a specific genre assigned, and if so, what is the teacher's definition of that genre? Is there a list that students can or must choose from?

Finding a book at a comfortable reading level is both an important and a delicate issue. A child who is looking for pleasure reading does not need to feel or be judged on his or her reading abilities. Children develop as readers at different rates, and you cannot assume that readers of a certain age read at the same level as other children their age. In fact children's librarians are more likely to interact with better readers, so their initial reaction may be to overestimate the abilities of a child based on his or her age.[2]

Grade level may be a more reliable indicator, but even in the same grade there is a wide range of abilities. The question "What was the last book you read and enjoyed?" is illustrative if not taken completely at face value. The child might have read that book for completely different reasons than he or she has for picking out a book today. If there is a question about the child's ability to read a book comfortably, ask him or her to *try it on.* Open the book at random and ask the child to read a paragraph to you. His or her ability to work through the words may speak volumes, both to you and to the child. If there is still doubt, ask the child if there are words he or she does not understand that you could define, and ask a question or two about the meaning of the paragraph. One approach that is always available is to offer several choices in a range of reading levels, and let the child pick the one most to his or her liking.[3]

With children, readers' advisory is often about selling not only an individual title but also the process of reading. The child's motivation in looking for a book may have nothing to do with a desire to read. The child may have an assignment to do a book report, or might be under pressure from a parent to get something to read. The child may want to read, but be frustrated by his or her own perception that he or she lacks the ability to read well. While addressing all these potential issues, do not forget to express your own love of reading, which is, of course, wholly separate from the idea that reading is good for you or important.

Popularity versus Quality

The question of popularity versus quality, so prevalent in collection development circles, is no less of an issue in readers' advisory. It is also a more heated question for readers' advisory work with children than it is with adults. We feel a greater responsibility to guide the reading of children, who we might feel are not as well equipped as adults to make good choices. We also feel that adults should be more able to live with the consequences of their choices. While we consider which books to promote to children, though, we should look not just to our goals but also to the practical results of our efforts.

We must first define, then, the purpose of readers' advisory. As little as ten or fifteen years ago, public librarians approached readers' advisory for children as if we were school librarians or reading teachers. More and more, we recognize now that we have a different and a complementary role: teachers teach reading; public librarians promote it. School personnel make sure children can read; we make sure they do it. We are less concerned with making children capable readers, and more concerned with making them avid readers.

The stated goals of readers' advisory for children have not changed much over the years. We seek to encourage children to read at higher and higher levels. We encourage children to read quality literature, which author Mae Benne once referred to as "special titles." We encourage children to diversify their reading, to experience books with different subjects, settings, and genres.[4] These aims, and the intentions behind them, are unquestionably noble, but we should consider what the effect has been of promoting such goals.

In the name of challenging children to read to their highest ability, we have often turned reading into a struggle. Instead of showing reading to be a pleasure, we have made it into a chore, and in the process have discouraged struggling readers and created vast numbers of reluctant readers. In the name of promoting quality literature, we limited our collecting of, and failed to promote, popular literature that might have brought a great deal of joy to many of our customers. Indeed, we have turned the very word *popular* into a derogatory term, setting us at odds with our customers. In the name of diversity of reading habits, we have avoided separating our fiction collections by genre and form for fear that children will never leave one section. This has made finding reading more difficult for browsers, and it has also stigmatized genre readers whose preferences are no less valid than anyone else's.

The change in focus from principles to outcomes is illustrated by Mae Benne's approach to the issue of dividing fiction collections by reader interest, as outlined in her book *Principles of Children's Services in Public Libraries.* She contends that such divisions are problematic because they discourage children from using the card catalog.[5] While good subject access is a real asset to a catalog, it is important to remember why certain collections are used. When it comes to fiction, libraries need to be promoting reading, not catalog use. The success of the large bookstores during and since the late 1990s should be instructive. Readers enjoy browsing, so making the experience simpler and more fruitful will attract readers.

The quality versus popularity debate is an intellectual freedom issue as well. This debate persists in adult collection development as well, but we would never think to argue that adults should be denied access to books because we think they are not well written. Adult service librarians are much more likely to create genre collections, and even to create finding aids that point to the next science fiction title, or another fun mystery author. Adult services librarians who do not want to alienate their customers would never think to tell one to put a novel back because he or she is capable of reading something more challenging or more worthy. If we are willing to feed adults' appetite for popular reading, we should afford children the same consideration.

Readers' Advisory with Parents

Children's librarians doing readers' advisory have one factor they must deal with that most adult librarians do not—parents. Sometimes parents come in alone, and the children's librarian must suggest books without the potential reader present. At other times, both parent and child come to the library together, and that has a dynamic all its own. Let us deal first with the parent who comes in to get a book for his or her child.

The first thing to realize is that the readers' advisory interview has become an exercise in hearsay. You can, and should, attempt to solicit the same information from the parent as you would from the child, but that information will be colored by the parent's perspective. This is not to say that parents will be misleading or purposefully unhelpful; they are clearly interested in their child's reading or they would not have come, and they are clearly open to suggestions or they would not have asked you. Parents are likely to be limited in their own knowledge of how children read, however, and may have received only filtered information from their own children. The child is likely to tell the parent what he or she thinks the parent wants to hear.

Parents, even those involved in their child's reading, may defer to the child's age or grade level when choosing the difficulty of a book simply because that is the level at which the child should be reading. On the other hand, some parents will have a rosy view of their child's ability, either through wishful thinking or the belief that to constantly challenge a reader is the best way to make him or her improve. Without the child there, you cannot ask him or her to read a paragraph at random, so you must rely more heavily on recent books the child has read. Of course, the parent is naturally going to suggest the titles that he or she most approved of, and if the parent makes a habit of picking out books for the child then the list will be somewhat stacked.

The same problem exists when choosing a genre or subject. You must rely on the parent's interpretation of what the child likes, which is likely to be filtered. Parents want the best for their child, and they will define that from their own perspective and likely project that perspective onto their children. They may also lack understanding across gaps of age and gender. Rely again on open questions, rather than narrowing the discussion to what you feel the child will like. After all, you are likely to be projecting yourself. Get the parent to talk about his or her child—what he or she does, enjoys, and talks about. Both you and the parent may be surprised by what the child's interests really are.

Speaking with the parent alone has the advantage of allowing the librarian and the parent to discuss issues that might affect the child openly and freely. Either a parent or a child can ask for an exciting or even a scary book, but a parent is more likely to be able to describe parameters of the child's comfort level. The parent may feel more free to discuss issues that he or she would like to see dealt with—or avoided—in a book. The parent who wants a book to jog his or her child's thinking or to stimulate a conversation delights most librarians. This use of books is a basic form of bibliotherapy, and we tend to believe that books can change lives; indeed, this is one of the main reasons we do our job. The parent who wishes to limit the issues a child can confront in his or her reading sometimes challenges our understanding and patience.

When parents ask that books not include some particular issue, many librarians feel shunted or distressed. We believe that all people, children included, should be free to read about anything they wish. We sometimes forget at this moment that we serve parents too, and one of our mantras in intellectual freedom is that parents have the right to guide their child's— and only *their* child's—reading. Parents may go to what mainstream thought would consider extremes. One example is the devout parent who insists that there be nothing *unnatural*—magic, talking animals, or imaginary creatures—in their four-year-old's reading. Whether we feel that such a parent is limiting a child or going overboard is irrelevant. Insisting that the child is missing out on a world of wonderful literature is not only unproductive, but it is also unprincipled, and it undercuts our arguments later when other parents insist that we protect all children from a certain title by taking it off our shelves.

In the end, when performing readers' advisory with a parent, or any other adult choosing books for a child, one principle should be clear. You must offer an even greater range of titles than you would with the child present. That means a wider range of subjects, reading levels, genres, and any other characteristic that comes up during the readers' advisory interview. Also, encourage the parent to take a range of books home for the child to choose from. In the end, it is the reader who must choose for himself or herself if the transaction is to be successful.

Parents and Children Together

The comic strip *Unshelved*, by Bill Barnes and Gene Ambaum (http://www.overduemedia.com), refers to the parent and child who come to the desk together as "the two-headed monster." As much as we as librarians insist we want to see parents involved in their children's reading, we all do from time to time sympathize with this characterization. On the other hand, we as librarians constantly emphasize that we want parents involved in their children's reading, not only when they are in the preliterate stage (See chapter 17, "Family Programs and Family Literacy") but also throughout their childhood. Performing readers' advisory for the parent and child together can be extremely rewarding or ultimately frustrating, depending on how well the librarian can communicate.

Always address the child as much as possible, and try to get the child to speak. This can be difficult when a parent answers every question put to the child. Remember that you are serving two different audiences here—children whom we want to develop into readers, and parents who want our aid in guiding their children's reading. If the parent insists on the latter service, then perform it graciously. If you can, though, try to address both needs, which will require a readers' advisory interview with the child. Recognize that the information the child provides may be colored by the presence of a parent; generally the child chooses answers that are clearly intended either to please or displease the parent, and that reveal if he or she is feeling imposed upon. Reading tone and body language are important; experience is invaluable.

A physical separation from the parent may be best for all involved if the dynamic seems unhelpful, but if the parent wishes to remain involved, suggesting that he or she do something else for a while might be taken badly. Understand that there is no guarantee of a clean and productive end to this or any other readers' advisory situation. You can guide and suggest, but the customer must ultimately make his or her decision, and it is always possible that two customers in the same transaction may not come to the same decision. As always, offering a broad range of titles and the value-added service of an effective booktalk for each is most likely to bring success. Be careful not to take sides; you are an advisor, not a referee. Your value rests in your ability to open the collection and give information.

Recognize some aspects of the dynamic, especially if there is disagreement between parent and child. Often parents focus more on quality, looking more for the best book than the most appropriate one. Children may focus more on popularity, responding to factors such as media tie-ins or peer recommendations, and ignore their own reading ability or interests. Parents will often choose books of greater difficulty over ones of less difficulty, even if the easier book is more appropriate to the child's actual ability and even when the book is intended for pleasure reading. Children may be discouraged by the look of a book, unsure of their abilities and reluctant to try something outside their experience.

Remind both parent and child that reading is a varied and lifelong pursuit. Children should expect (and be expected) to read above and below their level, to read both familiar and broadening books, and to read for pleasure as well as information. Remind the parent that adults do this when they choose their own reading, and that children should be allowed this liberty as well. When tension is greatest, the answer is often to take a variety of books, including one or more books for the parent to read to the child or the two to read together. If it is possible in your community, try to extend the one readers' advisory transaction into a regular conversation, inviting the parent and child back for the next round when the current choices are exhausted and emphasizing the ongoing nature of reading selection.

Bibliographies and Static Communication

Librarians can leverage their readers' advisory effectiveness by using indirect, or static, communication. This means preparing hints and suggestions, making lists and finding aids, and putting this information into a format that people can access on their own. Organizing the information does require extra time and effort, but librarians need only write down the suggestions they make in person and organize them into coherent tools. Personal service is best, of course, but such aids allow for a greater audience since a customer can later access the information independently.

When creating these tools, decide who your intended audience will be. Children's librarians serve a wide variety of customers (see chapter 3, "Whom Do Children's Librarians Serve?"), and one readers' advisory tool cannot hope to reach all of them. When designing a tool, make sure you know who will use it, and make sure the intended audience is clear to the reader. You can do this explicitly in a title or description (e.g., "Lions, Tigers, and Bears: Wild Animal Stories for Elementary School Students"). Placement can also determine an audience; a newspaper article suggesting summer titles is most likely to be read by parents and should be written for that audience, whereas a flier handed out in schools should target the child as reader. Layout can help differentiate an audience as well; cartoon characters and bright orange paper will tell readers that a particular tool is intended for a younger audience, just as a bibliography in small type on letter-sized white paper is clearly intended for an adult reader.

These tools include the bibliography (or discography, or filmography), an organized listing of titles. Bibliographies can vary in amount and type of detail presented, and these choices should be well thought out. Author, title, and publication date for each work are standard in even the simplest of bibliographies. Publication information is usually included, if for no other reason than to model good citation skills to students. Reading level is useful for many lists that are not, in their design, aimed at a single level. Annotations of some kind are often the most helpful feature. People currently have many sources of titles, too many in fact to make sensible decisions, so having a description to work with is as important as having an organized list.

Bibliographies can be printed and copied so customers have something to work with if the librarian is not available, or if they prefer to work on their own. These are especially helpful for the parent who comes to the library to pick out a book for an absent child; they can take the list with them and have the child choose books to be picked up later. These lists can then be re-created in many formats, such as an article for a newspaper or a newsletter (see chapter 21, "Public Relations, Promotion, and Marketing"). Lists can be posted on the library's web page, with titles linked to the library's catalog, if it is available online, or to a commercial website that features reviews. Many public access catalog programs allow the librarian to integrate a bibliography into the catalog itself, so that users can choose a pre-programmed list as easily as they can pull up the record for an individual title.

The physical manifestation of a bibliography is the display, which places a number of items together in a temporary location, sometimes accompanied by signs, decorations, and even a printed list of the titles. Individual annotations can be taken from the bibliography and added to bookmarks to be placed in each book. Displays have the advantage of allowing for easy mixing of formats—audio, visual, and print—highlighting connections that are not easily made within a library's organization. Any list of titles can be transformed into a display, and the display will likely increase the effectiveness of the list and the use of the materials.

Readers' advisory is a way of making the most of the collection and all the resources that are poured into it. Each of these formats represents a different way librarians can capitalize on the work we do every day—suggesting titles for hearing, viewing, or reading. Keep a notebook, note cards, or some other record of what you suggest and why, and the amount of extra work involved in preparing these tools will be minimal compared to the effect.

NOTES

1. Anitra T. Steele, *Bare Bones Children's Services: Tips for Public Library Generalists* (Chicago: American Library Association, 2001), 16.

2. Mae Benne, *Principles of Children's Services in Public Libraries* (Chicago: American Library Association, 1991), 86.

3. Ibid.

4. Ibid., 84–85.

5. Ibid., 85.

11
The Internet

I s the Internet a service? It is not really part of the collection, as there is no selection process and the library does not own, or even own the rights to, the information it contains. Calling the Internet a part of the library's collection disguises the fact that it is used more often for communication than for information. Yet it is often seen as a part of the collection by librarians because it is used for finding information as if it were. The way it is used in support of reference and homework help, and the fact that individuals initiate its use based on their own needs, make it a service. Librarians are prone to thinking of the Internet as a research tool; the majority of our customers think of it as e-mail, Instant Messenger, bulletin boards, and blogs. It does not serve us well to be so out of sync with our customers.

Levels of Service

It is not enough to say that the library will provide access to the Internet; rather, it must define what service or services it will provide and to what audience. In order to use the Internet, a customer must have access, a machine to work on, the skills to use the machine and to navigate the Internet, and a reasonable idea of what can be gained by using it. Libraries can and do provide anything from the barest pieces of the puzzle to full service. They also offer different levels of service to different populations, not always explicitly, but by their choice of services to offer. Children are an easily differentiated audience, and children's services staff should be aware of what services are being offered and how the needs of children are being met.

Providing Access

The basic decision a library must make is how it will allow customers to access the Internet. Most libraries these days offer, at some level, the two basic components: an Internet connection and machines (computers) in order to use that connection. How those components are situated and arranged is a question of fairness and equity. At hundreds and even thousands of dollars per workstation, machines tend to be expensive items for libraries that usually spend twelve to fifteen dollars for a book. In most libraries there is a general agreement that there are not enough machines to go around. Therefore the decision about where those machines are located largely determines who has access to this service.

Children may be intimidated by having to go into an adult area to use the Internet. The people there may be unfamiliar, they may be less inclined to be welcoming to children whom they are not trained to serve, and even the furniture may be uncomfortable for children. (Of course, these same factors might form barriers for adults who need to use a computer in a children's area.) If the Internet is seen largely as a research tool, then the machines may be concentrated in numbers near the reference desk, which is often one of the most intimidating parts of the library for a child. In addition, if the library chooses to filter children's room computers and not adult room computers, then children may be barred by policy from using adult room computers. (More on filtering a little later.)

Children's services staff have an interest in making sure that the Internet is seen as a service of its own, subject to the demands of the customer, and not narrowly defined as a research tool. If the library takes the broader approach, then there is a better argument for placing an equitable number of machines in areas where different populations use the library, the children's room being one of them. Also, libraries that view the Internet primarily as a research tool sometimes restrict the use of their computers for communication, banning e-mail and Instant Messenger, for instance. Older children are more likely even than adults to use the communication tools available on the Internet, and so are disproportionately hurt by such policies.

The advent of open wireless, a connection to the Internet that a customer can use through his or her own laptop while in (or near) the library, promises to radically change the relationship between libraries, their customers, and the Internet. Some librarians may see the concept as a money saver; by installing a relatively cheap piece of hardware, the library can rely on customers to use their own machines rather than paying for expensive and quickly obsolete machinery. If the library uses this as an excuse not to buy computers, then children—especially younger and disadvantaged children who are less likely to own laptops—will suffer. If, on the other hand, the library goes ahead with open wireless and recognizes this have–have not dichotomy, it may choose to buy the same number of computers, and put more of them in the children's room.

The narrow view of the Internet as a research tool often affects how the library uses its connection to the Internet as well. In its broadest use, the library can simply open the Internet connection to be used for whatever the customer wants. Many libraries restrict the use of that connection, defining some uses as unworthy, or at least less worthy than others. The most common limitations are for illegal or antisocial activities (such as threatening or obscene behavior), forms of communication (such as e-mail, Instant Messenger, as mentioned earlier), and the pursuit of commerce. Libraries must consider that barring certain uses of their Internet connections, even when that use is barred for everyone, will inevitably discriminate against someone, as different customers are more likely to use the Internet for different purposes. Deciding on and enforcing such restrictions will be taken up later under the topic of the acceptable use policy.

Providing Support

The best support the library can offer for its Internet access is clearly one-on-one personal assistance. This, of course, assumes that the helper has either knowledge or experience to offer the customer. Those who serve children must be effective users of the Internet, which is so pervasive today that children really cannot be expected to operate without it. But it is important that the staff member be able to relate to the customer as well as the tool. If Internet support is left to the reference department, usually under the umbrella of adult services, then children may not be as well served as they would be by a person trained to meet their specific needs. This is another reason why equal Internet access should be available in children's areas as often as possible: the support there will be more in tune with the customer.

The library can provide preemptive Internet support the same way that it anticipates customer needs for books, by creating finding aids that list the location of resources on the Web. These listings are most useful when accompanied by a brief annotation, and this value-added service is one that libraries have done well to offer. It mimics some of the personal service mentioned above, and it is reproducible across time and space. One staff member with an expertise in Web resources or some special topic can serve people even when he or she is not available in the library, and customers can take that wisdom with them to their own computers in their own homes. A printed resource will never be as effective as personal service, but it may help to bridge the gap between customer needs and library resources.

The ultimate finding aid for Internet sites is likely to be a web page itself. Rather than asking users to type an address into a location bar, which many users may not know how to do, the library can program a link to take the user to the resource with a click of the mouse. An internal web page that points in-library users to resources outside the library should be the first page that appears on library computers. This may differ from the library's public web page, which will probably be designed primarily to point users to information about the library itself, with a link to outside resources. Just as the library should consider having a welcoming public page designed specifically for children, it might consider creating a distinct internal page that appears on computers located in the children's room in order to lead young users out to the Internet .

Providing Instruction

When most libraries consider teaching Internet skills, they think first of adults, especially senior citizens. This comes from the outmoded belief that children are naturals with computers, that they know more than we do, and that there is little of value that they can or want to learn from us. The one exception to this belief often pertains to research skills, specifically search and analysis. While this is certainly a role we can fill, there is much more that we can do.

Perhaps the greatest need for the library to instruct children in the use of the Internet is safety and security. While children may be proficient in the use of computers and comfortable with navigating hypertext, they are often heedless of consequences. This continues largely because parents are more hesitant with the technology, and so are unfamiliar with the issues that children are likely to encounter. Teaching children and parents together about the safe use of the Internet is one of the greatest outreach opportunities for the modern library, and children's services staff almost certainly need to be involved in order to make such outreach a success.

Children and parents alike need to know about the presence and the methods of both financial and physical predators on the Internet. They need to be taught about how personal information is collected—electronically, yes, through downloaded software, but also through interactions such as forms, log-ins, registrations, and conversations via e-mail and in chat rooms. Children need to know how to protect information such as their full name, their parents' names, their address, their school, or even their approximate location, their phone number or e-mail address, and their age. Conversely, they need to know that any information about anyone online that they receive may be false.

Both children and parents need to know how to look up and analyze information effectively, not just to find information more efficiently, but to avoid information that is false or even harmful. Something as simple as differentiating between a government website (whose URL ends in *.gov*), an organizational website (whose URL ends in *.org*), or a commercial website (whose URL ends in *.com* or one of the many newer extensions) can be a huge boon to the individual customers. Any training on safety and security on the Web is likely to result in improved communication between parent and child, and between customer and librarian. On a public relations note, the library that can demonstrate that it actively teaches children how to protect themselves online may be less susceptible to a charge that, by offering Internet access, they are letting children loose who are unprepared for a world of pedophiles and predators.

Filtering

The debate over whether or not to filter Internet computers in the children's library was dramatically changed when the Supreme Court ruled that the Children's Internet Protection Act (CIPA) was constitutional and could be enforced. Libraries that accepted federal money had to filter computers to some degree. The question of whether to accept federal money with this stipulation is a management and administration issue and will be dealt with in chapter 18, "Budget and Finance."

Assuming that the need for federal money has not dictated an answer already, the question is still open: to filter or not to filter. Choosing (or being required by law) to filter children's room computers opens up a series of new questions: What level of blocking should be used? Who will choose which sites to block and what will be the criteria for these decisions? Who can turn off the filter and how will it be done (a requirement mandated by the Supreme Court in case an adult should wish to use a filtered computer)? How does one handle customer requests to block or unblock certain sites? How does the library answer concerned customers who feel that by filtering the library is curtailing free speech and the free flow of ideas?

Even if the library chooses not to filter, there are questions: What types of activities will be allowed on public computers? How will any restrictions be enforced? How does the library answer concerned customers who feel that by not filtering the library is encouraging the use of pornography, especially among minors?

One thing is clear; the Internet is adding new levels of complexity to the administration of public libraries, and pushing the children's librarian into the center of the action like never before. Another thing should be easily inferred; the people closest to the customers need to be involved in the decision making. If children are going to be well served, then children's specialists need to be involved in the decision making.

Acceptable Use Policies

The beginning of any approach to offering the Internet to children—via filtered or unfiltered access—is the acceptable use policy. This document spells out the purposes for which the Internet may be used in the library, usually by defining the purposes for which it cannot be used. In addition, it should clearly state how, or if, that use will be monitored, and what will be the penalties for noncompliance. Acceptable use policies should be posted near Internet computers so that it is clear what can and cannot be done.

Consider carefully how the acceptable use policy will be perceived by customers; it is likely to be the most widely read of the library's policies. In order for the policy not be seen as arbitrary or discriminatory, make sure that it explains the rationale behind the decisions that were made about the policy and the library's philosophy of service with respect to the Internet.

Why does the library choose to offer Internet access? This question should be addressed first. If the library sees it as a research tool, and will restrict its use to that function, then that needs to be made clear or restrictions on other uses will seem arbitrary or pointless. If the library offers it to provide equal access to those who cannot or will not have the Internet in their homes, then that should be spelled out, and the policy should be written in such a way as to reflect that view. If the library will impose safeguards against certain types of materials, people should be informed not just of the restrictions, but of the purpose of those restrictions as well. It should be clear who has the authority to make such decisions, and whom the public should address to appeal those decisions.

Once the philosophy is stated, the policy can then lay out the rules under which the Internet is offered. Those rules can include what is and is not appropriate in general, nondiscriminatory terms. If this task seems overly simple, try to imagine writing an acceptable use policy for your book collection. Would you restrict the use of a reference book for pressing flowers because the book was intended for research? Would you tell people that they could not talk to each other while in the stacks because that area was not intended for communication? Understand that, as ridiculous as these examples may seem, they are not, in the eyes of many of your customers, categorically different from restricting the use of games or Instant Messenger on library computers. The fact that these, and many of the other common library restrictions, apply to activities most common among juveniles may look, or even be, transparently discriminatory. Being involved in the development and writing of these policies will allow the children's specialist to bring the needs and the sensibilities of their particular constituency to the table.

Many acceptable use policies place restrictions on who may use a computer. Different rules may apply to in-town as opposed to out-of-town customers. Children may need to get special permission from their parents or guardians before using the Internet, or possibly before using adult room computers. Children may be prohibited from using adult room computers at all. Again, if the reasoning is not well thought out, or well explained, the impression made may simply be that adults are allowed to use kids' computers, but kids are not allowed to use adults' computers—preferential treatment, pure and simple.

The acceptable use policy should clearly state if and how use will be monitored and how rules will be enforced. Penalties should be clearly stated so they do not appear to be imposed for arbitrary reasons, such as age. If there is a filter on the computer, this should be made clear, as well as whether or not staff will monitor activity and intervene. People, including children, deserve the dignity of not being pounced on unexpectedly, and parents should not be allowed to expect that the staff will supervise their child's online activity if that is not the case.

ACCEPTABLE USE STANDARDS FOR INTERNET AND IMCPL (INDIANAPOLIS–MARION COUNTY PUBLIC LIBRARY) COMPUTERS

All electronic traffic originating from the Indianapolis–Marion County Public Library Connection shall be in accordance with these Acceptable Use Standards. Failure to abide by these standards may result in the loss of Internet, computer, and Library privileges.

Acceptable Use

Use of the Library's computers shall be guided by the following principles:

1. Respect for the privacy of others.
2. Adherence to the legal protection provided by copyright and license to programs and data.
3. Consideration for the security and functioning of computers, computer networks, and systems.
4. Adherence to Library policies governing the security and functioning of computers, computer networks, and systems. Library staff may limit PC access time if other library patrons are waiting for access to PCs.

Unacceptable Use

It is not acceptable to use the Indianapolis–Marion County Public Library Computers for:

1. Any purposes which violate U.S., state, or local laws.
2. Transmitting threatening, obscene, or harassing materials, including the use of profanity or offensive language.
3. Intentional disruption of network users, services, or equipment harm to other computer systems. Examples of such programs are computer "viruses" and "worms."
4. Distribution of unsolicited advertising.
5. Tampering with computer or network security.
6. Making unauthorized entry into any systems accessible via Library computers.

7. Representing oneself as another person.

8. Developing and/or propagating programs that harass other users or cause harm to other computer systems. (Examples of such programs are computer "viruses" and "worms.")

9. Copying, downloading, or distributing commercial software or other material (e.g., music) in violation of federal copyright laws.

10. Accessing or loading pornographic, obscene, or sexually explicit material.

11. Other uses deemed inappropriate at the discretion of Library management.

Illegal acts involving the Library's computers may be subject to prosecution by local, state, or federal authorities.

Source: Indianapolis-Marion County Public Library, http://www.imcpl.org/use.htm.

Is It Worth It?

For most public libraries there can be no question that the Internet is integral to their operations and would never be abandoned; however, it may be worthwhile to look at the cost-benefit balance in order to see how the Internet helps and harms the operation of a library. By doing so, libraries can decide what level of resources to plow into the Internet, and more important for children's staff, in what part of the library to place those resources.

Plus: The Internet allows the library to devote fewer resources to providing reference services. The Internet, as an information tool, eliminates the need for some print reference materials, and consequently for the time and space needed to collect them. Those resources can then be used in other ways. The independent nature of Internet searching means many information requests will never reach the reference staff, which means that less staff time is devoted to this function.	*Minus:* The offering and maintenance of Internet service requires resources, space for computers, and staff time (to un-jam printers, clear locked computers, and troubleshoot).

Plus: The Internet represents a huge resource of great information. Even the smallest and poorest libraries can offer access to information that, historically, could not have been stored, organized, and accessed in even the largest research libraries. This is especially beneficial to children whose views of the world are expanding, as opposed to adults who tend to specialize.

Minus: The Internet is choked with great quantities of information that is silly, misleading, or downright dangerous, including fraudulent come-ons, rabid hatred, and the basest and most psychologically harrowing forms of pornography. The overabundance of this type of material is not just a problem in its own right, but its presence also makes the search for useful information that much more difficult.

Plus: The Internet is an avenue for unfettered communication. It eliminates distances, borders, and almost any other obstacle to interaction. With the library's Internet connection, children can hold on to relationships with family and friends no matter where they are, and build new relationships that would be otherwise impossible. Whether it is following an explorer over wireless e-mail, or asking a counterpart in another country about cultural differences, the Internet brings new depth to the old idea of a pen pal.

Minus: The Internet puts children into two-way communication with people whom they cannot possibly identify, putting them at risk for abuse. Studies report wide ranges of statistics, but it is clear that many of the people communicating online are lying about their age, gender, location, and intentions.

Plus: The Internet represents an awesome avenue for public library outreach. People who have no interest in any of our other services find their way into our libraries to use the Internet. Many of these people will then become users of other services, but even those who do not will have a reason to

Minus: The Internet is potentially the largest source of conflict and embarrassment for public libraries. The flack about pornography on public library Internet stations stands to dwarf any intellectual freedom storms we have weathered in the past. In exchange for something that many people, even many

connect with, and support, their public library.

librarians, feel is at best tangential to our mission, we stand to waste a great deal of time, energy, support, and political capital.

None of the reasons against should be strong enough to convince libraries not to provide access to the Internet. The Internet is too important in today's world, and doubly so for children whom we must prepare for the future. Still, carefully looking at the pluses and minuses of Internet access will allow us to design, execute, and communicate our services to the best advantage.

Programming

Programs are events the library organizes for a group. Unlike services, which are available whenever a customer needs them, programs are scheduled. Historically, programming has been seen as an extra, something offered over and above core services, and many libraries still view programming this way. Other libraries see programming as one of their core services. Why the different approaches? To understand, we need to look at the reasons why libraries offer programming and some of the reasons why they do not.

Why Program?

Many parents walk into a new library for the first time and ask when story hours happen, not if. In the eyes of our customers, programming for children has now become central to what public libraries do. It has become integrated into most public libraries, both for the way that it supports and promotes other parts of the library's operation, and for the way that programming helps to place the library in the center of the community. Consider all the positive reasons to program for children in your library.

Programming promotes reading and the love of books. It also promotes the use of the library and its collection. Having books is not enough; modern public libraries are not warehouses. Effective programming brings people—children and their parents and caregivers alike—into the library, it increases the likelihood that the children who do come will read, and it ensures that the books do not simply sit on the shelves. One program then promotes the next program, allowing the positive cycle to perpetuate itself.

Increased circulation from programming helps to highlight the effect of the library's efforts, and can go a long way toward justifying a budget. (See chapter 18, "Budget and Finance," for more on justifying budgets.)

Children's programming is also a training ground for future library customers. It habituates children to regular library visits, and it allows library staff to model good reading habits and to educate parents about developing language skills in their children (family literacy). By preparing preschoolers for school, programming helps to build a link in children's minds between education, information, and the library, an association that will encourage them to return to the library when they are older.

Programming helps to build community. It turns the solitary activity of reading into a social one. In so doing, programming helps to socialize children and parents alike, especially those new parents who are most likely to feel isolated and ill prepared to guide their children to reading.

There is nothing so basic to a children's services librarian's job as sharing stories with children.

Of course, children's programming serves a public relations and marketing function as well. Programs provide an opportunity for the children's staff to network with parents and caregivers, something that comes more easily to adult services staff members who encounter more adults. More importantly, key customers get a chance to see the library operating at its best. Library administrators sometimes point out that libraries are the one municipal service that most people view as positive and useful to them. Most people only notice the police when they are pulled over or when they have been in an accident; people only think about road crews when the roads are impassable; and of course no one relishes a visit from the fire department. Libraries are used voluntarily because they have something positive to offer, and never more so than during children's programming.

Why Not Program?

Despite all the apparent good that programming does for the library and the community, there are many arguments for why libraries should not program for children, or should scale back their programming. The first and most serious of these concerns is that programming may take resources away from library services.[1] It is always important to keep in mind the total cost of programming (materials, performer fees, staff time, space use, public relations, planning, and evaluation) when deciding what and how many programs to offer.

Consider the space that programs require. Is that space adequate? Is it safe? Will using the space make it unavailable for other library uses that will then be unavailable? How much time will be needed to set up, break down, and clean the space? Will people not be able to get reference or readers' advisory help during the program? Would the cost of the performer or materials be better spent, say, on improving the collection?

These are very practical, nuts-and-bolts concerns that must be addressed whenever planning programs and services. Other issues may arise that are not so well grounded, but may still affect how to plan for and execute programs, and how these programs will be perceived by others. The first is the belief by many that promoting reading should be the responsibility of the public schools and the public school media centers. Public library children's programs, with the exception of preschool story hours and the summer reading program, may be seen as redundant and wasteful. Others will see a great amount of resources serving a small number of people, small relative to the number of adults who use the library, and small even compared to the number of children in most communities who do not attend library programs. This argument has become stronger in recent years due to competition from other activities, from sports to arts, music, dance, martial arts, and a hundred more. There is even growing competition from corporate entities, including large chain bookstores that offer story hours and chain restaurants that hold celebrations full of kid-friendly activities.

The last reason people offer for not programming is a bit more disturbing. Some libraries are tempted to cut children's programming to make a budgeting point. If the public cuts our funding, then we will take away what the public wants most. This is a dangerous game for public libraries to play. Budget cuts often come about when the public feels that the library lacks relevance. The catalyst is often a money crunch, but cuts are made and accepted because the library is not an immediate need. Take away the most relevant service the library offers, and instead of shocking people into action you might confirm their suspicions; libraries are not about serving the actual needs of the people.

This type of decision is usually made at the administrative level or higher, where children's librarians traditionally have little say, and it shows. If the library wanted to make a cut that would hurt the most people by eliminating a popular and visible service, it could just as easily stop buying all adult fiction. That would strike most adult services librarians as absurd, but cutting children's programming has the same effect on most children's librarians.

Types of Programs

Programs can be classified in two main categories— literature-based and non-literature-based. Literature-based programs have reading at the core. These are covered in chapter 12, "Story Hours," chapter 13, "Book Discussion Groups," and chapter 14, "Booktalking." Literature-based programs are the most recognizable and traditional of the library's programs for children. They are also the easiest to justify and the least likely to draw criticism. Who could argue with reading to children, or gathering children together to talk about books? Because of their history, though, literature-based programs can be the most stagnant and unresponsive programs as well. If we are going to promote reading as a lifetime pleasure, then we must show that literature and reading are fresh, adaptive, and fun.

Non-literature-based programs deal with ideas and information that are not directly tied to the printed word. These are covered in chapter 15, "Entertainment and Enrichment Programs." Many non-literature-based programs, because they are so new in public libraries, can be inventive, even revolutionary. They broaden the library's audience by challenging the narrow stereotype of libraries as collections of dusty old books. They can help bring the human component back into the world of ideas. Chapter 16, "Summer Reading Programs," and chapter 17, "Family Programs and Family Literacy," deal with variations and combinations of these other programs for special purposes. These chapters highlight the ways that programs can be combined and integrated into the larger workings of the library.

NOTE

1. Mae Benne, *Principles of Children's Services in Public Libraries* (Chicago: American Library Association, 1991), 97.

12

Story Hours

Reading to children is the first and greatest gift we can give our customers. By reading to children, we show them that reading is fun and engaging. We model the habits they will one day develop, of adding inflection, pace, and characterization to the words we take off the page. We teach them the physical manipulation of a book, how to move from beginning to end and turn pages. We introduce them to illustrations and help them to relate the illustrations to the language. Eventually they will take over all of these tasks, but we begin by showing children how reading is done. It is important to remember all of these factors when choosing books to read and presenting them. If our inflection is flat, if we fail to move through a book in an orderly manner, if we skip over illustrations as unimportant, or fail to connect the illustrations to the words in the story, then we will fail to instill these habits in children.

Story hours, though, are not just about books; they are about a greater experience of language and story. There are many activities we can use to reinforce the books we read and to show children that books are the doorway to a large, fascinating, and fun world. Planning a story hour requires the children's librarian to select a theme, an idea, or a concept, to choose books that address it, and then to use those books to enhance the experience. There are many books out there with canned story hours that lay out all these components, and they are a great place to start, but children's librarians need to tailor their programs to their audience, their collection, and their own skills and strengths.

Choosing Books

Not every book that is good to read is good to read before a group. Choosing books to read at story hour requires looking not only at the quality of the book but also at how it will be used. If the story hour has mixed ages, then the book has to be accessible and interesting to all the participants. One child who feels lost by the book being read can distract many others. Older children who find the book babyish can also become bored and act out.

A book for story hour needs to be engaging to a much broader audience than a book read to oneself. Books with clear humor, like Esphyr Slobodkina's *Caps for Sale*; with great action and visual appeal, like Maurice Sendak's *Where the Wild Things Are*; with progressive development through the story, or with music and song, like the many versions of "I Know an Old Lady Who Swallowed a Fly"; and with tension and suspense, like Virginia Lee Burton's *Mike Mulligan and His Steam Shovel*, are perennial favorites for good reason: they hold a broad audience's attention.[1]

RECENT STORY HOUR WINNERS

The following is a list of books that have proven useful in story hours. Not all children's books, indeed not even all very good children's books, translate well in this setting. For the new children's librarian, this list represents a useful starting point. For more experienced children's librarians, it can be used as a reference in order to add a few titles to a regular collection of story hour favorites.

Allan Ahlberg, *Mockingbird*, ill. Paul Howard (Candlewick Press, 1998)

Jim Arnosky, *Every Autumn Comes the Bear* (Putnam, 1996)

David Axtell, *We're Going on a Lion Hunt* (Henry Holt, 1999)

Judy Barrett, *Animals Should Definitely Not Wear Clothing*, ill. Ron Barrett (Aladdin, 1998)

Jan Brett, *The Hat* (Putnam, 1997)

Jan Brett, *The Mitten: A Ukrainian Folktale* (Putnam, 1989)

Carol Carrick, *Valentine*, ill. Paddy Bouma (Clarion, 1995)

Michael Coleman and Gwyneth Williamson, *One, Two, Three, Oops!* (Little Tiger Press, 1999)

Doreen Cronin, *Click Clack Moo: Cows That Type*, ill. Betsy Lewin (Simon and Schuster, 2000)

Margery Cuyler, *That's Good! That's Bad!* ill. David Catrow (Live Oak Media, 1996)

Julia Donaldson, *The Gruffalo*, ill. Axel Scheffler (Dial, 1999)

Jules Feiffer, *Bark, George* (HarperCollins, 1999)

Rhonda Gowler Greene, *Barnyard Song*, ill. Robert Bender (Atheneum, 1997)

Sheila Hamanaka, *The Hokey Pokey* (Simon and Schuster, 1997)

Dianne Dawson Hearn, *Dad's Dinosaur Day* (Simon and Schuster, 1993)

Will Hillenbrand, *Down by the Station* (Gulliver Books, 1999)

Alison Jackson, *I Know an Old Lady Who Swallowed a Pie*, ill. Judith Byron Schachner (Dutton Children's Books, 1997)

Laura Numeroff Joffe, *Dogs Don't Wear Sneakers*, ill. Joe Mathieu (Simon and Schuster, 1993)

Gail J. Jorgensen, Patricia Mullins, *Crocodile Beat* (Bradbury Press, 1998)

Helen Lester, *Tacky the Penguin*, ill. Lynn Munsinger (Houghton Mifflin, 1998)

Jonathan London, *Froggy Gets Dressed*, ill. Frank Remkiewicz (Viking, 1992)

Heidi Stetson Mario, *I'd Rather Have an Iguana* (Charlesbridge, 1998)

Julie Markes, *Good Thing You're Not an Octopus!* ill. Maggie Smith (HarperCollins, 2001)

Bill Martin Jr. and John Archambault, *Chicka Chicka Boom Boom*, ill. Lois Ehlert (Simon and Schuster, 1989)

Kate McMullan, *I Stink!* ill. Jim McMullan (Joanne Cotler, 2002)

Mary Elise Monsell, *Underwear!* ill. Lynn Munsinger (Albert Whitman, 1988)

Robert Munsch, *Alligator Baby*, ill. Michael Martchenko (Scholastic, 1997)

Richard Rogers, *Rogers and Hammerstein's My Favorite Things*, ill. Renée Graef (HarperCollins, 2002)

Allen Say, *Tree of Cranes* (Houghton Mifflin, 1991)

David Small, *Imogene's Antlers* (Crown, 2000)

Rob Spence and Amy Spence, *Clickety Clack*, ill. Margaret Spengler (Penguin Putnam, 1999)

Iza Trapani, *I'm a Little Teapot* (Charlesbridge, 1997)

Iza Trapani, *The Itsy Bitsy Spider* (Charlesbridge, 1993)

Iza Trapani and Bob Merrill, *How Much Is That Doggie in the Window?* (Charlesbridge, 1997)

Nadine Bernard Westcott, *I've Been Working on the Railroad* (Hyperion, 1996)

Jeanne Willis, *Earthlets, As Explained by Professor Xargle*, ill. Tony Ross (Dutton, 1989)

Karma Wilson, *The Bear Snores On*, ill. Jane Chapman (McElderry Books, 2002)

Audrey Wood, *Elbert's Bad Word*, ill. Don Wood (Harcourt, 1988)

Audrey Wood, *The Little Mouse, the Red Ripe Strawberry, and the Big Hungry Bear*, ill. Don Wood (Child's Play, 1994)

Audrey Wood, *The Tickleoctopus*, ill. Don Wood (Harcourt, 1994)

Jane Yolen, *Owl Moon*, ill. John Schoenherr (Philomel, 1987)

Bernard Zaritzky, *Little White Duck*, ill. Jane Paley (Little, Brown, 2000)

Reading to Children

Reading to children is not as simple as it seems. Indeed, a common request from would-be volunteers is to "just sit down and read to children during story hour." It is not that simple. You are not only reading but also modeling good reading to children who have never read but will do so soon, and to parents who may not know how to read to someone else, a skill few people practice. Sadly, few children's librarians get much practice reading to children through library school, but this activity then becomes the most high-profile part of their jobs. Among the issues to remember when reading to children are illustrations, inflection, and pacing; by focusing on these, you involve the audience and promote reading beyond a single book or story hour.

Children do not always associate the pictures in a picture book with the words on the page. Adults do nothing to help this when they read the words with the cover facing out, or if they show the pictures only after they are done reading the words. Ideally, the illustrations are visible to children while the words are being read. The reader can even use his or her free hand to trace the words on the page, showing that the words on the page, the words being read, and the illustrations are all connected. Making sure you point out the illustrator as well as the author is another way of reinforcing this connection.

How you read is important as well. Children will be influenced by the experience of listening to others read when they themselves become readers. These are considerations whenever someone is speaking to others in a formal setting. Pacing is important; read too slowly and the story is lost on short attention spans, but read too fast and no one has time to notice the details or take pleasure in the story. Pacing becomes more difficult when children want to make comments and ask questions. This curiosity is natural and a good indication that the child is involved in the story. Discussion should be encouraged by engaging the child, but too much engagement can bring the story to a screeching halt for all the other participants. Intonation is important, especially if the setting or some of the vocabulary is unfamiliar to the children. The tone of voice can convey much of the meaning, increasing the children's vocabulary without having to stop and explain every word.

Obviously, preparation is important. Reading a book for the first time in front of children, or even after a few cursory readings, is not likely to produce exciting results. Read books for story hour on your own, many times, out loud, before you have to do so in public. Understand the plot of the story and remember the sequence of events; this comfort with a book allows you to choose the most appropriate tone and pace throughout your reading. Understand what makes the story funny, interesting, or memorable, and then highlight that when you read in front of the group. Know the story well enough that, if need be, you can put the book down at any point and finish it as a storyteller. This may be the only option other than not finishing the story at all if the children seem to be losing interest.

Remember that every book is an opportunity to promote the next book. Say the name of the author and the illustrator before, and even after, the story. Have other books by the same author or illustrator, or on the same topic, available and on display. Emphasize that if the children liked this book, they can take out another one that is similar to it. If all you do is read a book to children, your impact is minimal, a fact lost on many well-intentioned volunteers who think reading to children is the least they can do. Reading to children is a way of promoting reading and helping children to become readers themselves.

Story Stretchers

While books should be the focus of story hours, it is often the related activities that make the greatest impact. Children do not make distinctions between mental and physical activities, between learning and play, or between written and oral language as clearly as adults do. Children also have shorter attention spans than adults do, so a variety of experiences are most likely to keep their attention; include activities other than reading in order to reinforce themes, ideas, or events from the story. The books are still the focus, but there is much more that can add to the experience.

Storytelling

Storytelling has great value as a program in and of itself (see chapter 15, "Entertainment and Enrichment Programs," for more on how to do storytelling), but it also forms an effective change of pace as a story stretcher in story hours. Storytelling, presenting a story without scripted language, illustrations or a book in hand, allows more interaction between the children and the story because, as long as the tale is progressing toward its end, the teller can alter the story. The teller can change pace, level of detail, characterization, and any other aspect of the story. Indeed, recounting a story in this traditional form can often keep an audience alert and engaged for longer than reading a book.

As a planned part of a story hour, storytelling can create a break between two books or a transitional piece between stories and some other activity. Introducing storytelling in story hours is a way to give children a measured exposure to the form early on, preparing them for longer storytelling presentations later. It is also a way to practice the skill in short spells, and in comfortable environments. Storytelling is a skill every children's librarian should develop, and story hours are the perfect opportunity to do so.

Storyboards

Storyboards are mechanisms to visualize a story without using the static illustrations of a book. The most common type is a felt board or flannel board, easily found in library supply catalogs or made by stapling a piece of felt or flannel to a sheet of plywood. Pieces can be made by creating a picture on heavy paper or oak tag and attaching felt or Velcro to the back. When the piece is pushed against the felt board, it sticks. You can use a whiteboard and pieces mounted on magnets as well, or if you are confident of your drawing skills, you can draw in the figures on a large sheet of paper. As the librarian reads or tells a story, pictures representing characters or plot development are added to the storyboard.

Backgrounds can be set up in advance or added as the story progresses. The teller can add these details, or he or she can make the story more inter-active by inviting participants to do so. There are many books of short tales that work well in storyboard form, and it is easy enough to create the pieces and backdrops using the illustrations in your favorite book. Never throw away a worn-out children's book without seeing if there are intact illustra-tions that could be used for a storyboard.

LIBRARY PROGRAMS AND COPYRIGHT

Copyright is the permission to use the fruits of someone else's intellec-tual labor. In order to understand copyright, you must first understand when someone has a claim to his or her work, and then when you are infringing on that claim. Michael Skinrud, writing in the *National Storytelling Journal*, claims that

> you infringe on someone else's copyright when you use their material to put money in your pocket. If you are telling your own version of a folktale, or if you are telling a literary work in an educational setting for no fee, you are not violating copyright.[2]

This is an obvious simplification; there are no hard-and-fast rules for when and how you can use someone else's work short of gaining spe-cific written permission. There are four significant factors should a charge of infringement be brought to court: the purpose and character of the use (for-profit or not-for-profit), the nature of the work (scholarly or commercial), how much of the work is used, and what affect the use might have on the sales or market of the work.[3] Keep these factors in mind when considering using someone else's work.

Still, Skinrud's observation clarifies a great deal of what the chil-dren's librarian may face. Folktales, stories of unknown origin that exist in many versions, cannot be claimed by anyone. Using a literary work in its unaltered form in an educational setting, with proper credit given to the work's creator, cannot be deemed infringement. A particular, copyrighted version of a work, even of a folktale, is the product of someone's work and should be treated as such. The creator should be credited, and you should not use the work in a commercial way. When doing storytelling, it is always safest to create your own version of a story from a number of sources.

When adapting someone's work into a new format, especially if that adaptation involves creating something new based on a literary work such as puppets or reproducibles, then it is necessary to get permission. In *Books in Bloom*, Kimberly K. Faurot suggests researching who actually has the copyright, usually a publisher, and sending detailed requests for permission outlining exactly how you plan to adapt the work months in advance.[4] Of course, the simplest way to be sure is to use works such as Faurot's which have adaptations that have already been cleared by copyright holders.

Crafts

Crafts allow children to reinforce the ideas, lessons, and themes of a story hour, especially if the child is a concrete learner. The physical component of producing something stimulates different areas of the brain, allowing for more cross-brain communication and better brain function. This is especially important for boys whose brain structure produces less cross-brain communication than girls' do.[5] The physical object produced acts not only as a reminder of what happened in story hour but also as a conversation starter, encouraging children to practice their language skills by explaining the theme, or even recounting the stories, from their story hour experience.

Music and Rhyme

Children's brains are absorbing both information and structures of thinking. Ordered structures, such as rhyme and rhythm, logical progression, pacing, and repetition are all present in music. Add lyrics to the music, and you have structured language that is simple enough for preschoolers to digest. Studies show that those people who practice or are exposed to music have better word recall and verbal memory, and babies exposed to music learn faster than their peers, the so-called *Mozart effect*.[6] And music is fun too.

Adding music to story time can be as simple as singing a nursery rhyme or doing a finger play. You can add percussion instruments like tambourines, maracas, and triangles, or even blocks of wood. You can make an instrument as a craft in one story hour that the children bring back for the rest of the series, or that the library can hold and give to children each story hour.

Babies and Toddlers

Story hours can be designed for those younger than three with some modifications. The focus here is clearly on language, not specifically reading. Jane Marino of the Scarsdale (NY) Public Library described her "Mother Goose Time" for babies and toddlers as a "language enrichment program that uses rhymes, songs, and books."[7] Read very simple books with bright and clear illustrations. Infants and toddlers are less likely to be able to pick an object out of a background than they are to recognize that object alone on a page. Repetition is important as these children are learning to imitate sounds in speech. Choose books with repetitive text, and use the same books often.

Do not neglect games; play is an infant's primary way of interacting with the world.[8] Talk continuously through play and encourage parents to do the same. Once children are engaged in play, their minds are more open; that is the optimal time to instill language. Group games are especially welcome in story time, which may be one of the few times that a child is in contact with so many other children.

The physical abilities of the participants are an important consideration when designing a program for infants and toddlers. Pre-walkers will sit still through numerous rhymes and stories, so use this time to practice coordination with hand and foot motions. Finger plays help develop fine motor skills.[9] Once these children find their legs, however, watch out! That is the time to introduce stories with independent motion components. Stand up, sit down, touch your toes. Introduce new characters to storyboard stories by having the children place the figures on the board.

BOOKS FOR INFANT AND TODDLER STORY HOURS

The following is a selective list of books that may be rewarding to use with infants and toddlers. Many are available in board or rag book format. Every attempt has been made to choose books that are still in print, but that status is always in flux. This list should be considered a starting point for those beginning to work with this age group.

Janet Ahlberg and Allan Ahlberg, *Blue Buggy* (Little, Brown, 1999)

Janet Ahlberg and Allan Ahlberg, *Peek-a-Boo!* (Puffin, 1984)

Dawn Apperley, *Nighty-Night* (Little, Brown, 1999)

Emily Bolam, *Sleepy, Sleepy!* (Price Stern Sloan, 1999)

Sandra Boynton, *Barnyard Dance* (Workman, 1993)

Sandra Boynton, *But Not the Hippopotamus* (Little Simon, 1982)

Margaret Wise Brown, *Goodnight Moon*, ill. Clement Hurd (Harper Collins, 1947)

Susan Canizares and Samantha Berger, *Babies* (Scholastic, 2000)

Nancy White Carlstrom, *Jesse Bear's Tra-La Tub*, ill. Bruce Degen (Little Simon, 1994)

Nancy White Carlstrom, *Jesse Bear's Wiggle-Jiggle Jump-Up*, ill. Bruce Degen (Little Simon, 1994)

Nancy White Carlstrom, *Jesse Bear's Yum-Yum Crumble*, ill. Bruce Degen (Little Simon, 1994)

Marie Torres Cimarusti, *Peek-a-Moo*, ill. Stephanie Peterson (Dutton, 1998)

Donna Conrad, *See You Soon Moon*, ill. Don Carter (Little, Brown, 2001)

Lucy Cousins, *Country Animals* (Tambourine, 1991)

Lucy Cousins, *Count with Maisy* (Candlewick, 1999)

Lucy Cousins, *Farm Animals* (Tambourine, 1991)

Lucy Cousins, *Maisy Cleans Up* (Candlewick, 2002)

Lucy Cousins, *Maisy's ABC* (Walker, 1994)

Lucy Cousins *Maisy's Colors* (Candlewick, 1999)

Jane Dyer, *Animal Crackers: Bedtime* (Little, Brown, 1998)

Jane Dyer, *Animal Crackers: Nursery Rhymes* (Little, Brown, 1998)

Rebecca Elgar, *Is That an Elephant Over There?* (Levinson, 1998)

David Ellwand, *Big Book of Beautiful Babies* (Dutton, 1995)

Denise Fleming, *Barnyard Banter* (Holt, 1994)

Mem Fox, *Time for Bed*, ill. Jane Dyer (Harcourt, 1993)

Phoebe Gilman, *Something from Nothing* (Scholastic, 1993)

Heidi Goennel, *What I Eat* (Tambourine, 1995)

Heidi Goennel, *What I See* (Tambourine, 1995)

Heidi Goennel, *What I Wear* (Tambourine, 1995)

Heidi Goennel, *Where I Live* (Tambourine, 1995)

Kathy Henderson, *The Baby Dances*, ill. Tony Kerins (Candlewick, 1999)

Kathy Henderson, *Bounce Bounce Bounce*, ill. Carol Thompson (Walker, 1994)

Kathy Henderson, *Bumpety Bump*, ill. Carol Thompson (Candlewick, 1994)

Eric Hill, *Hello Spot* (Putnam, 2004)

Eric Hill, *Spot Helps Out* (Putnam, 1999)

Eric Hill, *Where's Spot?* (Putnam, 2003)

Tana Hoban, *Black on White* (Greenwillow, 1993)

Tana Hoban, *What Is That?* (HarperFestival, 1994)

Tana Hoban, *White on Black* (Greenwillow, 1993)

Tana Hoban, *Who Are They?* (Greenwillow, 1993)

Patricia Hubbell, *Wrapping Paper*, ill. Jennifer Plecas (HarperCollins, 1998)

Cheryl Willis Hudson, *Animal Sounds for Baby*, ill. George Ford (Cartwheel, 1997)

Cheryl Willis Hudson, George Ford (ill.), *Let's Count Baby* (Scholastic, 1995)

Karen Katz, *Counting Kisses* (McElderry Books, 2001)

Tony Kenyon, *Pat-a-Cake* (Candlewick, 1994)

Lisa Lawston, *Can You Hop?* ill. Ed Vere (Orchard, 1999)

Jane K. Manning, *My First Songs* (HarperFestival, 1998)

Ron Maris, *In My Garden* (Greenwillow, 1988)

Bill Martin Jr., *Brown Bear, Brown Bear, What Do You See?* ill. Eric Carle (Henry Holt)

Bill Martin Jr. and John Archembault, *Here Are My Hands*, ill. Ted Rand (1987)

Flora McDonnell, *I Love Animals* (Candlewick, 1994)

Margaret Miller, *Baby Faces* (Little Simon, 1998)

Jan Ormerod, *Rock-a-Baby* (Dutton, 1997)

Helen Oxenbury, *All Fall Down* (Little Simon, 1999)

Helen Oxenbury, *Clap Hands* (Little Simon, 1999)

Helen Oxenbury, *I Can* (Candlewick, 1995)

Helen Oxenbury, *I Hear* (Candlewick, 1995)

Helen Oxenbury, *I See* (Candlewick, 1995)

Helen Oxenbury, *I Touch* (Candlewick, 1995)

Helen Oxenbury, *Say Goodnight* (Little Simon, 1999)

Helen Oxenbury, *Tickle, Tickle* (Little Simon, 1999)

Helen Oxenbury, *Working* (Little Simon, 1995)

Ant Parker, *It's Bathtime* (Harcourt, 1996)

Ant Parker, *It's Bedtime* (Harcourt, 1996)

Ant Parker, *It's Playtime* (Harcourt, 1996)

Ant Parker, *It's Snacktime* (Harcourt, 1996)

Jacqueline Reinach, *Little Owl, Here's Your Towel* (Random House, 2001)

Phyllis Root, *One Duck Stuck*, ill. Jane Chapman (Candlewick Press, 2001)

Phyllis Limbacher Tildes, *Baby Animal: Black and White* (Charlesbridge, 1998)

Phyllis Limbacher Tildes, *Baby Face* (Charlesbridge, 2001)

Jeanne Titherington, *Baby's Boat* (Greenwillow, 1992)

Nancy Van Laan, *Tickle Tum!* ill. Bernadette Pons (Atheneum Books for Young Readers, 2001)

Roy Volkmann, *Curious Kittens* (Bantam Doubleday, 2001)

Kaori Watanabe, *My First Taggies Book: Sweet Dreams* (Scholastic, 2003)

Nicki Weiss, *Where Does the Brown Bear Go?* (Greenwillow, 1989)

Rosemary Wells, *Bear Went over the Mountain* (Scholastic, 1998)

Rosemary Wells, *Bingo* (Scholastic, 1999)

Rosemary Wells, *Max's Breakfast* (Dial, 1998)

Rosemary Wells, *Max's First Word* (Viking, 2004)

Rosemary Wells, *Max's New Suit* (Dial, 1998)

Rosemary Wells, *Max's Toys* (Viking, 2004)

Rosemary Wells, *Old MacDonald* (Scholastic, 1998)

Sue Williams, *I Went Walking*, ill. Julie Vivas (Gulliver, 1990)

Vera B. Williams, *More More More, Said the Baby* (Greenwillow, 1990)

Audrey Wood, *Piggies*, ill. Don Wood (Harcourt, 1997)

Dan Yaccarino, *So Big!* (HarperFestival, 2001)

FURTHER READING

Ann Carlson and Mary Carlson, *Flannelboard Stories for Infants and Toddlers* (Chicago: American Library Association, 1999).

Robin Works Davis, *Toddle on Over: Developmentally Appropriate Literature Programs* (Fort Atkinson, WI: Highsmith, 1998).

Linda Ernst, *Lapsit Services for the Very Young: A How-to-Do-It Manual* (New York: Neal-Schuman, 1995).

Kimberly Faurot, *Books in Bloom: Creative Patterns and Props That Bring Stories to Life* (Chicago: American Library Association, 2003).

Valerie Marsh and Patrick Luzadder, *Stories That Stick: Quick and Easy Storyboard Tales* (Fort Atkinson, WI: Upstart Books, 2002).

Shirley C. Raines and Robert J. Canady, *More Story Stretchers: More Activities to Expand Children's Favorite Books* (Mt. Rainier, MD: Gryphon House, 1991).

Shirley C. Raines and Robert J. Canady, *Story Stretchers: Activities to Expand Children's Favorite Books.* (Mt. Rainier, MD: Gryphon House, 1989).

Shirley C. Raines, Karen Miller, and Leah Curry-Rood, *Story Stretchers for Infants, Toddlers, and Twos: Experiences, Activities, and Games for Popular Children's Books* (Mt. Rainier, MD: Gryphon House, 2002).

Rob Reid, *Children's Jukebox: A Subject Guide to Musical Recordings and Program Ideas for Songsters Ages Two to Twelve* (Chicago: American Library Association, 1995).

Rob Reid, *Cool Story Programs for the School-Age Crowd* (Chicago: American Library Association, 2004).

Rob Reid, *Something Funny Happened at the Library: How to Create Humorous Programs for Children and Young Adults* (Chicago: American Library Association, 2002).

Carrie Russell, ed., *Complete Copyright: An Everyday Guide for Librarians.* (Chicago: American Library Association, 2004).

Judy Sierra, *Multicultural Folktales for the Feltboard and Readers' Theater* (Phoenix, AZ: Oryx Press, 1996).

R. S. Talab, *Commonsense Copyright: A Guide for Educators and Librarians*, 2nd ed. (Jefferson, NC: McFarland, 1999).

Jane Yolen, ed., *The Lap-Time Song and Play Book*, ill. Margot Tomes (San Diego, CA: Harcourt, 1989).

NOTES

1. Esphyr Slobodkina, *Caps for Sale* (New York: HarperCollins, 1988); Maurice Sendak, *Where the Wild Things Are* (New York: HarperCollins, 1988); Virginia Lee Burton, *Mike Mulligan and His Steam Shovel* (Boston: Houghton Mifflin, 1939).

2. Margaret Read MacDonald, *The Storyteller's Start-Up Book: Finding, Learning, Performing and Using Folktales* (Little Rock, AK: August House, 1993), 72.

3. R. S. Talab, *Commonsense Copyright: A Guide for Educators and Librarians*, 2nd ed. (Jefferson, NC: McFarland, 1999), 26–27.

4. Kimberly K. Faurot, *Books in Bloom: Creative Patterns and Props That Bring Stories to Life* (Chicago: American Library Association, 2003), 6–8.

5. Michael Gurian and Patricia Henley, with Terry Trueman, *Boys and Girls Learn Differently! A Guide for Teachers and Parents* (San Francisco: Jossey-Bass, 2001), 177–78.

6. "Where Does Music Fit into the Curriculum?" *Curriculum Review*, January 1999, 4.

7. Jane Marino, "B Is for Baby, B Is for Books," *School Library Journal*, March 1997, 110.

8. Alice Sterling Honig, "A Passion for Play," *Early Childhood Today*, November/December 2000, 32.

9. Donna Celano and Susan B. Neuman, *The Role of Public Libraries in Children's Literacy Development* (Harrisburg: Pennsylvania Library Association, 2001), 34.

13

Book Discussion Groups

Book discussion groups are common among librarians that serve tweenagers and teenagers, and in many ways they can operate in the same way as book discussion groups for adults. You decide whom to target for the group, set up a meeting time and place, choose a book, make copies available, publicize early enough so that people can get a copy and read it before the actual meeting, and prepare some background information and questions to help spur on the discussion during the meeting.

Who's In?

The composition of a book group for children is more complicated than for adults. You have to consider the age range of the participants when deciding whether to make the group single-sex or coed (see "Service to Boys," in chapter 2, "Principles of Children's Librarianship"), whether to allow or require parents or guardians, and whether to market to a specific type of genre reader. By the time they reach middle elementary school, children are entering a stage of emotional and developmental upheaval. They are approaching the period when they will have to separate themselves from their parents in many ways, though they still feel the strong draw of the parent-child bond. They are discovering the opposite sex, but often do not know quite what to do about it. The world is changing rapidly for them, yet they lack the tools to understand, or even talk about, these changes. These struggles make the age nearly ideal for book discussions. Book discussions can introduce young people to literature as a means of sorting out feelings and understanding the world. They can also be a cover that allows topics to come up in a safe environment.

All this upheaval, though, can make the composition of a book discussion both vital and treacherous. Among the youngest of these groups, for nine- and ten-year-olds, the inclusion of a parent or guardian can be an unqualified good. The child will be looking for guidance, unsure of how to act or what to do. The child may also appreciate extra time with the parent, so the book discussion fosters a positive psychological connection between the child and reading. By the time you hand the child over to a teen discussion group, that dynamic has changed dramatically. Teens are looking to separate from their parents, and the topics they want to discuss are often ones they do not feel comfortable discussing with their parents. At this stage, the book discussion group becomes a training ground for teenagers trying to work out very personal issues, and a rehearsal for discussions with their parents or other adults. The younger the children, the more likely you will be to invite parents to join the group. By the time children turn twelve or thirteen, you should seriously consider marketing your program only to the kids.

Then there is the question of boys-only, girls-only, and mixed-gender groups. Girls will tend to dominate most open discussion groups because girls visit the library more often and the traditional book discussion group is better suited to their needs. Girls also read significantly more than boys, so they will naturally show up in greater numbers. Because of this, boys who do attend may feel uncomfortably conspicuous and outnumbered. A boys-only book group helps boys feel less self-conscious, and goes some ways toward removing the stigma of book groups as a girls' activity. As children get older, the reasons for a girls-only book discussion multiply as well. Group identity and social pressure become stronger, and boys will tend to be more aggressive in group activities. Even the presence of one boy in a group of ten can seriously inhibit open, active discussion.

Time and Space

Choosing the setting for a book discussion will have a huge influence on its success. The choice of when to hold it will determine the audience. Obviously you need to schedule a parent-child book discussion when parents—especially working parents—are available. This may mean a late afternoon, early evening, or weekend program, or a summer program when many parents make a point of taking time out to spend with their children. Conversely it is best to schedule a program for preteens without their parents for after-school hours. This reduces the likelihood of conflict, and parents may appreciate their children having some structured time when adults cannot be home.

The location of the program will seriously affect its tone. The standard placement, at a table in the children's room, has the advantages of being convenient and close to the library collection that the program should be promoting. It may have the disadvantage, however, of being public and noisy, especially if the library does not have a separate meeting room. It also is not very special; it is the same place the children come for everything else they do in the library.

There are other locations to consider. Holding a discussion group in the local school after regular school hours makes transportation a non-issue, especially if there is a late bus. You start with a much larger audience than you would have in the library: those children who are at school at the end of the school day rather than those kids who come to the library after school. You just have to convince them to stay and participate.

Inviting participants to a different location adds to the separateness and the uniqueness of the program, even if that place is the table in the adult library section. Some teen discussion groups meet in local coffee shops. Choosing outside locations can also alter the composition of the group by bringing the program to where certain populations are. The local gym, YMCA, or recreation center might draw more boys. Camps can give the program exposure to a broad range of kids in a single location. Even holding it outside on the grass might attract kids who feel cramped and confined being indoors. The great advantage of a book discussion group is that it requires few if any materials, so mobility is easier than with other programs.

Choosing Books

Choosing the right book can be the most important part of a book discussion group, but what that right book is will vary greatly. Many adult book groups have an open process of nomination, discussion, and agreement for choosing their books, but this will usually not work well with children's groups, especially the youngest of them. Nine-year-olds probably have not heard of many books, and they don't tend to read the book reviews in the local paper. Also, children's books are not publicized as widely as adult books, save a few blockbusters. Still, choice is desirable.

Librarians experienced at booktalking should prepare a broad selection of books to present to the group and reach a decision by discussion. Build your list with the broadest parameters of the group in mind. If the group has boys and girls, make an effort to include some books that appeal specifically to boys, others to girls, and some to both. If there are adults and children in the group, look for books with many layers so that the parents will not be bored. If the group is advertised as being for a specific genre, fine, but if not, throw in a sprinkling of genres in order to provide varied choices. Try to pick a number of books at a time, so that the group knows what they are reading well in advance. This makes the members feel obligated to the group over a longer period of time, and allows for more balance by assuring participants that the current book may not be exactly what they want, but there is one coming that is.

Be careful of the reading level. Make sure that the books you choose are accessible to everyone in the group. While some readers may be excited to plow on through a tome clearly above the average reading level of the group, they can always do so on their own. Book discussion groups are a social exercise, and everyone should feel included. Besides, discussions are not supposed to be work.

Leading the Discussion

Leading a book discussion—any book discussion—is an art, and with children it is even more difficult. The objective, of course, is to get the kids talking about the book, so ideally you, as a facilitator, say very little and do not interfere with the discussion. Few discussions, though, take off at the starting gun and move along happily through the end of the program. You, as leader, have to take an active role, and that role may change dramatically from one program to the next. Having a series of open-ended questions prepared ahead of time is a must. Beware the closed, yes-or-no types of questions, such as "Did you think . . . ?" The answer is usually a single word and a look saying, "What else have you got?"

Bring in relevant connections to film, music, television, and current events. Children tend to read to understand their world far more than adults, who often read for escape. Connecting reading to the broader world will make it more enjoyable and satisfying for children, and also help them to see that reading is their best tool for understanding the world around them.

As moderator, you must also keep out various elements not related to the book that could hurt the discussion. The long, unconnected tangent is common to all groups of all ages in all types of discussions. Be prepared for it, and prepare your group up front that sidetracks will be closed. You can do this softly, subtly, and even humorously. Allow for some sort of group decision-making process—a show of hands, or a code word, anything—that will signal it is time to reel in the tangent. More disturbing is the turn that some groups make toward the personal or hateful. This is only to be expected. Even adults fall into this trap often enough, and children are still learning the rules and expectations of such a group. Again, lay the ground-work early. You can discuss the rules of conduct at the first meeting and write them up as a contract. Make it a point of pride and group identity that these are the rules: if you want to be one of us you abide by them.

If your program involves a significant number of boys, you may want to include physical elements. Move around, make something related to the book while you are discussing it or hold the discussion on a walk. In many ways, you can replicate story hour, which, for many boys, was the last time reading and interacting around books was fun and enjoyable. Make a discussion of the plot and the action in the book a prominent part of the program. If your program is solely or predominantly girls, expect to focus the discussion more on the interplay between characters.

Book discussion groups are a way to promote reading in conjunction with others, an aspect of reading often lost as children take their books to their rooms and close the door. Reading socially brings new depth and breadth to reading, enriching the experience and using literature as a springboard to other forms of language and experience. Book discussion groups also allow us to make reading special—an event, something to get excited about. Careful preparation can make the most of these advantages while minimizing the negative effects that can arise from clashing personalities and different points of view.

14
Booktalking

One of the most basic items in the children's librarian's tool chest is the ability to stand before people and tell them why they would want to read a book. When it is done in private, in response to the needs of an individual, it is a component of readers' advisory. When it is done at a gathering of people, speaker to audience, it is a program called booktalking. First and foremost, children's staff must remember that booktalking is not book reviewing. You are not being asked to give a complete and critical evaluation of the book. Booktalking is promotion, and especially with children you must remember that you are not just promoting the book but also promoting reading in general.

There are any number of resources that give you short booktalks to promote books, and it is worth using these to build up a repertoire, especially if you are unused to booktalking. They give you a solid piece of material that has been tested by people who do this regularly. At the same time, you should work on developing your own booktalks; they will be more meaningful for you, and you also need to be able to do this on your own. The books you want to promote may not be in any of the resources that are published, and it takes time for booktalks on new books to become available. If you want to be able to pick the books to work with, or you want to be able to work with new books, then you must be able to write booktalks.

Whether you are writing your own booktalks or using someone else's, there are a few things you must keep in mind. Never booktalk a book you have not read. You are likely to face questions about the books you promote, and it is embarrassing and damaging to your credibility to have to admit that you have not read a book when you are telling people they should read it. Do not talk about reasons *not* to read a book; speak about what is positive instead. This does not mean you cannot booktalk a book you did not like. If there is something about the book that you think will appeal to someone else, you can focus on that. "If you like gory stories, you're gonna love this. . . ."

This is important to remember when you look at books that might appeal to the opposite sex. There is probably nothing that affects reading taste as much as gender. If you are a woman, be careful to include books that will appeal to boys. If you are a man, make sure you are booktalking books that will appeal to girls. Remember that the style of the booktalk has as much to do with whether a child will be hooked or not as the choice of the book itself. If a book will be appealing because of high action, focus on the plot. If the book's appeal is the interaction of fascinating characters, put them front and center. Include some humor and some serious books, fiction and nonfiction. Booktalk a few genre books, but also include some standard novels. Do not forget poetry, even though you probably will not do an entire program of poetry books.

A BOY-APPEAL BOOKTALK

Hudson Talbott, Safari Journal: The Adventures in Africa of Carey Monroe *(Harcourt, 2003)*

(Portions of the text have been omitted for brevity.)

Carey Monroe, on safari in Africa:

The road I followed leads to a little village on the other side of the creek. There's a kid over there watching me. He looks about my age. I wonder if he's ever seen a Frisbee. I took mine out of my pack and tossed it over the creek. He picked it up and threw it right back. The next time I threw it he caught it and sent it right back to me. We were tossing it back and forth until—SPLASH—it had to happen—it landed right in the middle of the creek. I started to wade in for it, but the kid went nuts!

> "No! No! Mamba! Mamba!" he was yelling at me. And I'm thinking, "Who's Mamba?"
> My newest Swahili word: Mamba = Crocodile!
> Out of nowhere two giant jaws chomped down on my Frisbee!
>
> One of many new words and many adventures in Hudson Talbott's *Safari Journal: The Adventures in Africa of Carey Monroe.*

Do always mention the author and title of the book, and the illustrator as well if there is one. The point is to encourage children to read the book, and you want to make it as easy as possible to find it. If possible, it is a good idea to have booklists to hand out, so that the children can simply mark off the books they want to follow up on. You are not likely to have enough copies for every child in a program, so inevitably they will need to wait for books. Print the booklists as bookmarks, and the children will always have an answer to the question, "What do I read next?"

Always try to have copies of the books you are booktalking. Telling children about a book they cannot see makes it very difficult for them to identify with it. If possible, have copies the children can check out right there. While this may be difficult if you are booktalking outside the building, at a school or a recreation center for instance, it is worth doing even if that means writing down the names of the children and the books they took and entering it all on your circulation system later. Booktalking produces a great deal of energy, and it pays to capitalize on it before it dissipates. If you cannot let the children take a book right then, take names and place the books on reserve so that you can continue the contact that booktalking creates.

Types of Booktalks

There are as many ways to booktalk as there are combinations of books and readers. Do not feel constrained to make all your booktalks fit some mold. Kathleen Baxter and Marcia Kochel, coauthors of *Gotcha! Nonfiction Booktalks to Get Kids Excited about Reading*, remind us that sometimes you do not need to talk about the book at all, but only to hold up a picture for the children to see.[1] Still, some basic methods have stood the test of time. Good booktalkers tend to use many different types of booktalks, sometimes more than one for the same book. The following are some of the most common types of booktalks.

Plot summaries are the most basic, straightforward booktalks. Explain what happens in the book, but only up to a point. The best plot summary booktalks are cliff-hangers, especially if there is a tipping point early in the story. Regardless of where in the story the critical moment comes, do not give away too much. If the audience begs you to reveal the ending, then you know you have them. A similar approach is to use a question that arises in the book, a choice or a point of fact that the characters must work out. Put it before the audience and let them try to figure it out. Once again, do not reveal the answer to the question or the choice the character makes.

The character sketch is a simple way to draw children into a book. If they come to know a character, even briefly, then they will care about what happens to him or her. You can also sketch out the relationship between two or more characters, building up the tension without giving away too much of the plot.

You can read a vignette, a short scene directly out of the book. This gives the audience a taste of the writing style, and can be very dramatic if done right. Practice reading this out loud; the same words will sound very different from when you read them to yourself. Often, the first page of a book forms an excellent booktalk. If the author is attempting to make a strong statement right out of the gate, you can use that to your advantage. You can use a cross between the vignette booktalk and the character sketch booktalk by reading the introduction to one of the more interesting characters as presented by the author himself or herself.

Great dialogue writers can delight kids and create faithful fans. Pick a snappy exchange between a few characters and you have a short, effective booktalk. This is also a great chance to bring in a second person—an assistant, the teacher, or even a plant in the audience—so you can recite the dialogue as if you were in a play. This produces a refreshing change of pace in the middle of a string of more conventional booktalks.

One way to capitalize on popular books is to present similar titles or other titles by the same author ("If you liked . . . , then you will want to check out . . . "). This is one way to introduce a number of titles quickly, and have a large number of books for the audience to borrow on the spot. Use this same basic approach for multiple titles in a genre or a series. You can present a challenge to children to figure out what three books have in common, such as past Newbery Award winners, easy enough if they all have the seal on the cover but much harder if only one does. Building on thematic elements, like all the protagonists being dogs, works well also.

Take advantage of the omnipresence of the media to sponsor a "Have you read a good movie lately" booktalk, highlighting all books with media tie-ins. This is especially effective if you have movie tie-in editions that feature artwork from movies, television shows, or computer games. This is a great time to incorporate comic books and graphic novels; you may even surprise a number of children who did not know you carry these. Make sure to check with the teacher if you are booktalking in the classroom; he or she may prefer that you stay away from media connections.

Try to mix in various formats when you booktalk, just as you usually combine various types of books, unless you are speaking to a very homogenous audience. Not only do different types of books appeal to different people, but different types of booktalks also appeal to different people, and everybody likes a little variety. Do not read the first paragraph of six books in a row and expect to have anyone's attention by the end.

Break up booktalking programs. Presenting books for twenty or thirty minutes straight will challenge your ability to hold an audience, even if you are very good at it. Instead you might try to booktalk a joke book by sharing some of its humor, ask children a riddle and hold up the book where you found it, challenge a volunteer to read a tongue twister in front of the group, or demonstrate a magic trick or science experiment from a hot new nonfiction title.[2]

EXAMPLES OF DIFFERENT TYPES OF BOOKTALKS

Plot Summary Booktalks

Avi, *Crispin: The Cross of Lead* (Hyperion, 2002)

Can you imagine having no family, no home, not even a name? What do you have left? Well for this orphan boy in medieval England, all he has is a simple cross about his neck and a terrible secret that he doesn't even know that makes him a hunted animal. This is a story of going out on the road and finding strange friends, and trying to find yourself in a harsh world. It's *Crispin: The Cross of Lead*, by Avi.

Christopher Paul Curtis, *The Watsons Go to Birmingham—1963* (Delacorte, 1995)

Take to the open road with the Weird Watsons in an old Plymouth called the Brown Bomber, complete with an onboard record player blaring Yakkety-Yak all the way. You'll go from the neighborhood antics of downtown Flint, Michigan, to the explosive center of the

Deep South in the midst of the Civil Rights Movement. Travel with Daniel, Wilona, Kenny, Joey, and Daddy Cool through the everyday adventures of growing up, and the once-in-a-lifetime experience of being smack-dab in the middle of history. From Christopher Paul Curtis, it's *The Watsons Go to Birmingham—1963*.

Anthony Horowitz, *Stormbreaker* (Philomel, 2000)

Alex Rider is a spy, but he's no James Bond. He's fourteen years old and his cool gadgets come looking like yo-yos and zit cream. There's a bigger difference, though, and he knows what it is. "In the end," he tells himself, "the big difference between him and James Bond wasn't a question of age. It was a question of loyalty. In the old days, spies had done what they'd done because they loved their country, because they believed in what they were doing. But he'd never been given a choice. Nowadays, spies weren't employed, they were used." That makes Alex one unlikely spy, but when his uncle, the man who raised him, is killed on a mission for MI6, the British Secret Service, Alex finds himself in the family business, picking up where his uncle left off, trying to get to the bottom of a terrorist plot, and to get out of it alive. It all revolves around a new type of computer that's being delivered to every school in England—a very generous gift. So why is MI6 so interested, and Alex's uncle so dead? Alex needs to find out before the clock strikes 12 noon in *Stormbreaker*, by Anthony Horowitz.

A Character Sketch Booktalk

Andrew Clement, *A Week in the Woods* (Simon and Schuster, 2002)

One of these guys is the gung-ho cheerleader type, you know, rah-rah-rah, let's show some spirit and all that; the other is sullen and moody, and way too bored with school. One of these guys is a go-get-em science teacher; the other is a slacker student with a bad attitude. One is an outdoorsy environmentalist type; the other is more comfortable in a New York penthouse than he is in a tent in New Hampshire. One lives on a schoolteacher's salary; the other gets driven to school in a limousine. Oh yeah, these guys are going to get along great when they spend a week in the woods. Read *A Week in the Woods*, by Andrew Clement.

A Vignette Booktalk

Will Hobbs, *Wild Man Island* (HarperCollins, 2002)

(Portions of the text have been omitted for brevity.)

Wilderness. Under the circumstances, I couldn't imagine a more ominous word, unless it was bears.

What else did I know about Admiralty Island? "All three of the ABC Islands have brown bears," Julia had said early in the trip. I knew for an awful fact that the bear I'd just seen was a monster grizzly. Brown bears, the naturalist had gone on to explain, were the same animal as grizzlies— *Ursus arctos.* Brownies, as Julia called them, got a lot bigger in southeast Alaska than the grizzlies in the interior because of all the extra protein that salmon added to their diet. Some topped a thousand pounds.

Tell me about it.

Julia said there was another name for Admiralty, the Indian name. The Indians called it the Fortress of the Bears.

I felt sick, remembering what she'd said next. "Admiralty Island has the densest population of brown bears in the world. One per square mile."

And Andy Galloway had just washed up on the shore of Admiralty Island, the Fortress of the Bears.

It's a scene from *Wild Man Island*, by Will Hobbs.

A Dialogue Booktalk

Wendelin Van Draanen, *Swear to Howdy* (Knopf, 2003), 17–19

(Portions of the text have been omitted for brevity.)

While Sissy's handing the cokes over to mama and dad, Joey's face is all frantic, trying to tell me something.

"What?" I whispered.

He just kept twitching at the face.

"What?" I asked again, and then it clicked. He hadn't put bugs in just Sissy and Amanda Jane's drinks. He'd put them in all the cups. My eyes shot back and forth. From my parents to my sister. From my parents to my sister. And when I was sure no one was looking, I mouthed, "Bugs?"

He nodded.

I whispered, "Why?"

"Didn't want 'em to go to waste!"

. . . We were almost out of the park when the screaming started.

Read Wendelin Van Draanen's *Swear to Howdy.*

A Theme Booktalk: Unbelievable but True

John Fleischman, *Phineas Gage: A Gruesome but True Story about Brain Science* (Houghton Mifflin, 2002)

Phineas Gage was a normal man, a hard worker, a construction kind of guy who worked on the railroad. True, he had a somewhat dangerous job; he was a tamper, meaning that he would tamp down the explosives just before they were set off, blowing rock out of the way so that the railroad could lay tracks. One day, the explosives went off early, and the metal bar Phineas used was shot out and through his head, a fatal wound. But where most people's stories would have ended, Phineas's had just begun: the wound may have been fatal, but it took seven years for it to kill him.

Roger Highfield, *The Science of Harry Potter: How Magic Really Works* (Viking, 2002)

Harry Potter is a fantasy, right? It isn't possible that any of those amazing things could happen, is it? Could all the wonders of Hogwarts have a basis in real life? Consider this: the Marauders Map might be a form of GPS tracking, and the Sorting Hat bears a striking resemblance to a CAT scan. Now ask yourself, could NASA be working on their own version of the invisibility cloak? And where do you suppose the legends of dragons came from if there never were dragons in the first place? Find out the truth in Roger Highfield's *The Science of Harry Potter: How Magic Really Works.*

Ken Silverstein, *The Radioactive Boy Scout: The True Story of a Boy and His Backyard Nuclear Reactor* (Random House, 2004)

He built a what? He built it where? How? Didn't anybody notice? How can an ordinary kid working in a potting shed do something that generations of scientists with their PhD's and fancy laboratories have failed to do? How did he even think to try? This one is just too amazing to miss.

A Media Tie-in Booktalk

Joss Whedon, Karl Moline, and Andy Owens, *Fray* (Dark Horse Comics, 2003)

For the fans of *Buffy, the Vampire Slayer* comes this graphic novel from Buffy creator Joss Whedon. It's hundreds of years in the future, and the demons have all been vanquished; no slayers have been called in generations; the watchers have lost their purposes and their minds. But when the blood drinking *lurks* begin to rise up, the world needs a hero once again, and one is called. Her name is Fray. Read this new take on the Buffy legend, *Fray*, by Joss Whedon, Karl Moline, and Andy Owens.

Building a Booktalk Repertoire

Booktalking is something you will likely do every day of your career; it pays to preserve your booktalks for later use. This does not mean developing ten booktalks and using them all the time; you will always be adding new ones, but you want to be able to recall those you used successfully in the past. Whenever you read a book, take the time to write a booktalk; it is a great deal easier while the book is fresh in your mind. Writing booktalks on cards allows you to take them out, pick the one you want, and slip it into the book for a quick check. This way, it is even possible to tape the booktalk to the back of the book so you can read it as you hold the cover up to show your audience. Building up a computer file of booktalks allows you to reproduce them in various formats any number of times. You can also organize them and sort them by various criteria, which can be helpful as the collection gets larger and larger.

What do you include? The author and complete title are a must, as well as the text of the booktalk itself. Booktalks can be read word for word, usually when using a vignette from the book itself. You might copy the passage and read it while holding up the book, or add a little drama by opening the book with a flourish and reading from a marked passage. In either case, remember that it is easy to lose an audience when you stop making eye contact. Know the passage well enough to be able to look up occasionally as you are reading.

Booktalks can also be presented more informally, related as a story or with a conversational style. It requires no less preparation, and probably more, to put the notes aside and just speak to the audience. If you do an informal booktalk well, children see your personal connection to the book. If you do it poorly, you appear disorganized and the book seems uninteresting. Write out what you want to say ahead of time and practice your talk, so that even if you present it with different words, your message will be clear. After your booktalk, save it for reuse later.

Also include the publication information in your records of booktalks. You probably will not share this when booktalking, but it will help you keep track of when a book was published and when it was in print. Booktalking books that are hard to find is ineffective. Review the publication information periodically in order to stay abreast of new editions and cover art. You can also include lists of similar titles or other books from the same author, making it easier to build that type of a booktalking program.

Include notes on preferred audiences. This includes age, reading ability, interests, gender, and any sensitivity an audience may have. If you offer programs at a shelter for temporarily displaced families, you might want to be able to find a title that deals with homelessness in a sensitive manner. If you do programs at a religious camp, you might want to know when a book includes something that might be offensive to the community. A detailed booktalk record allows you to have impact while being sensitive.

FURTHER READING

Kathleen A. Baxter and Marcia Agness Kochel, *Gotcha! Nonfiction Booktalks to Get Kids Excited about Reading* (Englewood, CO: Libraries Unlimited, 1999).

John Thomas Gillespie, *The Newbery Companion: Booktalk and Related Materials for Newbery Medal and Honor Books*, 2nd ed. (Englewood, CO: Libraries Unlimited, 2001).

NOTES

1. Kathleen A. Baxter and Marcia Agness Kochel, *Gotcha! Nonfiction Booktalks to Get Kids Excited about Reading* (Englewood, CO: Libraries Unlimited, 1999), xiv.

2. Ibid., xvii.

15

Entertainment and Enrichment Programs

Enrichment programs are ones where information is presented in either a formal or informal setting, and where people come together to learn something new or expand their outlook. For children, they are usually exploratory, general overviews of topics that go beyond what they generally learn in school. They give a nod to the idea that books are not the only way that libraries can fulfill their mission to inform and to educate. Entertainment programs promote community and the use of the library by drawing people into the library to socialize and enjoy themselves while at the same time viewing or sampling the library's resources and services.

Enrichment programs in the library present information and ideas in a literature-rich context, and promote the use of the collection by developing an interest in new areas of inquiry. This makes them especially important for reluctant or poor readers who need the extra encouragement, and especially useful for elementary-age children who have learned to read but are not yet proficient enough to really explore unfamiliar topics in text alone. Entertainment programs are instrumental for those potential customers who have less of an immediate need for the library. Teenagers and tweenagers, for example, may have access to good school libraries, and thus may not need to visit the public library to do their school assignments.

These potential users, then, may not be exposed to all the other things the library has to offer. As with all library programs, job one is to get people in the door, and job two is to put library resources in their hands.

Outside Presenters

Many of these programs require booking a speaker or performer to come into your library and present a program. There are some basics that you should always remember when making these arrangements. First, make sure you know what your administration requires for you to book a program—how to reserve space, how to get on a calendar, or how to get spending approved. Who has the authority to do any of these things? Make sure you know the method of obtaining payment, too, and how far in advance you need to start the process in order to get your performer paid on time.

Second, make sure everything is in writing. If you are going to advertise a program, tie up space and staff time, and possibly make payment, you want to be sure that the program is offered where and when you expect it. Oral agreements can be misunderstood, misremembered, and even misrepresented, by you or the presenter. Make sure both parties have a written agreement that spells out the time, place, content, length, and anticipated audience for the program. List all the costs, including travel, materials, and other expenses; if the library is not paying the presenter, state that as well. Include directions to the program site and contact information on both sides in case of unforeseen circumstances. Many presenters will have this type of form, especially if they perform regularly, and the library may also have a standard contract. If neither is the case, create a form or simply write a letter with all of these components, keep a copy for yourself, and make sure your presenter has a copy too. Check with your administrator to see if he or she would like a copy of the documentation as well.

If possible, see performers in action before you book them. A knowledgeable person may not be an effective presenter, a great presenter may not be suitable for a smaller audience, and a program that does well for one age group may be completely unsuitable for a different age group. You cannot get a good feel for a performer from a brochure, a letter, or a résumé. If you cannot see a performer in person, it is perfectly acceptable to ask for references; be sure to check them. Call or write to others who have hosted or seen a performer. Ask around among colleagues. First-hand knowledge is the best way to judge whether a performer is right for your needs.

If the person is not a regular performer but a local expert, then your job is much harder. It is best to use a professional who has done this before and knows what to expect, and whose performance at your library may help him or her make other bookings in the future. You have to judge a non-professional far more closely. Always meet such a person before you book him or her. See if he or she has the personality to perform, especially for children. Knowledge is necessary, of course, but if the presenter cannot engage an audience, no one will ever benefit from his or her knowledge. Go over exactly what they wish to present; obtain an outline or synopsis if you can. If the expert is not used to presenting, this collaboration will be a big help to him or her as well.

Many experts, even expert hobbyists or weekend practitioners, forget what it is like to be ignorant, and will quickly talk over an audience's heads, especially if those heads are only a few feet off the ground. Make sure that the presenter is willing to use common language, or at least define any words of jargon he or she is going to use. Ask the presenter to create hand-outs or visual aids to explain key terms or concepts. You might even offer to make these yourself.

Library Skills

The most traditional and recognizable enrichment programs are those that teach library skills. These are most common in school libraries, but the public library children's librarian may offer them for visiting classes, for homeschool families, or for new residents. This is your chance to show off your specialty, and to become a little more real in the eyes of students. It is also a great time to build bridges with your local school librarians, by setting up joint programs that emphasize the ways school and public libraries are arranged in a similar fashion and the types of resources that are unique to each type of library. Scavenger hunts and other contests can reinforce library skills such as the Dewey Decimal System or reference book use, and also present the library as a place where learning can be fun.

Crafts/Arts

There is a strong feeling in our society that children are not exposed to enough art, be it decorative or performance art, participatory or observational. Meanwhile, money-strapped school systems are cutting art out of their curricula and nonprofit art agencies are feeling the effects of a bad economy and fiscally skittish national government. This is not the time for libraries to forget that they provide access to information *and* ideas. Entertainment and enrichment programs can expose children to arts that are as simple as drawing, or as grand as drama.

Some arts, like drawing, painting, and other handicrafts, will be a part of most story hour programs. This is a great start, and sets the stage for more advanced programs as children age. Those hands-on, manipulative activities should not be forgotten when children enter school. They are something that children identify with the library, and it pays to remind them of how much fun they had at the library as preschoolers. Is preparation and planning time short? Use the same crafts you offer to preschoolers for after-school enrichment programs.

Often you can simply skip some of the preparation steps and use more raw materials to transfer a preschool project into one that is more fitting for a ten-year-old. Instead of reading picture books and using the craft to reinforce the story, offer the craft and have books out to reinforce the craft. Include books not only tied to the completed project but also about the methods and materials used in the craft. Do not abandon story hour techniques at any age.

You can also expose children to art at a higher level by bringing in artists to inspire and instruct them. Artists, like any other group, include those who can teach as well as those who cannot. Do not be discouraged by an artist who feels uncomfortable teaching. It is often enough to set a time when an artist will set up and work in the library so children can see him or her and maybe ask a few questions. Of course, if you can get an artist to teach, then you are really capitalizing on the good work you did in story hour and bringing it all full circle. The same children who gazed at pictures can then actually make them.

Performing Arts

The performing arts are more difficult to integrate into a library setting because they require more room and freedom of motion. Specialized surroundings are also often necessary—like floors appropriate for dancing and acoustically viable rooms, both for the quality of the performance and for the comfort of other library users. If you can bring the performing arts into your library, onto the library lawn, or, if necessary, into the library parking lot, the payoff can be enormous. Performing arts are events that get people excited. They can draw entirely new audiences to your library; they can make it clear to everyone that the library is about a lot more than books, and they demonstrate that books are part of a much greater world of discovery.

The advantages of bringing performing arts to children in a library setting include children's exposure to appropriate behavior in a performance venue. This is not a natural skill, and children who have been exposed to nothing more than a movie theater do not know the first time they attend a concert that it is not acceptable to go in and out of the auditorium or move around in seats. Introducing children to live performance in a setting as comfortable and intimate as a library allows them to enjoy this new experience without disrupting others or being turned off by the negative reactions of their fellow audience members.

Music promotes learning and brain development, and it is unfortunate that it is often abandoned in library programming for children who have completed preschool. Music helps to stimulate both the analytical and the emotional portions of the brain, encouraging higher-level thinking. Lenn Millbower, a trainer who specializes in using entertainment to enhance learning, writes that "music is a tool for reaching beyond language. It awakens the recesses of the mind and calls emotion to attention."[1] This is very much the goal of entertainment and enrichment programming.

Storytelling

Traditionally, storytelling, oral presentation of a story without illustrations or a written text, was the primary method of educating, entertaining, and transmitting culture. This was true when reading material was scarce, and literacy was limited to a relative few. Today those roles are shared by a combination of media including print, movies, television, music, and video games. The nonprint vehicles do not tend to use language well, and print vehicles are still beyond the reach of those who cannot read, so traditional storytelling makes sense for preschool children, for children struggling with language skills, and for adults who have limited skills in English, whether because they never learned them or because English is not their native language. For many others, traditional storytelling has lost its immediate usefulness, but it remains a pleasant and expansive way to interact with language.

Storytelling sparks the imagination by allowing listeners to make their own mental pictures. It gives the storyteller the flexibility to change pace and focus to match the mood of the audience and to interact with them, drawing them into the story. Traditional storytelling is pure story line, so it exposes children to the structure of story in concentrated form, and as such forms a building block to developing literacy. Eventually, telling stories interests children in books and reading. Children who were told stories three or more times in the last week are more likely than those who were not to show at least three signs of emerging literacy—such as recognizing all the letters of the alphabet, pretending to read, and being able to write their names (44 percent versus 34 percent).[2]

You can either bring storytellers into your library or you can tell stories yourself. The first option brings high quality and makes storytelling seem more special. It makes storytelling an event. The second option makes storytelling a part of what the library does. It also makes storytelling comfortable and commonplace. Each approach has benefits for children, and ideally they will be exposed to storytelling both as an everyday occurrence and as a performance art.

If you are going to tell stories yourself, either as a separate program or as a component of a larger program, you can be comforted to know that storytelling is not meant to be difficult. Storytelling is simple—and the simpler the better. The best advice any storyteller can receive is to get out

The author telling stories in Brookline, Massachusetts

of the way and let the story tell itself. This means not overembellishing with a lot of words or wild gyrations, props, or sound effects. Many storytellers find that they discover the real core of stories after many years of retelling them, so their narratives tend to get shorter and simpler. This is in fact how traditional folklore developed.

How do you begin storytelling? There are any number of books that will give you a solid overview of the art. The following will give you a quick outline to begin with. Start with a traditional story that is very short and that you and your audience know well. Something like *The Three Little Pigs* or one of Aesop's fables is a good place to begin. Locate a number of different versions; you may find them in both picture-book versions and in folklore collections. Read them through and note what is common to all the editions; then use those elements to establish the very basic plot line, literally how to get from the start to the end. Focus on the action and the setting. This is the beginning of your story; look it over and try to describe the story from beginning to end, adding just enough words to make the story flow.

The next step is to start practicing your storytelling. That means putting the paper down and saying the story out loud without memorizing the words. Tell it over and over to yourself, and then go back to the story as you have it written down and add the phrases and details that sound good to you. As you continue to rehearse and revise, some elements will become a regular part of your telling and others will fade away. This is what storytellers call *living with a story*. When you feel comfortable with the story, tell it to someone you know well—not looking for criticism or critique because most people are not able to do this well—but just to hear yourself say it out loud in front of someone else and to see his or her reaction.

After this step you are ready to tell a story in front of children. It may seem a bare shell you have to work with, but that is what you really need. Build it into a story hour or other program, or just gather a few children who are spending time in the children's room and ask if they would like to hear a story. Tell it as simply as you can, slowly and in a normal voice. If the children want to join in on the parts they know (and he huffed, and he puffed . . .), let them. Be aware of the reaction of your audience; when you look at your story again afterwards, you will want to remember which parts had their attention. Congratulations, you are a storyteller!

Of course there is much more to learn and practice, but storytelling never gets too far from that simple plot line. Costumes, funny voices, props, and even morals are extras that can be used when they enhance the story but should be avoided if they detract. Learn stories one at a time, and tell them over and over. Many children would prefer to hear stories they know, even if you just told them the same story a week ago. Go and see story-tellers whenever you can, and ask them questions about how they choose stories, how they prepare, and how they present. Get in contact with local storytelling organizations where you can practice telling stories and get some critique from people who know what they are talking about. If you have trouble finding local storytellers, start with the members of a regional or national association.

Local storytelling organizations can also be the starting point for bringing storytellers into your library for special performances. This is best done after the children have been exposed to some storytelling in regular library programming. Children who have not been exposed to storytelling may not know how to react—and may either interfere with the program or hang back shyly when asked to participate. You do not want a performance interrupted by a five-year-old who stands up and insists loudly and repeatedly that he or she wants to see the pictures. On the other hand, if children are regularly exposed to traditional storytelling, they will be better prepared for other types of performing arts, such as dance and theater.

If possible, see a storyteller perform before you book him or her for your library. Storytelling is a very personal art with no real hard-and-fast rules. The range of styles among storytellers, even those in the same small region, can be immense. Not all styles speak to all audiences, and there is really no objective way to rate a teller. If seeing a teller perform is impractical, however, you have no choice but to rely on personal references.

Storytelling Organizations

International Storytelling Center
   http://www.storytellingcenter.com

League for the Advancement of New England Storytelling
   http://www.lanes.org

National Storytelling Network
   http://www.storynet.org

Talks and Lectures

Bringing in experts to talk about what they do is a sure way to expand the use of your nonfiction collection, create relationships with people you can call on later for specialized information, increase the profile of the children's program, and attract new customers to the library. One of the advantages of this kind of program is that local experts often want to talk about their interests, and will do so for free or at a nominal cost. One of the disadvantages is that special interests may attract just a specialized (spell that *small*) audience. Librarians planning adult programs are very familiar with the concept, whether they choose to offer these types of programs or not. Children's librarians can benefit from children's interest in what *big people* do.

Ask the local fire chief to send a firefighter over during National Fire Prevention Week, held every October, for a special story hour. You supply the stories and crafts; the firefighter provides the interest. The children will benefit from seeing a firefighter put on his full bunker gear, the protective outfit firefighters use when they enter burning buildings, while keeping up a steady dialog with a group of preschoolers. The point is to make the children comfortable with what looks like a Halloween costume and to keep them from hiding from firefighters who might try to rescue them in an emergency. Important information is presented, and the children make a connection between learning, books, and fun.

The list of local presenters is nearly endless. Police officers, especially canine units, are always a hit; doctors and dentists, hobbyists from stamp collectors to model airplane fliers to short-band radio operators often elicit enthusiasm. Look around your community to see who is doing something interesting. Poll the local teachers and see if they have a closet specialty that they never get to fully indulge in the classroom. They have the advantage of being extremely familiar with standing in front of children. There are teachers out there who give special lectures and demonstrations on roadkill, large animal husbandry, and the chemistry of explosions. The more frustrated they are by a lack of outlets for their specialty, the more appreciative and enthusiastic they will be when you open a door for them.

FURTHER READING

Margaret Read MacDonald, *Shake-It-Up Tales: Stories to Sing, Dance, Drum, and Act Out* (Little Rock, AK: August House, 2000).

Margaret Read MacDonald, *The Storyteller's Start-Up Book: Finding, Learning, Performing and Using Folktales* (Little Rock, AK: August House, 1993).

Katy Rydell, *A Beginner's Guide to Storytelling* (Jonesborough, TN: National
   Storytelling Press, 2003).

Ruth Sawyer, *The Way of the Storyteller* (New York: Viking, 1942).

Marie L. Shedlock, *The Art of the Story-Teller* (New York: D. Appleton, 1915).

NOTES

   1. Lenn Millbower, "Turn Up the Music: Rev Up Participants' Emotions through
Song," *Training and Development*, March 2004, 20.

   2. C. W. Nord, J. Lennon, B. Liu, and K. Chandler, *Home Literacy Activities and
Signs of Children's Emerging Literacy: 1993 and 1999* (Washington, DC: U.S.
Department of Education, 1999), 8.

16

Summer Reading Programs

Remember the goal of the reading program. A positive experience in the public library where reading, books, and fun are connected. No rule or issue is more important than a happy child that [sic] will always think well of the library and the staff.

—Virginia State Library,
*Up and Running: A Step-by-Step
Guide to Managing Your Summer Reading Program*

Summer reading programs are really a collection of programs that run the gamut of program types, but form a special and distinct experience. The goal is often to combat aliteracy, the ability to read but not the motivation.[1] Summer reading programs encourage reading for fun and in vast quantities, and the goal is fairly universal. American Library Association (ALA) statistics show that 95 percent of public libraries in America offer a summer reading program, more even than the 89 percent who offer story hours.[2]

Summer reading programs are also crucial to the development of young readers; these offerings help to offset summer reading loss, the slippage in language skills that children experience from the end of one school year to the beginning of the next. This loss can be up to two months of reading achievement, and those losses accumulate over the years. Disadvantaged children are most at risk, largely because they have less access to summer reading programs since libraries in poorer areas are more likely to restrict hours and services in difficult budget times. Also, poorer children are more likely to encounter transportation barriers that keep them from taking advantage of the programs that are offered. Children in wealthier communities also have more options for enriching summer activities, so they are less dependent on summer reading programs.[3]

A 2001 Los Angeles County Public Library study showed that summer reading program participants were 10 percent more likely to read at least fifteen hours per week. That is a vital gain, since reading just six books over the course of the summer can be enough to offset any summer reading loss.[4] Summer reading programs can be the difference-makers for many of the children in our communities.

Theme

Summer reading programs are often held together by a general theme, comprised of a slogan or catchphrase, a logo or some set of visual graphics, and symbols or objects that reappear during the length of the program. Themes help in publicizing a summer program because they give a focus to what might otherwise be just a collection of unconnected events. Themes aid in cross-promotion by creating natural ties between one program and another. They also make a program special, memorable, and unique. The effect may be greater on parents than on the kids themselves, but parents are customers too. In addition themes may motivate the staff to remain focused throughout the busiest time of the year.

Theme packages can be bought from library supply vendors, are often created by state libraries or statewide children's services organizations, or are sent out by corporations as canned programs. Every year, more and more of these programs are created, so if you are looking to choose a theme it is worth contacting a state library—yours or any other—to see what programs they have archived. A quick search of the Web for *summer reading programs* will produce a list of themes, including where and when they were first offered and how to get the necessary materials.

Reading Logs/Incentives

Logging what children read is the most basic component of most summer reading programs. The structure is simple: The child keeps track of what he or she reads on some sort of a log, and either periodically or at the end of the summer shows the log to a librarian. The librarian may then offer an incentive in the form of a prize, the child may add a piece or pieces to a progressively growing display that highlights how much children in the community have read, or the child's reading may be credited toward some communal goal. Those too young to read for themselves may be offered a read-to-me alternative; these children keep track of the books that someone reads to them. Their log can either function in a separate program or on equal footing with those completed by independent readers. The log itself is often part of a canned theme and carries the logo and graphics peculiar to the theme.

Incentives have been a touchy issue since summer reading programs first began in the late 1800s and early 1900s.[5] Many librarians stand firmly against any competition or reward structure, preferring to promote reading as a pleasure and a reward unto itself. Such a stance is certainly reasonable and works for many children in many communities, but it is shortsighted to see the issue in just this one way. Good readers certainly see reading as a pleasure, but these also tend to be the readers we do not have to reach out to in the summer. They will be in the library and reading on their own regardless of what we do. More reluctant readers may be enticed by prizes, and many children, often boys, will be attracted by the competition. On the other hand, poor readers might be intimidated by contests where they are likely not to do as well as others. But incentives need not mean one person wins and gets the big prize. Incentives can be given out to all children who reach a certain goal, or even some personal goal worked out with a children's librarian. It is important to design a program that addresses the needs of as many participants as possible, however they present themselves, and not to blindly follow a narrow principle based more on theory than practice.

Incentives, should you choose to use them, can be based on how many books a child reads, how many pages a child reads (to guard against one child reading many small books that are well below his or her reading level just to get a prize), or some other measure. More and more, libraries are clocking in the number of hours a child reads, rather than the productivity of that time, in order to level the playing field and allow even the poorest readers to benefit from a little extra push to read during summer break.

One inventive summer reading theme is *Read a Ton*. Instead of counting the number of books or pages or hours read, weigh in the books children read on a postal scale. For every pound read, the child can add a construction-paper weight to a huge scale display on a wall, adding pound after pound to offset the giant cutout of an anvil labeled *One Ton* on the opposite side of the scale. Such innovations highlight the spirit of a summer reading program—that reading is fun and rewarding for everyone, not just those voracious readers who will read all year round, and who are probably plenty visible in the library anyway.

Displays of the cumulative reading of all the children involved in the program add a level of wonder and accomplishment to a summer reading program. Likewise, a communal goal can build camaraderie, and even positive peer pressure to come together in order to achieve a goal. Conversely, allowing children to write their name on the incremental piece of the display that they add can produce a healthy level of competition. Boys especially respond to incentives that are tied into the program.

The ways of displaying cumulative reading are as varied as the imaginations of the librarians. The Mount Lebanon Public Library in Allegheny County, Pennsylvania, once had children write the names of the books they read on paper links, then put them together to form a paper chain of 3,500 links that wrapped around the entire children's section.[6]

Supporting Programs

Offering regular programming and special library events at the same time as the summer reading program incentives creates a positive feedback loop. Children coming in for the incentive program learn about programs, and the programs in turn give the library a chance to draw attention to the incentive program. Summer programs attract families together, as summer is often when parents take time off from work to be with their children who are out of school. If nothing else, a library can continue its regular programming schedule through the summer, benefiting from the added business caused by the incentive program and the broader audience of school-age children. Beyond that, the library can offer enrichment programs tied to the summer reading theme, reading programs that help children read the books for their reading logs, or entertainment programs designed for families to enjoy together. Programs need not be directly related to reading. Within the framework of the summer reading program, even nonreading

Summer is a great time to get families together for a program, like this storytelling and origami program in Alton, New Hampshire.

programs that promote library use will result in literacy gains for children, according to a 2001 Pennsylvania Library Association study.[7]

Administering a Program

Planning for summer reading is important because summer reading itself is important—to the community, to children's services, and to the library as a whole. The library's administration must be involved at an early stage to determine the broad goals of the summer reading program. These goals will almost certainly be closely tied to the goals of children's services, which in turn should support the goals of the entire library. See chapter 19, "Planning," for more on goal setting. Some goals that are prominent specifically during the summer reading program that you should consider include: reaching a wide new audience of children that does not regularly use the library, strengthening relationships with other community agencies, ensuring that children will not lose the reading skills they developed throughout the school year, and welcoming families into the library together.

Scheduling

The summer reading program is often the most intensive period of activity for children's services, and for the library as a whole. Careful planning is needed to minimize the impact on staff and the library's other services. When scheduling, make sure you know when staff members, both in children's and adult services, are taking vacations. Increased traffic and circulation during major programs can put a terrible strain on skeletal staffs. See if schedules can be adjusted to concentrate staff at times when traffic will be heaviest—when programs are in session and when children need their reading logs to be checked.

Also make sure that your programs and events do not conflict with other events in your community. By late winter you should be in contact with sports and recreation organizations, religious groups, camps, and child care facilities to determine who will be holding regular weekly events on certain days and at certain times, and who will be doing special events on certain days. A summer scheduling summit is a grand idea, but not always practical. You may need to simply contact these other groups in order to create your own calendar of times when not to schedule. Try to avoid the frustration of having audiences gutted for the final week of summer reading because another local program starts a week earlier than it has in previous years. You do not want to waste time, resources, and energy planning events that will not be well attended. Once you have set your schedule, make sure to circulate a calendar to other groups so that they will know not to set their programs against yours.

Publicity

Plan your entire program ahead of time, and have it all laid out in a single flier; then take that flier to classrooms and day cares before school gets out. What you do there to get the children's attention can vary widely—from presenting a goofy skit based on the summer theme, to booktalking some of the new books that are or will be available during the summer, to promoting key programs. Whatever you do, get their attention. Go to sign-ups for other summer activities such as sports or day camps, with fliers in hand, and talk about how to round out the summer with library activities. Make sure every child in your community has a copy in his or her hands at some point, and do your best to make sure the library publicity gets home to parents. There are few purposes more appropriate for a mass mailing than to announce a summer reading program.

Some libraries are now promoting summer reading through special websites. As is usual for emerging trends in libraries, it is in urban areas where this development is most visible. The New York Public Library (http://summerreading.nypl.org) and the Hennepin County Library (http://www.hclib.org/kid) outside of Minneapolis were among the groundbreakers.[8] Summer reading websites can be used to attract new participants by posting games and links to author sites and recreational reading sites. They allow interactivity by letting kids review the books they read. They are new and exciting, and they reach out to children in a format that children are increasingly comfortable using.

Do not stop publicizing once the summer begins. Make publicity part of your planning; put aside time every week to write press releases, hang posters, and visit sites where children and parents congregate. Make sure, too, that at each program you promote the next program. Programs during the summer may come more quickly than at other times of the year, so pay special attention to keeping your website current. If you do not have time in your schedule to promote, then you have too much scheduled and will be wasting energy on programs that will not be well attended because of a lack of exposure. For more general publicity ideas, see chapter 21, "Public Relations, Promotion, and Marketing."

Sign-ups

There are advantages to signing up children for summer reading, the biggest being the ability to analyze and report on who participated. Depending on what information you collect, you can determine how many children participated, what their ages were, what schools or classes were represented, and where they live. This will allow you to quantify the impact on the community, the impact on neighborhoods, and the impact that different forms of publicity, such as class visits, had on participation. All of these factors affect decisions about reading programs for the coming academic year and summer.

Signing up children can also help them feel responsible to the program, which encourages regular attendance and participation. It also helps in planning for programs by showing how many children may be around. If you collect phone numbers or e-mail addresses, then these can be used to remind participants of upcoming programs. (These lists can also be used for the same purpose after the summer reading program is over and all year long.)

The disadvantages to signing up for summer reading are the same as for any other program. If the sign-up system makes children or parents not planning to be around all summer hesitate to register, then it has discouraged casual participation. Some parents are leery of giving out personal information, either because they do not want phone or e-mail solicitations (from the library or anyone they fear may obtain the list from the library), or because they are distrustful of giving information to a government organization. This latter fear is common among immigrants, some of whom may not be fully legal, but many of whom come from cultures where the government is not to be trusted.

Whether to sign up participants is a decision to be made at the local level, but if you know the advantages and pitfalls of either decision you will be prepared to head off trouble and make the most of opportunities.

Evaluation

Determine before the beginning of summer reading how you will evaluate the program. Statistics are a simple way to evaluate, whether you are counting the number of participants who sign up, the number who complete the program (however you might define completion), or the amount of reading done. A simple comparison between the current and past years can show progress or decline. Surveys done before or after the program can include polls to determine child or parent satisfaction, or they can be used to identify changes in behavior, such as the number of hours children spend reading as opposed to watching television. Teachers can be enlisted to help determine participation by having them ask students to produce their reading logs and counting how many can do so. Circulation records, broken down by day or even hour, can show the impact of programming on library use.

Once you have determined the impact of the summer program on the participants, the library, and the community itself, do not keep it a secret. Prepare an end-of-summer press release thanking volunteers, donors, and parents, and also pointing out the highlights of the program. Use an end-of-summer review as a reason to speak to the board of trustees, and presumably to library administrators as well, to remind them of the impact that children's services have. Then use your evaluations to begin planning next year's program.

FURTHER READING

Donna Celano and Susan B. Neuman, *The Role of Public Libraries in Children's Literacy Development* (Harrisburg: Pennsylvania Library Association, 2001).

Carole D. Fiore, *Running Summer Library Reading Programs: A How-to-Do-It Manual* (New York: Neal-Schuman, 1998).

NOTES

1. Donna Celano and Susan B. Neuman, *The Role of Public Libraries in Children's Literacy Development* (Harrisburg: Pennsylvania Library Association, 2001), 11.

2. Celano and Neuman, *Role of Public Libraries*, 10.

3. Katy Benson, "Summer Reading Loss: What Once Was Lost Can Now Be Found @ Your Library," *Onondaga County Public Library News*, Summer 2004, 1–2.

4. Ibid., 3–4.

5. Carole D. Fiore, *Running Summer Library Reading Programs: A How-to-Do-It Manual* (New York: Neal-Schuman, 1998), xv.

6. Celano and Neuman, *Role of Public Libraries*, 36.

7. Benson, "Summer Reading Loss," 3.

8. Walter Minkel, "Summer Reading Season," *School Library Journal*, August 2002, 33.

17

Family Programs and Family Literacy

Family literacy begins with the theory that librarians have much less direct influence on children's reading ability than do parents. The aims of family literacy should be to instruct the parents on how to be their children's guides to literacy, to model good literacy habits, and to create a community of readers. Preliteracy skills are a vital part of family literacy; they are central to the process of learning to read, and they are habits best formed in the context of family relations. Preliteracy skills were enumerated in 2000 by the Preschool Literacy Initiative, a joint venture of the Public Library Association and the National Institute of Child Health and Human Development. They include vocabulary, print motivation, print awareness, narrative skills, letter knowledge, and phonological sensitivity.[1]

In everyday terms, this means showing a child how to handle a book, teaching young people to associate reading with meaning, exposing children to the structure of story, and immersing children in a sea of language that is delivered in story, rhyme, song, and creative play. These are things librarians can do well, but that parents can do with more consistency. Teachers, too, have a great influence on the reading of children due to the amount of time they spend with children, but their primary goal is to teach children how to read, not necessarily how to love to read. In the words of Myrna Machet and Elizabeth J. Pretorius, "school practices tend to focus on teaching decoding skills rather than teaching children how to take meaning from text or the ways in which literacy will be meaningful in their lives."[2]

Ken Haycock, a library science professor at the University of British Columbia, asks:

> If youth literacy is a priority, are we better served by children's librarians serving children directly or by reorienting their role to train others—daycare supervisors, community centre leaders, and preschool and primary school teachers—in selecting literature, telling stories and programming around quality books?[3]

The ideas behind family literacy go beyond the parent-child-librarian relationship; they ask us to step back and look at results rather than methods, at what we hope to accomplish rather than what we expect to do in order to achieve that goal. The mind-set of family literacy, once established, should then be turned outward to include the entire world of the developing child.

To accomplish its specific aims, the library needs to bring families in together, and to engage children and adults and get them working together. Programming is the ideal vehicle for promoting family literacy, and the library is the perfect venue. Family programming is more a style of programming than a category unto itself. As Machet and Pretorius put it, "family literacy encompasses a wide variety of programmes that promote the involvement of both parents or other family members and their children in literacy enhancing practices and activities."[4]

Why Do Family Programming?

Family literacy is most essential among disadvantaged families or communities, for whom literacy is less likely to be a legacy and by whom preliteracy skills are least likely to be passed on. Parents who themselves have low literacy skills are not likely to pass on literacy to their children. In this respect, training and encouraging parents with low literacy skills to read to their children helps both the child and the parent, who is likely not to have many opportunities to practice his or her literacy skills at a manageable level.[5] Indeed, in an Ogden City, Utah, program called Project Even Start, it was found that low-literacy adults who participated in a family literacy program gained more reading skills than the children who accompanied them.[6]

While literacy skills need to be a focus of attention, you should not discount the social effect of literacy training. As Machet and Pretorius point out, "literacy is not taught or learnt in a vacuum but takes place in a social context that either fosters or fails to support the development of literacy in the child."[7] In even our most disadvantaged areas, the inability to read (illiteracy) is not nearly as great a problem as the unwillingness to read (aliteracy). Programming across the generations helps form a supportive and encouraging atmosphere where children see reading, not as a solitary endeavor, but as a value shared within a community of readers.

What Makes a Family Program?

Think about the timing of your programs. If you want to get working parents to a program, you cannot schedule it during the regular workday. If you want to include young children, you cannot schedule a program late at night. If you wish siblings of different ages to be involved, then do not schedule programs during the school day; instead design programs during school and summer vacations. Weekends are usually a more open time, but be aware of activities such as sports that will draw away elementary-age children. The early evening is often family time and a good time to try to bring in a wide range of ages. Of course no time will be agreeable to everyone, and local circumstances can dictate timing that is different from the norm. If a single employer dominates the local economy, then that employer's schedule will impact on yours. Robust after-school programs or evening arts programs would have the same effect—splintered audiences and limited impact.

Broaden your audience by designing programs for multiple ages. Traditional story hours are often designated for children of certain ages, and the development of baby lap-sit programs separate from preschool and toddler story hours is increasing this division. The advantage of such division is the ability to focus on a specific developmental stage, but there is a disadvantage as well. Parents with more than one child may not be able to participate because they are caring for a sibling. There is also the loss of shared experience between the siblings themselves. In smaller libraries, story hours tend to be a come-one-come-all affair; larger libraries may want to leave some room in their schedules for this broader approach as well.

The other effect a broad audience will have on your planning is in subject matter. It is much simpler to plan a program that is for four-year-olds than one for four- to eighty-year-olds. By necessity, your family programs will need to be more engaging than traditional programs to keep the interest of all participants. Parents will be discouraged from participating if there is nothing in the program that appeals to them. You need them involved; otherwise you have gone to a lot of extra work when you could have just done a children's program.

Programs with a strong performance element work well (see chapter 15, "Entertainment and Enrichment Programs"), and you can also go the other direction and make a very informal, hands-on program where people come and go, and decide how and when they will participate. This can mean a program with a number of stations all connected to a common theme, each with its own activities. It can mean a large-group physical activity, such as painting a mural or constructing something out of craft materials. It can also mean something as simple as a drop-in craft where a person can come at any time during a stretch to mingle with whoever is there, get directions and discuss the project with a staff member, and do the project at his or her own pace.

The most distinct form of family literacy program is the caregiver-training program, a chance to explicitly address the issues of emerging literacy with parents and caregivers in an instructional setting. These can be done as separate, stand-alone programs, or in conjunction with other programs. An evening parents-and-caregivers-only program can be offered before the beginning of a story hour series or summer reading program. Such a preview program can offer the children's librarian a chance to explain what will happen in the coming weeks, which skills will be emphasized, how the various adults can help during the programs, and what the adults can do at home to reinforce what is done in the library. The Enoch Pratt Library in Baltimore made such caregiver programs a regular part of their highly successful Mother Goose on the Loose program in order to explain the theory behind the program, and to extend the impact of the program into the home.[8]

Family programs are more time consuming and complicated than other forms of programs, largely because developing family programs requires the facilitator to anticipate a very diverse audience. Integrating elements of family literacy in your more traditional programs will reduce your workload while making the family programs special. If you accept the idea that family programs leverage the librarians' efforts by training parents in teaching literacy skills, then the extra work may be well worth it.

How to Do Family Programming

Family programming need not impose a huge financial burden on the library. Indeed, much of the programming that most libraries do have important elements of family programming already. We need only make a few adjustments in our story hours, book discussions, entertainment, and enrichment programs to make them more family friendly. Often, all we really need to do is to invite (or allow) parents and siblings into our regular programs and to make a few adjustments to integrate them. We may need to adjust the timing of our programs so that more members of the family can participate, as discussed above. We need to promote our programs as family programs. People who are used to the way things have always been done may expect to drop off children for a program and pick them up when it is over.

Changing our intentions will not necessarily change their perceptions. Adding phrases such as "parents and caregivers are encouraged to stay and participate" and "siblings of all ages are welcome" to each poster, press release, information sheet, or other outreach tool will make clear the intent of the program, or at least generate some questions. Be open about what you are trying to do. Tell the adults that the program is as much for them as it is for the children, and that the point of the program is to help them help their children. Parents, grandparents, and others adults will feel more secure in their roles if they know exactly what is expected of them and why. Older siblings may react positively to being assigned a responsible role in the program—that of a mentor or guide to a younger sibling.

There are any number of special programs, services, and activities that the library can offer to encourage reading and learning for the whole family. The parenting collection, which is common in many libraries, is an example. Its placement in the children's area allows parents and children to share reading time together and encourages parents to model good reading habits. The Rock Island (Illinois) Public Library had children and parents produce a book together and then placed these books on display.[9] The Nichols Memorial Library in Center Harbor, New Hampshire, hosted a family field trip to a nearby science center for a tour of the facility and a hike through the grounds. Libraries can promote read-together programs with logs and incentives similar to those used in summer reading programs, except that the reading tracked is done by family members in concert. This could be parents reading to children or children reading to parents. Libraries can stock games, toys, and manipulatives designed specifically for parents and children to use together. The Illinois State Library even suggests creating a parent and child advisory board, drawing in both generations to help develop new programs.[10]

When promoting programs aimed at families, take into account the fact that the real target is likely to be families that do not already have a relationship with your library. In fact, an Illinois study of people in adult literacy programs found that 33 percent of participants never use the library.[11] Understandable, given that those who struggle with literacy are not likely to be avid readers, but sad when one considers how much more the library has to offer, especially nonprint materials for entertainment and enrichment. Partnering with groups that address adult literacy is a necessary first step. Remember that low-literacy skills tend to be passed down from parents to children, so an entire family can benefit from the library's effort. Advertise in places like Laundromats, playgrounds, and pediatricians' offices, where children and parents are likely to congregate together.

While these are simple enough accommodations, they will have a significant effect on the flavor and feel of our programs. In the long run, they will also have a great effect, as behaviors that are modeled and explored in our programs are replicated in homes. If you would like to start a new program specifically with family literacy in mind, there are outside sources you can tap for support. (See chapter 18, "Budget and Finance," on the use of public funds.) The William F. Goodling Even Start Family Literacy Program is the source of federal money for family literacy programs, although those monies are now administered mainly by state governments. Begun in 1988, family literacy appropriations reached $250 million in 2002.[12]

FURTHER READING

Illinois State Library, *Read Together, Grow Together: The Family Literacy Initiative*, Illinois State Library Special Report Series, 1995.

National Center for Family Literacy website, http://www.famlit.org.

NOTES

1. Renea Arnold, "Public Libraries and Early Literacy: Raising a Reader," *American Libraries*, September 2003, 48.

2. Myrna Machet and Elizabeth J. Pretorius, "Family Literacy: A Project to Get Parents Involved," *South African Journal of Library and Information Science* 70, no. 1 (2004): 39.

3. Ken Haycock, "Literacy, Learning and Libraries: Common Issues and Common Concerns," *Feliciter* 49, no. 1 (2003): 36.

4. Machet and Pretorius, "Family Literacy," 40.

5. Ibid.

6. "Family Literacy Project / Project Even Start," *WSU/Standard Examiner*, Ogden City School District, http://departments.weber.edu/chfam/html/literacy.html.

7. Machet and Pretorius, "Family Literacy," 40.

8. Betsy Diamant-Cohen, "Mother Goose on the Loose: Applying Brain Research to Early Childhood Programs in the Public Library," *Public Libraries*, January/February 2004, 43.

9. Cyndy Colletti, "Family Literacy: A Definition," *Read Together, Grow Together: The Family Literacy Initiative* (Springfield: Illinois State Library Special Report Series, 1995), 6.

10. Ibid., 20.

11. Ibid., 5.

12. National Center for Family Literacy, "The History of Even Start," http://www.famlit.org/ProgramsandInitiatives/EvenStart/History.cfm.

Management, Administration, and Leadership

This section will include everything not connected to direct service that a children's specialist has to do to make service possible and effective. It includes activities that many children's librarians try to avoid. Most people who go into children's work do so because of a desire to work with children and a belief that this work is vitally important. It is not surprising, then, that children's specialists prefer to leave such issues as budgeting, public relations, planning, and policy writing to administrators. They may begrudge the time spent away from their *real* work.

The problem with this approach is that the *other* work has a direct impact on the effectiveness of children's services. It all needs to get done, and if children's services staff leave it to administrators, then the administrators will perform these tasks from their own point of view. If the administrator has no background in children's services (and few do), then the needs of children's services will not be reflected. This is the case in far too many libraries today. One way to address this is for children's librarians to step up and be counted when policies are being written, when budgets are being developed, and when the library is communicating with the larger community. Another way is for children's specialists to step into administrative roles to help lead the profession in ways that acknowledge the importance of children's services. In either case, it is important for children's specialists to understand these aspects of management and administration, and how they affect children's services.

Administration is primarily about matching resources to needs. Chapter 18, "Budget and Finance," is all about securing resources. Chapter 19, "Planning," is all about the identification and prioritizing of needs. Chapter 20, "Policy and Procedures," talks about how to connect the resources with the needs in a way that brings results. It is inefficient to allocate resources without a clear understanding of both how and why those resources will be used. It is ineffective to identify needs without securing the resources necessary to address them.

Chapter 21, "Public Relations, Promotion, and Marketing," is all about getting the most for the library's efforts. Too often our services, though well-intentioned, well-planned, and well-executed, fail to have a great effect because we fail to engage our customers. Librarians are famous for assuming that the world should know our value and appreciate our work—and this is most true of children's librarians. Consequently, we never tell our customers what we are doing and why it is of value. We put up posters in our libraries or make a display of books that we think should be popular but are not. We call this marketing, and we are surprised when these things do not spark any new interest. We are prone to reaching out to those who are already in our libraries, and thus the underserved in our communities stay that way.

Finally in chapter 22, "Professional Development," we look at the central, and so often overlooked, component of our service, the talents of the children's librarians themselves. We work so hard to better our spaces, our collections, and our technology, all to better the lives of the children we serve, and we ignore the fact that the most valuable resource we have to give is ourselves. By making ourselves stronger we make our libraries, our communities, and our profession stronger as well. Professional development is not selfish; rather, it is as selfless an act as any public servant can perform so we need to honor the pursuit of professional development.

18

Budget
and Finance

While money never read a child a story, or helped a student do his or her homework, the lack of money has at times made these operations impossible. In recent decades, the public and public officials have increasingly demanded accountability from governmental organizations. People want to see results, and they want to be able to understand where their money is going. Gone are the days when librarians could count on the argument that public libraries are an inherent good, but libraries today often lack the skills to justify our actions beyond such arguments. As Ken Haycock wrote in the Canadian Library Association publication *Feliciter* in 2003, "We are oriented to providing service, which is certainly laudable, but we are less oriented to assessing outcomes and impact beyond the anecdotal 'I enjoyed myself and it made a difference.'"[1]

Competition from the large chain bookstores and the proliferation of the Internet have led many to question the need for libraries at all. Libraries must now demonstrate their effectiveness, and the popularity and wide use of children's services can help this cause. The children's service specialist must also defend his or her worth inside the organization in order to secure the resources needed to do the job. It is a question of increasing both the size of the slice and the size of the pie.

Justification

Justification is a process that every library administrator knows well; it is one-half of the process of securing resources. Planning is the demonstration of future needs, and will be dealt with shortly. Justification involves being accountable for the resources entrusted to you in the past and demonstrating how those resources were used. We are looking here specifically at securing public monies, but many of the same principles apply when looking for private funds as well.

Justification requires you not merely to determine your worth but also to communicate that worth to others, and communication requires both speaking and listening. It is important to speak in words that your audience understands, and also to tailor your message to the concerns of your audience. When justifying the need for resources to library administrators, you can use library-specific language, but you must focus on issues that mean something to them. Specifically, you need to consider what information they can use when they have to, in turn, defend their requests to their superiors. If you find yourself speaking directly to representatives of funding sources who, presumably, are not librarians, then you need to remember to speak in a language free of library jargon that they can easily understand. Also, consider what information they need to satisfy their constituencies, whether that be taxpayers or a corporate board that must approve a charitable contribution.

Statistics

Many children's specialists despise statistics, claiming that a number cannot ever measure the true result of great children's service. How do you measure the joy a child finds in a story, or the lifelong benefits of hooking a child on reading? The answer is, you cannot, but if you want to continue serving children, you must somehow communicate the value of what you do. One approach is to use anecdotal evidence, as will be discussed later, but people are naturally wary of this type of justification on its own. The effect on one child may seem priceless, but there is a real price tag on service, and a great deal of pressure to spend wisely. People want answers to hard questions: how much, how many, who is being served, and how are they being served? The greater question is how to do the greatest good for the greatest number of people because no one can afford to do all the good that is possible. The answers to these questions begin with statistics.

For the moment, put aside the benefits that you cannot measure and focus on activity that you can. Circulation is a number most administrators keep a close eye on because it is a good way of assessing how busy a library is. Certainly, many of the services a library provides do not result directly in circulation, but if people come to the library for one service, they are likely to take advantage of the collection as well. Also, circulation by adult versus children's collections is a fair way of comparing the business and impact of the respective departments. Get those numbers; your administrator probably has them monthly, weekly, or even daily. You can also measure in-house use of materials by periodically gathering materials left on tables or other surfaces, pulled out of order, or left for reshelving. This gives a sense of what materials were used but not circulated.

Reference surveys, which count and classify reference questions over some period of time, are a regular part of most libraries' data collection. Unfortunately, too often these surveys are performed entirely by the reference staff. While adult reference is counting questions, including those that come from children, the children's staff is probably fielding many similar types of questions under the guise of homework help and readers' advisory that are never recorded. For reference departments, these surveys are their primary form of justification; children's services should use them as well.

Related to the counting of reference questions is the measuring of fill rates. A fill rate is the number of times a person looking for something in the library actually finds it, and it is a first measure of customer satisfaction and service effectiveness. There are any number of fill rates you can measure: customers looking for a specific title, for pleasure reading, or for information on a specific topic; or fill rates for picture books or audiovisual material; and the list goes on and on. The only way to gather this information is to ask people. A survey should be done in an ordered fashion under established procedures to ensure that the information is meaningful. There are many sources for how to do a fill rate survey, the most established of which is probably *Output Measures for Public Library Service to Children*, by Virginia A. Walter.

Most children's departments keep track of the number of programs and attendance at those programs, numbers that are then turned over to the administration. It is important to make sure those numbers are used to identify the impact of children's services. Count the people served by a program, including the adults who attend and are learning along with the children (see chapter 17, "Family Programs and Family Literacy"). You can count each attendance by each child at a program; if a child comes to five programs in a series, count it as five attendances. This measures use of your programs.

You can also measure impact by counting the number of children who attend any program. In this case each child is counted only once no matter how many programs he or she attends. These two methods of counting, when put together, allow you to say that *x* number of children attended programs at the library, and the average child in your community attended *y* number of programs. Make sure children's program numbers are not grouped together with adult programs and passed on to governing bodies as simply *library programs.* If they are, then the impact of children's services is lost. The numbers are usually far greater for children's programming than for adult programming in most public libraries.

Measure the amount of contact children have with the library. If the library does a periodic head count of persons using the library, or persons using furniture or equipment, make sure the numbers are broken down to include how many used the children's section, furniture, or computers, and how many people using each resource are children. If children's room computers are more heavily used than adult room computers, then there is justification for increasing the number of computers in the children's room. If children are found to be using adult room furniture or equipment at a significant rate, then there is reason to consider adding more of these resources to the children's library to lure the children back.

Count the number of contacts with community groups, such as visits from Boy Scouts or Girl Scouts, day-care centers, school classes, or camps. Count how many people participated in these visits. Count the number of times the children's staff goes outside the library to interact with any of these groups and the number of people present when they do.

Keep track of the traffic on any children-specific pages of your library's website. Whether your library hosts its own website or has someone else host it, site-use statistics should be available. If there is no breakdown for how much traffic exists on which page, then a counter that is discreet—even invisible to the public—can be placed on any individual page. If your site gets a thousand hits a day, and the children's page gets five hundred of them, then it is clear that many of your online users are either children or caregivers. The children's page may even be contributing greatly to the use of other pages on the site. Many website management programs allow you to see referrers, the last pages visited before users landed on any specific page. Tracking referrers allows you to see how a site is navigated, where a user first goes on a site, and what pages are found only later. If the children's page is the entry point for the majority of users, and other pages are the beneficiaries, then it makes sense to expand the resources for children on your web page.

Analysis

Circulation, reference questions, programs and program attendance, community contacts, and Web traffic are all good measures of children's library use, but they are raw measures that neither speak clearly to the public nor measure impact. Comparison is the key to making the most of statistics. Compare each of these numbers to the same number from the previous year or years and state the change as a percentage: if circulation is ten thousand items in year one and eleven thousand in year two, there is a positive change of 10 percent. Are you circulating more materials? Offering more programs? Drawing more audience members? Hosting more class visits? The next step is to compare the children's services budget for these same years. If children's circulation went up 10 percent and the children's services budget went up 3 percent, then you are proving yourself a good steward of resources and you have the beginnings of an argument for increased funding.

There are any number of comparisons you can use to make your raw statistics more meaningful. Useful numbers to collect include the cost of children's services (staff, collection, programming, supplies, all the facets of the children's department budget, both per line item and as a total), the number of items in the children's collection, and the number of children in your service area (town or city clerks should be able to provide this information). Use these factors to add meaning to your raw numbers.

Per capita comparisons show impact on the average persons you are serving. Divide each of your service numbers by the number of children you serve to get a per capita number and a picture of what the library means to the average child. Circulation figures might mean little to a budget committee member without exposure to the library, so make sure to show that the average child in his or her district checks out six books, attends two programs, asks four reference questions, and visits the children's page on the library website eight times each year; that committee member might start to understand how important the library—especially the children's department—is to the community.

Cost-per-use numbers show the efficiency of your department. Determine cost per circulation by dividing the total children's services budget by the amount of children's material circulation. This is not a particularly *clea*n number because circulation is not the entire output of the children's room, and money goes into many services other than circulation, but this is still a useful number. Administrators regularly use cost-per-circulation figures for the entire library as a measure of efficiency; it is a concept they understand. When you justify your budget to your administrators, use their language. If the cost-per-circulation ratio in the children's department is lower than that of the entire library, and it almost invariably is, then your administrator should recognize that children's services, as an investment, get excellent results. The same goes for cost per program participant (program budget divided by program attendance), which is usually significantly lower for children's programs than it is for adult programs.

The turnover rate (circulation per volume) measures the use of a collection. Most automated circulation systems can easily produce both circulation and holding numbers broken down by various parts of the collection. Divide the total circulation of children's materials for a year by the number of children's materials in the collection, and you have the turnover rate for children's materials. Again, in most libraries this number will be significantly better, in this case higher, than the adult materials' turnover rate.

Each of these numbers is useful when requesting funding for the children's department. Children's services often produce more results with fewer resources than is true in other parts of the library. Given more resources, children's services could often create a better return on investment than monies spent anywhere else. These numbers may also be useful to the administrator who has to defend the entire library's request for funding. Not being primarily concerned with children's services, he or she may have never considered producing numbers that show the impact of the library so clearly.

Anecdotal Evidence

While isolated examples of the good that libraries do may not be effective arguments in and of themselves, once a solid statistical basis is created, anecdotal evidence can then be a powerful tool. The argument goes like this: the library impacts the average child every day in these ways, and here is an example of just how that works. Gather this type of information by asking any customer who is particularly happy with your service to write down why he or she is happy and to give you the note, or to send it to the library's governing board, to the governing board of your town or city, to the press, or to all of the above.

Too often we accept the premise that the people who are happy will say nothing, while those who are unhappy will be vocal. Those with the power to grant or deny us resources—to support or undercut our efforts—may not accept that argument and feel that the complainers are representative of how we are perceived in the community. Counteract this by encouraging the happy and well-served majority of your customers to speak up and be heard. Explain to them that the services they appreciate will be better supported if they speak out.

Collect any positive feedback you get, any positive press coverage you receive, and a few well-chosen photographs of children enjoying your services and add these items to your presentation anytime you are promoting the library or defending its budget—or defending your own budget for that matter. Anecdotal evidence, on its own, will seem shallow and unprofessional. Statistics alone will seem cold and impersonal. Put the two together for the most impact.

Outcome Measures

Statistics and analysis comprise what we know as output measures, or measures of what the library produces. Recent attention has been paid to so-called *outcome measures*, which study the effect of library service on the people who are to be served.[2] This approach sets as the benchmark the expectations of customers, rather than the library's view of what constitutes quality service.[3] In the words of Martha Kyrillidou, it means going from "the user in the life of the library to the library in the life of the user."[4] One way of accomplishing this is to measure changes in the life of library users and then to relate those changes to library service by, say, correlating preschool story hour attendance with success in kindergarten. Another way is by polling library users about their satisfaction with a particular experience, such as a reference transaction. Outcome measurement may also mean quantifying the economic impact of library services by calculating their replacement cost in the commercial market.[5]

This outcome-based approach has the promise of refocusing library service on what really counts—the meeting of needs—rather than on the gathering of resources, which is more often measured.[6] The downsides, however, are numerous: This type of analysis takes a great deal of time and resources itself. Correlations between library service and life results may always be called into question. The opinions expressed in user surveys are subjective and often skewed by the fact that they present the perspective of current users, who are likely to feel favorably toward the library. This last objection can be countered by going out into the community and specifically targeting those people who do not use the library, and whose experience might shed light on the limits of library service.[7]

Outcome measures are a new and emerging reality in libraries, spawned by the recent push to impose a business model of accountability on library service. Everyone in the library world will need to accommodate this new approach, and children's services specialists can hope to raise their status and usefulness within the organization by being at the head of the curve.

Outside Sources of Income / Grant Writing

There are great advantages to securing money for the library without having to justify it before a budget committee, but there are usually strings attached. The classic example now is the E-Rate and CIPA. Starting in 1998, many libraries became dependent on E-Rate money, federal discounts of 20 to 90 percent on the costs of providing electronic telecommunications services paid for by levees on telecommunication providers. Because the level of discounts was determined by the affluence of the community, poorer areas became the most dependent. Then in 2000, Congress passed CIPA, which required public libraries that receive federal money to filter Internet access to protect users under the age of seventeen from adult-oriented materials. In 2004, Baltimore's Enoch Pratt Public Library received $2 million in E-Rate funds out of a $30 million annual budget. The library had never filtered its computers, but when CIPA was upheld, Enoch Pratt instituted filtering.[8]

Grants, whether governmental, corporate, or private, often come from organizations with strong agendas. Make sure you know what restrictions the granting institutions are going to place on using the money. If the grant is an ongoing one, remember that those rules can change. If a company offers you big money, and you design services based on the expectation of that money, will you later be able to resist its pressure in a controversy?

Look at the time involved. Time is money. Will you spend thirty hours researching, writing, defending, and reporting on a grant that gains you $250? Consider the cost to your library of your time. A trustee in Laconia, New Hampshire, explained to a reporter why his library would not be accepting $1,700 annually in E-Rate money, with its CIPA strings attached.

The library considered not only the cost of applying for and administering the grant but also the cost of buying and maintaining the filters, and even the amount of staff time required to turn off the filters when an adult requested it, as required by the Supreme Court. It just was not worth it.[9]

Sometimes applying for a grant is indeed worth it, even if the payoff is less than the resources you put into it. Winning grants can show governing bodies, trustees, town councils, mayors, and school boards (in the case of school libraries) that you are looking for money on your own. A library director in Massachusetts was poring over stacks of paperwork a couple of feet tall, separating out telecommunications costs to claim for E-Rate funding. It was, she admitted, a week's worth of her time. When asked how much the library paid her in a week, she admitted that it was more than the library would gain. Why do it then? Because, she pronounced, every member of the city council would be aware that there were thousands of dollars to be had, and if the library did not get its share, they would be upset.

These are the pressures that administrators feel, and you should be aware of them. No topic is more dangerous for a library director than money. Of course, even a very lucrative grant may not be worth working for if the governing body then deducts the grant from the tax money your library receives. In this last case you have used valuable library resources and made no net gain in money.

FURTHER READING

Virginia A. Walter, *Output Measures for Public Library Service to Children* (Chicago: American Library Association, 1992).

NOTES

1. Ken Haycock, "Literacy, Learning and Libraries: Common Issues and Common Concerns," *Feliciter* 49, no. 1 (2003): 37.

2. Roswitha Poll, "Impact/Outcome Measures for Libraries," *Liber Quarterly* 13, no. 3/4 (2003): 329.

3. Peter Hernon, "Service Quality and Outcome Measures," *Journal of Academic Librarianship*, January 1997, 2.

4. Martha Kyrillidou, "From Input and Output Measures to Quality and Outcome Measures, or, From the User in the Life of the Library to the Library in the Life of the User," *Journal of Academic Librarianship*, January–March 2002, 42.

5. Poll, "Impact/Outcome Measures for Libraries," 336–37.

6. Kyrillidou, "From Input and Output Measures," 43.

7. Peter Hernon, "Service Quality in Libraries and Treating Users as Customers and Non-users as Lost or Never-Gained Customers," *Journal of Academic Librarianship*, May 1996, 171.

8. Robert S. Anthony, "Shhh! And Cover Your Computer Screen," *Black Issues Book Review*, January–February 2004, 17.

9. Annmarie Timmins, "Libraries Pass Up Computer Money, Local Officials Reject Internet Filtering," *Concord Monitor Online*, June 13, 2004, http://www.concordmonitor.com/apps/pbcs.dll/article?AID=2004406130343.

19
Planning

The planning process is one that takes place for the benefit and effective management of an entire library. If your library has not done any planning, you cannot realistically drive the process from children's services. On the other hand, if your library does go through a planning process, it cannot hope to do so effectively without strong input from such a vital component as children's services. Ideally, the library will go through a planning process, and children's services can do its planning within that framework. But you can also use these techniques to plan just for children's services.

While there are any number of approaches to planning, most consist of four broad segments: visioning (What do you want to be?), role setting and goal setting (Where do you want to go?), activities (How will you get there?), and evaluation (What were the results?). This book is not the venue to give an exhaustive description of the planning process; there are entire books on the subject, some of which are listed under "Further Reading" at the end of this chapter. What you will see here is an overview of the process with special emphasis on the areas that most concern children's services.

Why Plan?

Why would any library take on the added task of planning when there is already so much to do? Why especially would a children's specialist want to take time away from actually serving his or her customers in order to join in a planning effort, especially in a larger library where children's staff could so easily keep their heads down and be overlooked? These questions must come up, especially near the end of a long look at all the things that children's services staff do.

Planning helps a library respond to state laws or regulations that might require a long-range plan; changes in population demographics, funding (up or down), laws and regulations that might affect library service, the information and technology environment, the business climate of the community; and any number of other events that might make the effective library of today the obsolete library of tomorrow. Since these factors are always in flux, many libraries continually engage in planning processes every three, four, or five years.

One reason for children's librarians to get involved is to represent the needs of the children's room's clientele. Go back to chapter 3, "Whom Do Children's Librarians Serve?" and look at the list. How many of these people are likely to be on a community planning committee? Surely not a number proportional to the number of people who actually use children's services. Actually, when it comes time to pick members of the committee, children's staff should make sure that their customers *are* well represented. There is likely to be a great deal of interest in the needs of children on any committee of involved community members, but that interest in no way guarantees any understanding of the true needs of children.

Another reason for children's librarians to be involved in planning is to help reconstitute a system that has traditionally not listened to the voices of children's specialists. Sandra Nelson, in *The New Planning for Results*, points out that "planning, by its very nature, is about organizational change."[1] If it is done well, then the planning process may reveal how much children's services add to the actual service the library provides, especially considering the small share of library resources that generally fund children's services. Effective planning can bring a clear vision, where once there was only tradition and perception, and this knowledge is bound to benefit children's services.

Vision and Mission

Visioning is seeing things as they could be. A vision statement lays out an ideal, a future toward which to work. The library must decide how big a vision it wants to begin with. The *Planning for Results* process suggests gathering a community planning committee in order to create a community-wide vision statement. This certainly entails much that is beyond the scope or control of the library, but these efforts will help to identify areas where the library could cooperate with other community entities to benefit the whole community.[2] Certainly, the library can express a vision describing what the community and the library can be.

Mission statements describe what business an organization (or a person) is in. In broad terms, they say what the organization will do. Where visions describe ends, missions describe means. Where visions should be lofty and inspiring, mission statements must be practical and grounded in reality.[3] Mission statements are useful for any organization that wants to focus itself on what it really wants to accomplish. And having a clear picture of what it wants to accomplish is the best way to assure that it will be effective, relevant, or in force years down the road. You, as an individual, can write a personal mission statement, children's services can write one for itself, and children's staff should be involved in the writing of the library's mission statement. An effective mission statement can be a public relations tool to tell your customers what you, your department, or your library is all about. It can be a touchstone for making decisions about priorities, policies, and resources. It can be a unifying force within the organization to inspire, motivate, and focus everyone.

Information Gathering

Gather as much information about your community as you can. Demographic data in all its forms is a great place to start, and it can be gathered from government sources—from the local town or city clerk to the Federal Census Bureau. How many people live in the community? How old are they? Specifically, how many children live in the community and what is their age breakdown? What are their family situations? What are their housing situations? What languages do they speak? What is their citizenship status? Are there neighborhoods where any of these characteristics are pronounced? Where are these neighborhoods in relation to the library or its branches? Physical location is especially important to children who do not drive and who do not have easy access to public transportation.

Business and economic data is important too, and what cannot be found in census data can usually be obtained from local Chambers of Commerce or Economic Development Councils. How much do people make? What is the average family income? This is often a very different matter from personal income as it affects the resources available for children. A community with an average family income of $50,000 and an average household size of 2.5 persons is a very different community than one with the same family income and an average household size of 4.2 persons. The library will want to know about businesses in the community and the general business climate. This affects the stability of the children's population—and can be an indicator of how transient or permanent it is. It will also affect how much donation money may be available for special projects.

There are also questions about individuals to be answered. Who are the stakeholders in the community? Who feels connected with the community and with whom does the community identify? Who are the power brokers? Who can influence others? These people will need to be contacted in order to find out what people in the community think about the library, what needs the community has, and how the library can help to fill those needs. If these questions are asked among people who have no stake in children, then the answers may be very limited.

It is not unusual to have a community operating almost as two separate entities, those with school-age children and those without. These two entities may have separate social networks and social organizers, as well as separate power structures and leaders. In short, they may have completely different stakeholders and power brokers. Children's staff can help to ensure that the group most interested in children, whose focal point is likely to be a school or a recreation field rather than city hall or the Rotary Club, does not get overlooked.

Finally, there is much information to gather about the library itself. Detailed breakdowns of services, resources, and abilities need to be made and presented in a way that nonlibrarians can understand. How many materials does the library own and circulate, and what are the characteristics of those items? How much of the library's business is children's materials, *E* level, *J* level, or young adult/teen? Who uses the library services such as reference or readers' advisory, and how much service is offered? Who attends programs, and how many of those are offered? How are resources such as space, money, staff time, and administrative oversight allocated? Who is answering these questions?

Role Setting and Goal Setting

Once there is a vision of what the community and library should be, and what the current status of both is, it is time to formulate the steps needed to bridge the gap. Here is where the focus turns to what the library can do, either on its own or in conjunction with other community resources. These are not actions or tasks (those will come later), but priorities, paths of service, or general roles that the library will take on to serve the community better.

There are, in fact, two primary approaches to role selection that are currently in use. The first comes from *Planning and Role Setting for Public Libraries*, by the Public Library Association), and the second is PLA's new approach, laid out in *Planning for Results* and *The New Planning for Results*. Regardless of which approach the library takes, the setting of priorities is vital to children's services because the needs of the adult customers and the needs of children are often not the same. If priorities are set by adult services people exclusively, then resources will flow toward those priorities, and the needs of children may not be met.

The Old Method: Goals

Planning and Role Setting for Public Libraries identified eight roles that public libraries might adopt, and encouraged libraries to choose three roles to focus on through a planning cycle. Some of these roles applied directly to children's services (one of them exclusively to children's services). Those eight roles are Preschooler's Door to Learning, Formal Education Support Center, Reference Library, Popular Materials Library, Community Activity Center, Community Information Center, Independent Learning Center, and Research Library.

Obviously, Preschooler's Door to Learning has the greatest impact on children's services. If the library adopts this as one of its priorities, then it is committing itself to supporting the picture book and first reader collections, to holding story hours and family literacy programs, and to maintaining a well-trained children's staff to assist both children and parents in developing reading skills. Libraries that choose Formal Education Support Center as a key role should put resources toward a juvenile collection that meets the needs of the local schools' curricula, build homework support services, and encourage cooperation with local schools and homeschool families.

Libraries that choose to emphasize the Reference Library role should remember that children ask more reference questions than adults do, and build a reference collection at reading levels accessible to children, train reference staff to work with children, and teach children's staff to do reference. If one of the key roles is Popular Materials Library, the library needs to put funding into current juvenile materials—including popular culture titles and emerging formats—not just into bestseller adult fiction.

Libraries that make it a priority to be Community Activity Centers have the advantage of a long tradition of children's programming in public libraries, but if they wish to fulfill this role they must reach beyond the preschool level to older children and tweenagers. Libraries that wish to be Community Information Centers need to invest time and energy into building relationships with recreation departments, schools, day-care centers, and social service agencies to make sure that the library is the center of information for children and parents.

Obviously, most or all of these activities go on in a public library regardless of the roles chosen for emphasis, but none of these activities happens without resources. If a role is not made a priority, then time, energy, money, and attention will flow in other directions. Even if one of these roles is chosen, children's services must make a case for the needs of children within that role; otherwise the needs of adults may simply take precedence.

The New Method: Service Responses

Planning for Results reconstitutes the eight roles into thirteen *service responses*, most of which can conceivably be applied at all levels, but none of which focus directly on children's services. Those service responses include Basic Literacy, Business and Career Information, Commons, Community Referral, Consumer Information, Cultural Awareness, Current Topics and Titles, Formal Learning Support, General Information, Government Information, Information Literacy, Lifelong Learning, and Local History and Genealogy. The idea of this newer approach is not to choose priorities, but to rank them; a nod to the idea that libraries serve, and are asked to serve, most or all of these needs to some degree.

Basic Literacy encompasses much of the goal of Preschooler's Door to Learning, as well as addressing the needs of adult learners with low literacy skills. Because these adults often use the children's collection (as discussed in chapter 3, "Whom Do Children's Librarians Serve?"), this service response is of particular interest to children's staff. Commons carries many of the same implications as Community Activity Center; Community Referral is analogous to Community Information Center; Formal Learning Support to Formal Education Support Center; General Information to Reference Library; and Current Topics and Titles to Popular Materials Library

The inclusion of Information Literacy as a service response emphasizes the teaching role of librarians, and could have a profound impact on how both children's librarians and reference librarians see their work. Should a library choose to put this high on its priority list, children's services staff must push to be included: information literacy skills are best learned early in life. Children must be taught the skills needed to access information, not just in the library but also in the information-rich world all around them. Reference librarians may be well trained to access information, but that does not directly translate into the ability to pass these skills on.

Children's librarians already have a relationship with children, and are used to explaining things at an elementary level. Indeed, it may make more sense to use children's staff to teach adults information literacy than to use reference staff to teach children. It is not unusual for children's services staff to teach Internet classes, which are attended almost exclusively by elderly customers who are trying to keep up with their grandchildren. If this service response is emphasized, and children's staff is included in its execution, then children's librarians should be prepared to increase their teaching and speaking skills. (See chapter 22, "Professional Development," for more on this.)

Objectives and Activities

Mission statements and goals or service responses help to show what needs to be done, and the next step is to determine how to get these things accomplished. Objectives are outcomes that have measurable results and mark progress toward those goals. *The New Planning for Results* advises that objectives should have three components: a measure, a standard against which to compare the measure, and a date or time frame at which the measure will be evaluated.[4] Notice that the how and when of evaluation are decided on early in the process, before the plan is even put into effect. Activities are short-term actions; they make up the to-do list of the planning process. The follow-up on goals and objectives marks the difference between a plan that is useful and positive, and one that gets released and slid into a drawer never to be seen again.

Evaluation

Evaluation means going back to check the progress that has been made once the plan has been put into action. Evaluation begins early in the process with decisions about how progress will be measured, what output measures will be used, how the progress will be reported, and when the progress will be reported. The book *Output Measures for Public Library Service to Children* lists specific measures that can be used for each of the eight roles from *Planning and Role Setting for Public Libraries,* and much can be adapted to the thirteen service responses of the *Planning for Results* approach. More important, *Output Measures for Public Library Service to Children* gives practical suggestions for interpreting the different output measures.[5]

Evaluation results need to be checked against stated goals and objectives, and the results need to be distributed as widely as the planning document, both within the library and to the larger community. This reporting will assure all those involved that the considerable effort of planning was not a mere academic exercise. Planning doesn't end with a completed plan, or even with a completed evaluation. One planning cycle leads directly to the next, and if people are to be recruited into working on a new plan, you must prove to them that the last cycle produced real results.

FURTHER READING

Thomas Hennen, *Hennen's Public Library Planner: A Manual and Interactive CD-ROM* (New York: Neal-Schuman, 2004).

Ethel Himmel and William James Wilson, *Planning for Results: A Public Library Transformation Process* (Chicago: American Library Association, 1998).

Charles R. McClure and others, *Planning and Role Setting for Public Libraries: A Manual of Options and Procedures* (Chicago: American Library Association, 1987).

Sandra Nelson, *The New Planning for Results: A Streamlined Approach* (Chicago: American Library Association, 2001).

Douglas Zweizig, Debra Wilcox Johnson, and Jane Robbins, with Michele Besant, *The Tell It! Manual: The Complete Program for Evaluating Library Performance* (Chicago: American Library Association, 1996).

NOTES

1. Sandra Nelson, *The New Planning for Results: A Streamlined Approach* (Chicago: American Library Association, 2001), 31.

2. Ibid., 46.

3. Douglas Zweizig, Debra Wilcox Johnson, and Jane Robbins, with Michele Besant, *The Tell It! Manual: The Complete Program for Evaluating Library Performance* (Chicago: American Library Association, 1996), 15.

4. Nelson, *New Planning*, 86.

5. Virginia A. Walter, *Output Measures for Public Library Service to Children: A Manual of Standardized Procedures* (Chicago: American Library Association, 1992), 9–14.

20

Policy and Procedures

It is important that children's specialists understand not only what the policies and procedures of the library are but also how and why they are developed and what their purposes are. Too often, children's specialists see policy and procedure as an obstacle—something that must be overcome in order to do their jobs. This can mean that the children's specialist is out of tune with the workings of the larger library, and that policies and procedures are developed without an appreciation of the needs of children's services. The easiest way to address these problems is for children's services staff to be involved when policies and procedures are being developed.

Policies are usually developed by library administrators in conjunction with an overseeing board or body, such as trustees, commissioners, or, in the case of school media centers, a school board. They help to assure that services today are still available in the future. Continuity of service is important; people are more likely to use services that they trust will be there in the future. Policies allow these governing bodies the opportunity to fulfill their mission of setting broad guidelines for expected outcomes.

Procedures are usually developed by library administrators, in conjunction with mid-level administrators whose departments are directly affected by the procedures. If the library is not large enough to have a middle management level, the administrator may or may not consult with frontline staff. Procedures help to assure that services offered now are also offered during the next shift. Again, continuity of service is important if the customer is to feel secure in what is being offered. Procedures allow the administration the opportunity to fulfill its mission of defining levels of service and setting priorities.

Together, policies and procedures give the organization a base for explaining to the public what it does. Theoretically, they should protect the staff member when he or she follows the rules, and protect the organization when he or she does not. If children's specialists are not involved in development, then bad policies and procedures could put children's staff in the position of deciding between giving good service and protecting their standing in the organization. No one wants to be put in that situation. By participating in the development of policy and procedure, the children's specialists can ensure that the needs of children, parents, caregivers, and teachers are addressed. Administrators and adult services staff, however well-intentioned, may not have the expertise or experience to know how policies affect these segments of the community.

Some policies have been addressed earlier, such as the collection development policy in part 2, "The Collection," and the acceptable use policy in chapter 11, "The Internet." The following policies also affect children's services directly; children's staff members should understand them, and children's specialists should be involved in their creation and maintenance.

Interlibrary Cooperation

Gone are the days when interlibrary cooperation meant simply interlibrary loan. Cooperation may be as informal as a personal relationship between staff members at different libraries, or as formalized as a consortium. Cooperation can take the form of resource sharing, shared cataloging, cooperative buying and discount negotiation, reciprocal borrowing privileges, or joint program development. Children and adults are affected differently by these relationships. Children in the service areas of many different public libraries may attend the same school, which means that without cooperation among libraries, classmates may have distinctly different levels of library support.

Reciprocal borrowing agreements can be a real boon to adults, but are less advantageous to children who do not drive and may not be able to get to other libraries. On the other hand, a healthy interlibrary loan system can save children who are in the unique position of needing the same informational materials as twenty, sixty, or a hundred other individuals at the exact same time. When a really large class report is assigned, no individual library can fill the need.

Children's specialists can sometimes experience isolation within their libraries because of the distinctiveness of their audiences. An interlibrary cooperation policy that allows for plenty of interaction among specialists, as well as joint programming between libraries, can help to combat this isolation and spread new ideas and methods.

Circulation

Children and adults use libraries very differently, yet too often there is a single set of rules governing the basic component of library use—circulation. An adult pleasure reader is unlikely to want to check out fifteen books at once; a child is very likely to want just that. An adult looking for information on a specific scientific topic is not likely to be in competition with many other individuals looking for the same resources at the same time, but a child will be in this situation often.

Circulation policies should recognize a different set of needs among juvenile customers than exist among adults. Policies can be written to handle different collections differently, so that limits on the circulation of adult books are different than those on the circulation of children's books. Policies should not be written setting different rules for different customers based on their ages; this amounts to unequal access and is in opposition to one of the basic principles of children's librarianship. Ideally, policies should be written flexibly enough to allow different users with different needs to access the library in ways that serve them best. In this way, children's services can lead the way to more open and less restrictive rules for all library users. After all, a person's a person no matter how *big* as well.

Most restrictions placed on circulation are imposed to guard against some future rush of demand that never seems to appear. Libraries are more likely to be short of space than short of materials, and the shelves are never really empty. When considering circulation rules for the children's area, try a less restrictive period as a test to see if a shortage appears. If none does, then relax the rules even further and watch the results. This approach may make adult services staff uncomfortable if they feel that they cannot relax their rules in a similar fashion. This is the time to assert the need for different rules for different parts of the collection.

At other times, restrictions are put in place to dictate behavior. These restrictions are marked by justifications such as, "Well, nobody needs to read more than five books at once," or "They shouldn't be watching more than three videos a week anyways." This is a dangerous path for a public service entity to tread. Libraries should not dictate to customers how they will use the materials we provide, and if children's behavior should be modified, it is the parent or guardian who needs to do it. The best-intentioned efforts of librarians to use policy to modify behavior will frustrate customers whose use of the library is perfectly justifiable, even if it is beyond the use that we, as librarians, expect.

Intellectual Freedom

Intellectual freedom is so central to the mission of the library that it has been addressed in virtually every section of this book. It is entwined in how we choose and organize our collections, how we provide services, and how and why we plan programming, and it is a central theme when we talk about the ethics and responsibilities that underpin our profession. One of the major challenges to intellectual freedom is discrimination based on age. When developing an intellectual freedom policy, the library must take a stand based on the Horton Principle: "A person's a person, no matter how small."[1] Furthermore, this principle must be translated into the practical, day-to-day operation of the library. Children's services cannot hope to preserve the rights of children without being at the table when intellectual freedom is discussed.

School Curriculum

School media specialists would have to consider the curriculum as a policy. The curriculum is the ultimate policy of a school, and if the media center is to be an integral part of the organization, then the voice of the media specialists should be heard when that curriculum is being developed. This goes for more than the just the library skills portion of the curriculum. How the school promotes reading, the emphasis on research skills, and intellectual honesty all affect virtually every subject, class, and grade. Plus, being involved in curriculum development gives the media specialist more information earlier in the process, which makes planning, resource buying and sharing, and cooperative efforts more effective. This also affects the public library children's specialist, who must work with the school media specialist to have the maximum impact on students.

NOTE

1. Theodor Seuss Geisel, *Horton Hears a Who!* (New York: Random House, 1954).

21

Public Relations, Promotion, and Marketing

You have built a great collection. You have designed a dynamite set of programs. You and the rest of the staff are trained, and willing and able to help customers. The question remains, how do you bring the people through the door? Certainly there are those who already know you are there, and there are always those who come looking for the public library. But for many people today with hectic lives and access to commercial sources of information and reading materials, such as home access to the Internet and easy access to large bookstores, the library is just not a presence in their lives. You can grow a library either by convincing your current customers to use more and more of your services, or by introducing yourself to new customers. This chapter is about doing both.

Before setting out on your own, it is important to understand how public relations, promotion, and marketing are done in your library. There may be rules in place that require all press releases to go through the director, the trustees, or even the city. Much of the work may have already been done—building media relations, collecting lists of media outlets, and performing the remaining background chores. There may be other staff members who have responsibility for publicity, so leaping forward blindly can cause hurt feelings. In addition, all of these efforts require the allocation of resources, if only your time. Outreach is an important part of the library's service program, and it is the most visible. The library as a whole— its governing body and administration—has the right to oversee any outreach efforts.

That being said, outreach is important enough to demand your attention. You should be proactive in reaching out to your community and especially your specific constituency. Your success is dependant on positive, aggressive outreach, and if the larger library's outreach efforts do not adequately promote your programs and services, then you need to take on the responsibility yourself. If you do this well, other parts of the library, or even your city or town, may want to use your outreach vehicles to promote their services. This places children's services at the center of activities in your library and your community, and everybody wins.

Building Media Relations

The media is a vital tool for publicizing the library, its programs, and its services. In-library marketing is not enough, because it fails to reach those people who do not already use the library. Press coverage reaches out to this new audience, and it makes the library more of a presence for everyone. The primary goal has to be to place the library, and specifically children's services, in the minds of as many people as you can, as often as you can. This means that communicating with the press should be done regularly and often. Do not wait for the biggest event of the year to reach out to local media outlets; they will have no relationship with you impelling them to cover your story, and their audience will not be expecting to find information about you in the newspaper, on the radio, or on the television screen.

The second goal is to control your message. The press is a powerful force, and power is always as dangerous as it is useful. An inaccuracy or misrepresentation can leave the wrong people in the wrong place at the wrong time looking for a program that is inappropriate for them or just not what they were expecting. The best way to eliminate these possibilities is to convince the press to run your copy with as little editing as possible. That means providing press releases that can be used word for word, in formats that can easily be incorporated into the final product. It means providing pictures that show the library in the light in which you want to be broad-

The Annual Parlin Library Scholastic Chess Tournament in Everett, Massachusetts, makes for great publicity.

cast. It might mean going so far as to produce your own audio and video product.

A side benefit of having a regular and positive relationship with the press is that when someone expresses something negative about the library, the press will have an impetus to come to you for your perspective. If that other account involves children in some way, a single press report can undermine literally years of good work and community building. And even if the original story proves to be false or misleading, the damage is done. You do not want to be in the position of building a new relationship with a press outlet when that outlet is about to announce that the library is not a safe place for children.

Press Releases

Writing an effective press release is difficult because the audience is so broad. Any other outreach you do is targeted at a specific audience; the media broadcasts its message to all: children and adults, adults with children and adults without, the working and the retired, the single and the married, those who use the library regularly and those who never set foot through your door. Because of this, the information you send out will be mixed in with information aimed at all these different audiences. Your first job is to get noticed in all that background noise.

Write your own headlines. Never send out a press release simply under the heading *Press Release*. If you make a newspaper write its own headline it is likely to focus on some aspect other than the one you would choose. Keep it short and eye catching; you have only the briefest moment to get a reader's attention. Once you do, you may keep it for no more than a few seconds. Newspaper writers talk about the pyramid approach to writing: put the vital information, in condensed terms, right at the beginning of the article. This is the top of the pyramid. Get the who, what, where, when, and why down clearly and quickly. Once you have articulated the basics, start expanding your focus to include description, exposition, and background. Below that, add tangential information. This is where to mention other activities and services that a person interested in this particular program might like as well.

Using the pyramid approach helps your readers by letting them decide when they have enough information, at which point they can simply stop reading without missing the major thrust of the article. It helps the newspapers by giving them the choice of how much space they can devote to your article; they then cut at any point, and the top of the pyramid stays intact. It benefits you by letting the papers make their cuts from the bottom without altering your primary message. It is also a format they understand and are comfortable working with. If you use the pyramid approach, you can go ahead and make your press releases long and rich. Take the opportunity to cross-promote services and programs. Always add phone numbers, e-mail addresses, and Web addresses so that an interested person can seek more information.

Pay attention to submission guidelines. Most newspapers print them somewhere in each paper or list them on their websites. If there are restrictions on length or format and you ignore them, all your efforts will go to waste. Even the smallest of newspapers are likely to have a number of addresses and contact people. Sending to the wrong place or person can cause a delay that might mean your press release does not arrive where it needs to be in time to be printed. If the paper accepts electronic submission, use it. There is no better was to control your message than to allow the paper to simply cut and paste your press release into their format. Also, newspaper people tend to be a harried bunch; if they do not have to retype your submission, they are more likely to run it, and run it in its entirety.

Check the preferred format for electronic submission. Does the paper prefer it in the body of an e-mail or as an attachment? If as an attachment, what programs and versions are compatible with their system? Can you submit pictures electronically? In what format? Black and white or color? What size and resolution are preferred? The less intervention required on their part, the more likely you will be to see your message in print. If these details are not printed in the publication itself, call and ask. Not only will this build goodwill by avoiding troublesome incompatibilities, but it is also a great excuse to introduce yourself to someone at the paper.

There is nothing wrong with sending out two press releases for the same event, one well in advance and the other just before the event. Promote every event, every story hour series, and every ongoing program. You want the papers to count on content from you on a regular basis, and if they get it they will reserve that space for you. If the public gets used to seeing your activities on a regular basis, they will know where to look when they want to know what is going on, and they will think of your library as a place where there is always something happening.

The children's services department has the potential to craft an extremely positive picture of the library as a whole. You do not want the first thing someone reads about your library to be an intellectual freedom challenge or a budget battle. If people see ten pictures of smiling children for every negative message about the library, they will be more circumspect about naysayers. This is a point you need to make to administrators if there is any resistance to your publicity efforts. Good public relations from the children's room benefits everybody.

SAMPLE PRESS RELEASE

Cow Day Is Greenland Library Tradition

Greenland, NH

The Weeks Public Library in Greenland celebrates a long-standing tradition this month as once again it holds Cow Day on Wednesday, June 23, from 2:00–4:00 p.m., complete with crafts, stories, butter making, and yes, a real live cow to meet (just a little one, actually). Bring along your favorite cow joke too! Young children especially enjoy this close-up and friendly encounter with a four-legged reminder of our rural heritage. There is no registration needed, so just bring the family for an afternoon of fun. This program is free and open to the public.

Cow Day traditionally kicks off the library's Summer Reading Program, and this year's summer reading theme is Check Out a Hero. There will be many exciting opportunities all summer to get to know your local heroes and what they do. The library will hold a field trip to the Greenland Fire Department on Thursday July 8, at 1:00 p.m. The Portsmouth Police Department will present a police dog demonstration at the library on Monday, July 19, at 7:00 p.m. The Greenland Emergency Medical Technicians (EMTs) will bring an ambulance to the library on Tuesday, July 27, at 1:00 p.m. for tours and a demonstration.

Of course, the library's regular programs continue all summer long. Story hours for all ages are Tuesdays and Wednesdays at 11:00 a.m., Open Chess Night is Thursdays, 6:00–8:00 p.m., and Cribbage Night is Mondays, 5:00–8:00 p.m. Schedules are now available from the library, the Greenland Central School, and many local merchants.

The library is located at 36 Post Road, two doors down from the Greenland Central School. Contact the library at (603) 436-8548 for more information, or by e-mail at weekspl@comcast.net. For directions and more information on all the library's programs, visit us on the Web at http://www.weekslibrary.org.

Public Service Announcements

A public service announcement (PSA) is a recorded statement that is then broadcast over television or radio airwaves. It is basically a commercial for your library. All stations run PSAs in partial fulfillment of their public responsibilities as required for licensing by the Federal Communications Commission (FCC).[1] They might as well run them for you.

PSAs are a good way to raise awareness and create positive feelings. They are not the best way to get across large amounts of information. PSAs are run—and repeated over a long period of time—whenever they fit into a programming schedule. They are not the right approach for promoting small, individual programs. PSAs can be created to be run for months leading up to a huge program, but they are best for promoting ongoing services. Everything else belongs in a press release.

Your local television or radio station may be willing to help you produce a PSA. Find out who is in charge of community relations and approach him or her with your idea. Be clear about the purpose you have in mind, without being either too general or too specific: how great the library is will not translate well, but you also should avoid having a script. Ask what the station would be willing to produce, and how they wish to do it. Some stations will ask you to provide the personality; others prefer to use their own people. Be flexible and acknowledge that these people do this for a living, and are doing it for you for free.

Consider cooperating with other libraries, or other libraries' children's services departments, to create a unified message for the public libraries in your area. Media outlets may be more receptive to helping you promote to a larger audience, especially if their listeners cover a broad geographic area. If you do a regional or statewide summer reading program, this may be the perfect opportunity to get together and do a series of PSAs.

If you have confidence in your skills, and you really want to control your message, you may choose to create your own PSAs. Many colleges, technical schools, and even high schools these days have media labs capable of producing broadcast quality audio and video. Teachers and students alike may be appreciative of the real-life practice. Another advantage is that you can make one clip and distribute it to a number of outlets. The disadvantages are that the quality of the production may be amateurish, and you still have to conform to the requirements of length and technical format that are required by the stations you want to reach. If different stations have different requirements, one PSA may not work for all. If you are going to create your own PSAs, research the requirements of your primary station or stations. Ask them what they will accept, and make sure that those producing the PSA understand these requirements.

Newsletters and Other Publications

Direct mail is still the most effective means of reaching new customers, at least if the piles of junk mail that flow from mailboxes these days are any indication. Broad distribution of fliers and literature is an effective outreach tool; that's why people always want to leave handouts at the library for their organizations. You need to distribute information outside the walls of your library because in every community there are people who never walk through your door.

Newsletters are not newspapers; this is not an exercise in journalism. Newsletters are outreach tools, and though we would be loath to use the term propaganda here, it is important to remember that you are sending out a concerted message. Newsletters and fliers should be visually attractive. They should include small bits of information, not long blocks of text. Promote programs that are coming along in the future rather than reporting on things in the past. While a wrap-up of former programs may induce positive feelings, it gives the reader no direct reason to use the library. Do not use these formats primarily to warn, cajole, or educate your audience on procedural matters or mundane policy issues. The purpose of any promotional material should be to encourage a person to walk into the library.

Remember that people are bombarded these days with information; you must stand out. Before you produce any publication, take a draft to your library's literature rack and stuff it in among the other fliers. Does it catch your eye? Make it visible. Use larger type, especially for headlines, and break up text often with headings, subheadings, excerpts, and quotes. Never shrink a font to make something fit; shrink the number of words instead. Break up pages into columns, and columns into boxed text. Graphics are easily integrated into word processing programs these days, and free clip art is everywhere. Children's services specialists should be creative enough, and aware enough, to be able to produce something better than your average community organizations' outreach tools, and that is appealing to a broad audience.

When possible, arrange to insert your newsletter or a flier into a mailing from some other organization. Not only does this save money in postage while broadening your audience, but it also connects you in people's minds with an organization that they already support. You may even tailor a flier to match the interests of those in the other organization. Offer to do the same for other organizations when you are sending out a mailing or distributing a newsletter in your community. It never hurts to give people a psychological reminder that the library is involved in the community, not just a stand-alone entity with its own interests.

E-mail has created a new avenue for reaching out to your current customers and making them feel more connected with your library. An e-mail distribution list is a way of entering e-mail addresses once, and then sending copies of an e-mail to all the addresses on the list with the push of a button. Sending an e-mail newsletter requires nothing more than copying newsletter information into an e-mail and sending it to this type of list. It has much the same effect as direct mail to an established mailing list, but it is very quick and quite affordable. The only cost involved is the time you put into it.

Building an e-mail newsletter distribution list can be as simple as putting out slips of paper asking for e-mail addresses. Children love to get mail, electronic or otherwise, and many parents like first knowledge of upcoming programs and new releases. Without the concern of mailing or printing costs, you can send out an e-mail newsletter more often; by doing so, you increase the number of contacts the library has with its customers and give the recipients the pleasant experience of having news far in advance of other library users. When sending to a list, especially one that includes children, remember to use the blind carbon copy (BCC) feature on your e-mail system. That assures that recipients do not see the names or e-mail addresses of other recipients, protecting the safety and privacy of your customers and making sure that your list is not just copied into someone else's list to be used for electronic junk mail.

What do you put in a newsletter, print or electronic? If you collect information regularly for one, recycle it into the other. Take community information from your bulletin board, or any other outreach tool you have. Cut and paste the text and graphics from any posters you produce in-house. The chances are that you already have a good deal of the information; you just need to fit it into a new format. It is useful for people to see the same information many times in different formats; reinforcement is the best way to make sure your message is not just heard but also retained. Add lists of books and other materials that have either just been released or are expected to be released soon. Promote your programs heavily; you want the newsletter to be the first of many contacts the recipient will have with your library.

Web Writing

Children's librarians, especially frontline children's service specialists, are often among the youngest and newest members of the library staff. Because of this, they are often among the most technologically savvy. Children's librarians also serve audiences that tend to be more technologically advanced and focused than other library audiences. It is natural that children's specialists be asked to develop web pages for the library. If this is not a strength of your skill set, then make it one. Web writing is an opportunity for children's services to become central to the workings of the greater library.

Even if someone else is responsible for the library's website, children's services may be responsible for a specific children's page. An effective web page can be a doorway into library services such as databases, an online catalog, and renewing or reserving items electronically, if the library provides such resources over the Internet. At the very least, it can be a guide to more traditional library services such as collections and programs.

The great advantage of a web page is that it can be updated quickly. There is no reason for a web page to be static over time, especially a children's web page. There will almost always be more going on in the children's room than in the adult room, so children's pages should always be fresh and up to date, promoting programs, activities, and services. Any poster that you display inside the library can be reproduced on the website, either by reformatting the document from which the poster was produced or by scanning the poster and adding it to the web page as a picture. As with a newsletter, focus on coming events and reasons for people to use the library in the future, not just on feel-good stories about past events.

More and more, libraries will rely on outreach to remain relevant in an increasingly busy and disjointed world. Children and parents will need constant reminding that the library is there and relevant to their lives. Also, the library will increasingly be judged on its technological relevance. People will expect more from our web pages as they rely less on other methods of getting information. This is especially true for children, who know no other methods of accessing information. All our good work is for naught if we are not effective in saying to people, "Here we are, and here is why we matter."

NOTE

1. The Museum of Broadcast Communications, "Public Interest, Convenience, and Necessity," http://www.museum.tv/archives/etv/P/htmlP/publicintere/publicintere.htm.

22

Professional Development

We strive for excellence in the profession by maintaining and enhancing our own knowledge and skills, by encouraging the professional development of co-workers, and by fostering the aspirations of potential members of the profession.

— *Code of Ethics of the American Library Association*

You must not neglect to increase your skills and add to your value— professional development—whether you are a library school graduate and have twenty years' experience, or you are a trainee in your first week of work. Remember that libraries are not buildings full of books but systems for delivering service to your community, and the most important part of those systems is the people who make them work. That means that, as important as collection development may be, professional development is even more so.

The reasons for professional development are varied, as are the methods. Children's specialists must keep in touch with current and changing issues in order to provide the most up-to-date service. By strengthening children's services you will strengthen the entire library and, by extension, the profession. Great children's service benefits all libraries by increasing impact and reflecting well on our profession. Many professional development activities give children's specialists a chance to practice valuable leadership skills, opportunities they may not have within their own organizations, that will allow them to rise to administrative positions in the future in order to influence the direction of their libraries and the profession as a whole. Finally, professional development will improve both your visibility and your market value in the library world. Librarians are reaching for pay equity with other professions, and children's librarians' salaries lag behind those of others within the profession. One way to address both of these issues is for individual librarians—children's specialists in particular—to increase their own value.

Conferences and Classes

Conference attendance and formal training are the basic ways of improving your skills and value. Library conferences offer concentrated periods of exposure to very specific issues, while formal classes and workshops offer broader coverage of more general issues. Each requires support from your organization, and this support is worth fighting for. Continuing education is vital to librarians who are in a field that deals with information and public service, both of which require constant training and updated skills. If the organization expects you to do your job well, it must support your continuing education. That support can come in the form of financial means to attend classes or conferences, time off, preferably with pay, and incentives for those who continue to improve themselves.

Library classes and workshops, as well as conference attendance, should be a component of periodic performance evaluations. Many states require continuing education hours for certification or recertification; sadly this professional development is not often required for children's librarians, although it may be a basis for salary increases or promotion. Classes and conference attendance are the most commonly accepted forms of continuing education for recertification, so they should be a significant part of any personal continuing education plan. There is financial aid available for continuing education. Check with your state, regional, and national library associations for lists of scholarships and grants.

National Conference Scholarships

American Association of School Librarians (AASL) Frances Henne Award
http://www.ala.org/Template.cfm?Section=awards

Demco New Leaders Travel Grant
http://www.ala.org/ala/pla/plaawards/planewleaders.htm

EBSCO (ALA) Conference Sponsorship
http://www.ala.org/Template.cfm?Section=awards

Penguin Young Readers Group Award
http://www.ala.org/ala/alsc/awardsscholarships/profawards/
penguinputnam/penguinputnam.htm

Professional Reading

Professor A. J. Anderson of the Simmons College Graduate School of Library and Information Science would repeatedly remark in his management classes that librarians today have no excuse not to be up on their professional reading. The online, full-text magazine index, a basic tool available in most of the libraries where we work, brings an almost limitless supply of new ideas, new ways of looking at things, and best practices suggestions. He would urge his students to find a few minutes every day to look up one article of interest and read it. The simple exercise would further our own education indefinitely.

Professional reading is self directed, requires no travel and minimal to no expense, can be done at any point in the day or week, and offers limitless variety. In short, it has none of the obstacles that librarians commonly blame for failing to pursue professional development. On top of that, if we are to present ourselves as advocates of the power of reading, not just for pleasure but also for the betterment of the individual, then how embarrassing is it if we do not read about our own profession? Yet children's librarians seem to lag behind other specialists in this area, as in other professional development opportunities. Reference librarians often defend time spent reading at public-service desks, saying they are doing their professional reading, which in turn helps them provide better service. Children's librarians are too fond of saying they read children's literature as their professional reading. While this is important, it does not change the fact that professional reading helps children's specialists use their knowledge of children's literature more effectively.

Children's librarians should read not just about children's librarianship but also about other fields that affect children, such as education, child welfare, and child psychology. They should also read the wider library press to see what trends are affecting their libraries and might affect the clients they serve. Children's specialists must always keep an eye out for issues that affect children, but on which children's advocates have as yet failed to be heard. And if children's librarians are going to rise in influence within their organization or the profession—and if someday they may be administrators so they can have an even greater impact on the quality of services to children—then they must take on the responsibility of learning what affects the greater library world. Children's librarians cannot claim that their needs are not being met, that children's services are not valued adequately, or that their contribution is underappreciated, if they fail to understand the workings of the library or the profession as a whole. They will also be less effective advocating for the needs of children within their organization if they do not understand the needs and challenges faced by adult services or the administration.

Library-Related Journals on the Web

Some journals have at least some of their content available online. On many of these sites, some of the content is only available to subscribers.

American Libraries (the magazine of the American Library Association)
http://www.ala.org/al_onlineTemplate.cfm

Computers in Libraries
http://www.infotoday.com/cilmag

The Horn Book Magazine
http://www.hbook.com

Information Technology and Libraries (the journal of the Library and Information Technology Association)
http://www.ala.org/ala/lita/litapublications/ital

Knowledge Quest (the journal of the American Association of School Librarians)
http://www.ala.org/ala/aasl/aaslpubsandjournals/kqweb

Library Journal
http://www.libraryjournal.com

Public Libraries (the journal of the Public Library Association)
http://www.ala.org/ala/pla/plapubs/publiclibraries

School Library Journal
http://www.schoollibraryjournal.com

Teacher Librarian
http://www.teacherlibrarian.com

Voice of Youth Advocates
http://www.voya.com

Young Adult Library Services (the journal of the Young Adult Library
Services Association)
http://www.ala.org/ala/yalsa/yalsapubs/yals

Committee and Organization Work

There are almost endless opportunities for children's librarians to join committees that do valuable work on behalf of the larger library community, and that afford the children's specialist a perspective outside his or her own organization. Committee work can expose children's librarians to new people and ideas, and make them consider an aspect of their jobs more closely then they otherwise would. Isolation is a major problem among children's librarians who often work physically separated from their colleagues in adult services and separated by decades in age from most of their clientele. The problem is worse in small and rural libraries where the children's librarian is likely to be a department unto him or herself. Committee work can fight that isolation by letting the children's librarian connect with adults, colleagues, and people who share their area of expertise. It also raises the value of a staff member by offering networking opportunities, and by allowing him or her to show off skills and build a base of contacts with specialized skills to call on when the need arises.

Committee work gives the children's specialist a chance to expand his or her leadership and management skills, and it also offers a different perspective on how to motivate, articulate a vision, set goals, and evaluate progress. If the planning in his or her library takes place at a higher level, this experience is even more valuable to the children's specialist who is not likely to get much similar experience within his or her own organization. If the children's specialist has aspirations to a position of greater responsibility or an administrative career, then committee work is an excellent way to gain exposure and recognition.

Most local, state, and regional library associations have children's issue sections, or at least roundtable-type groups that meet informally. Start small, with committee membership at the most local levels, in order to build experience and contacts. Both background and connections will help as you move up to committee chairmanships and larger organizations, and eventually to officer positions. As with conference and class attendance, it is vital to inform your organization of your committee work and to get support. If committee work improves your skills and effectiveness, then the organization benefits. Committee work also benefits the profession as a whole, so libraries should be interested in seeing that committee work gets done. Your committee work also reflects well on your library, both in the library community and in the local community. If this work benefits the library, then the library has an obligation to support you with flexibility and time out of the building.

Children's specialists can be involved in non-children-specific parts of library organizations as well. Certainly a strong voice for children is needed in intellectual freedom committees, public library advocacy groups, and even reference and cataloging subsections. All of these entities do work that affects children, but they are usually populated by adult services or technical services specialists. The point of view of a children's specialist is often lacking.

The ALA is, of course, leadership practice on a grand scale. While the payoff for working nationally is greater in all the aspects mentioned above, support from your administration is even more important. Involvement in such a role demands a greater commitment of time, money, and energy. Meeting attendance often means significant travel. ALA has divisions devoted specifically to youth services specialists; the Association for Library Services to Children (ALSC; http://www.ala.org/ala/alsc/alsc.htm); the Young Adult Library Services Association (YALSA; http://www.ala.org/ala/yalsa/yalsa.htm); the Public Library Association (PLA; http://www.pla.org); and the American Association of School Librarians (AASL; http://www.ala.org/aaslhomeTemplate.cfm) are all places where children's specialists can have a great impact.

Mentoring

The term *mentoring* has taken on a number of meanings over the years. For some today, it is a formal relationship within an organization where a more experienced member does a form of ongoing training and orientation for a newer colleague. Mentoring relationships are also created across organizational lines by library associations that seek to strengthen networking opportunities among their members. The most basic form of mentoring, though, and the most traditional one, is the informal relationship built between one experienced person and another person who is looking for knowledge.

Library school tends to lay a theoretical groundwork for a career, and policies and procedures shape much of day-to-day activity, but to excel in any field there is little that can make up for experience. The new children's specialist can either gain that expertise by trial and error, or benefit from someone else's years in the field. But mentors do more than help a new practitioner integrate knowledge into practice; a mentor is also a sounding board and advisor. A mentor can help with career decisions and can introduce a mentee into established networks.[1] A mentor enables a newcomer to give more to the profession and also to gain from the profession as much and as soon as possible.

There are advantages to formal mentoring programs within an organization. A formal program helps in matching up mentors and mentees, and can provide for time off for mentoring partners to meet, resources for joint conference attendance, and generally provide resources and support. It also helps if the organization makes it easy for both mentoring partners to view the other at work.[2] A formal mentoring program also affords training and support to the mentors, as mentoring is not necessarily a skill we come to naturally.

One difficulty with a formal, in-house mentoring program is that there are usually relatively few children's services specialists from whom to draw mentors. If the personalities in any given mentoring relationship do not work well, there are likely to be few options. The most logical, and possibly the only choice of a mentor for a new librarian may be that person's immediate supervisor. No matter the formality of the mentoring relationship, it is important that the exchange be confidential and nonjudgmental.[3] Indeed, in a nursing profession guide, one of the core competencies of a good mentor is the ability to work outside established and patterned methods, to take risks, and to work well with ambiguity and a little chaos.[4] All of this is, of course, much easier when there are no direct lines of responsibility; therefore formal, library-sponsored mentoring programs are less than ideal.

It is probably best to find a mentor outside one's own organization, but how? State associations and library schools' alumni organizations are a great place to start. Many have established mentoring programs, and you need only list your name with them. If not, these outlets hold events, publish newsletters, and have websites where one can identify persons who have the kinds of backgrounds that the new librarian finds interesting. It may take more work than participating in a formal mentoring program, but mentors are out there to be found and cultivated.

It is sometimes harder for mentoring partners to observe each other at work when that work takes place in two different organizations, both because of distance and time. You must either convince your own organization that time observing your mentoring partner will benefit your library, or you must make the time on your own. However you arrange this piece of the puzzle, remember that it is vitally important. Moving beyond abstract discussion, such observation gives the newer librarian valuable exposure to real-life children's work, and allows the mentor to offer very practical advice.

This discussion has focused on the benefits of the mentoring relationship to the newer librarian, but there are advantages to the mentor as well. Everyone benefits from the smooth integration of new talent into the field, and on a personal level, mentoring helps to develop management skills such as communication and coaching. It can be refreshing, and it can remind someone who has been in the trenches for a while what it is like to come into the field fresh and excited. Mentoring is also an avenue for effecting change, not just in the individual, but in the organization and the profession as well.[5] Mentoring is a way of extending one's influence and impact. Mentoring relationships benefit the mentor and the mentee, and it is both possible and desirable to be in different relationships so you can be both the mentor and the mentee throughout your career.

Writing, Speaking, and Teaching

Writing, speaking, and teaching fall in a single category for the simple reason that they all share a vital component; they all require you to put yourself and your ideas before others. This is important to do for two reasons. First of all, the presentation of knowledge, ideas, and experience is how the profession progresses. If you do something well, then others will benefit from knowing about it. None of these activities requires you to be super-librarian. You do not need to be better at all aspects of your job than all members of your audience to be effective. You only need to offer some small thing that is of practical use to others.

And it is important that children's specialists take this step. Writing, speaking, and teaching all bring recognition and respect. Reference librarians and administrators understand this; academic librarians in tenure-track positions base their careers on it; and children's librarians often fail to see it. These activities not only help to train your fellow children's librarians, but they also expose non-children's specialists to the importance and complexities of your specialty while showing off the fact that children's specialists possess talent as writers, speakers, and teachers. Sadly, too often articles are written, speeches given, and classes taught for children's librarians, not by children's librarians, but by professors, administrators, or other specialists. The voice of working, frontline children's staff is being lost because that voice is not being raised.

The other reason to write, speak publicly, or teach is more personal. If you want to strengthen your own knowledge and understanding of a subject, then the prospect of putting yourself forward before others who are knowledgeable is a powerful motivator. Before you say anything, orally or in print, you will check your facts, consider your positions, and look at the matter from several angles. In addition, once you do make your presentation, you will receive feedback that will help guide your further study. You may think you thought of every possible angle and checked every available fact, but in truth there is an almost endless supply of opinions and research, and someone is sure to have studied, considered, or researched something you missed.

The most challenging aspect of presenting is fielding questions and hearing the critiques of one's work, but this experience is seldom as negative as most of us fear. Most librarians are committed, inquisitive, intelligent people whose feedback will be positive and reasonable, making the few who are not so professional less memorable. Do you need a thick skin? Absolutely, but you can develop that just like any other skill—with practice.

Writing

Writing for the profession can be as simple as submitting an article to your state association newsletter, or as major as writing a book. You can publish reviews, bibliographies, research pieces, and the always-appreciated piece on best practices that details something you do well. Start small and work your way up, gaining experience as you go. Remember to do your homework. Be familiar with a publication before you consider submitting something to it. Read through a number of issues, noting the focus of the articles, the level of depth, and especially the audience. Writing a piece on the effective use of puppets for a journal that caters to library administrators is not likely to be a productive exercise. On the other hand, an article submitted to that same journal on the public relations impact of having a puppet program versus the costs involved probably would be productive, and would speak to administrators in their own language about an element of children's work.

Most publications have editorial guidelines that spell out the length, format, and tone that are expected from a manuscript. The guidelines will speak to the timing of submissions, the process of selection and publication, and other factors that should be considered. These are guidelines, not mere suggestions. If you want your article published, then take them seriously. Most publications also list their editors and staff. Read closely to find out which person is most likely to handle your piece. You can always contact an editor by mail or e-mail (do not call someone directly if you want your request to be met with sympathy) to inquire about the appropriateness of your idea. An editor can tell you to go ahead and submit, to find a more appropriate publication, or to modify your idea to make it more appealing. Listen to editors and do what they suggest, both before you submit and afterward. Editing and writing are two completely different skills; let editors do the job they are trained to do. Your writing will almost certainly benefit.

When writing, especially for a professional publication, stay brief and stay focused. While some professional writing is witty and entertaining, that is not the purpose but a pleasant bonus. People read professional literature to gain information and insight into their work. It is not a literary exercise. Tell your audience what you know and what they need to know, and do it as concisely and clearly as possible. Start with a point, illustrate that point, then confirm that point. Readers are short on time; publishers are short on space. Make sure that every draft of your piece is shorter than the one before, and you can be reasonably sure the piece is getting better and better. Most publications have strict limits on the number of pages or words a manuscript can be. Again, these are rules not suggestions, and neither do they imply that every article needs to be within five words of the limit.

Publishing for Children's Services: Where to Find Submission Guidelines

Magazine Publishers

American Libraries (the magazine of the American Library Association): http://www.ala.org/ala/alonline/submittingal

Children and Libraries (the journal of the Association for Library Service to Children): http://www.ala.org/ala/alsc/alscpubs/childrenlib/guidelinesforauthors

The Horn Book Magazine http://www.hbook.com/articlesubmissions.shtml

Knowledge Quest (the journal of the American Association of School Librarians): http://www.ala.org/ala/aasl/aaslpubsandjournals/kqweb/aboutkq/authorguide.htm

Library Journal: http://www.libraryjournal.com/index.asp?layout=forReviewersLJ

Public Libraries (the journal of the Public Library Association) http://www.ala.org/ala/pla/plapubs/publiclibraries/editorialguidelines.htm

School Library Journal: http://www.schoollibraryjournal.com/index.asp?layout=SubmissionsSlj

Teacher Librarian http://www.teacherlibrarian.com/about_us/write_tl.html

Book Publishers

ALA Editions: http://www.ala.org/ala/ourassociation/publishing/alaeditions/forauthorsonly

Libraries Unlimited (Greenwood Publishing Group) http://lu.com/manu.cfm

McFarland and Company, Inc. http://www.mcfarlandpub.com/autproposals.html

Neal-Schuman Publishers http://www.neal-schuman.com/submission.html

Upstart Books (Highsmith Press) http://www.highsmith.com/webapp/wcs/stores/servlet/Production/UPB/pages/upb_submissions.jsp?storeId=10001&catalogId=10040&langId=-1

Speaking

Speaking and presenting should be the most natural activities in the world for children's librarians. We regularly stand before audiences with short attention spans, wide ranges of knowledge, and high expectations. If we can speak to two-year-olds, we can speak to librarians. The opportunities exist, from giving a short workshop at a local gathering of children's librarians to standing at a podium at a library conference.

How do you get yourself to a podium? Often, you need only volunteer. Local workshops and cooperatives are always looking for presentations that are short and practical. Write up a brief outline of a presentation on something you feel you do well and send it to the contact person for the organization. Read newsletters and electronic discussion lists carefully for calls for proposals. These are advertisements for possible speakers at future conferences. Most have guidelines much like those for written submissions, and these, like those, are rules to be followed exactly. Conferences are usually run by volunteers, librarians like yourself who do this for their own professional development (committee work) and the good of the profession. The rules make it possible for them to perform their duties quickly and effectively, and then get back to their jobs.

Once you have a speaking engagement, remember to keep in mind the comfort and interests of your audience. If you are planning on doing some speaking, go to a few speeches yourself with the specific purpose of watching what the speaker does and how the audience reacts. You will usually see that good speakers tend to restate and rephrase in order to emphasize important points. People actually take very little information away from a presentation. Much of what a speaker says is useful for illustration and clarification, but what an audience remembers is really quite small. Also notice an audience's attention span. Good speakers break up a presentation with changes of pace and tone, punctuate it with illustrative stories or activities, and conclude before an audience gets bored. Never go over your allotted time when you speak; indeed it is perfectly fine to go significantly under if by doing so you emphasize what is really important. Most audiences appreciate a chance to ask questions, make their own points, and even challenge yours. Ending your presentation early to allow more time for questions and answers shows respect for your audience.

When you do present, try not to read a speech from notes. That is writing for the profession, which belongs in a journal article (and is dealt with above). If you are going to read a document, you might as well hand it out and let people read it for themselves. Speaking differs from reading by being interactive; it invites the audience to influence the speaker. Think of the times in story hour when you put down the book and just tell the children the story. Try to work from an outline or broad notes to keep yourself on task, but speak to an audience directly. You must know what it is you want to say, or you would not have volunteered to speak in the first place. If there is too much detail for you to remember, even with an outline or notes, then you have planned to use too much detail and you should reconsider. The points you want people to remember—the walk-away or take-home points—will probably be lost.

Remember your natural advantage as a children's librarian when you speak. You do this all the time. You speak to audiences and hold their attention even when they are squirming in their seats, a fire truck is rolling by, and it is getting on toward snack and nap times. Do not trade that skill for a more formal style in hope of being more impressive. Instead, convince other speakers to imitate you in hope of being more accessible.

Teaching

Teaching requires a greater amount of experience and a broader range of knowledge, as courses generally are longer and cover larger topics than a speech or a workshop would. Still, the emphasis is on what you have to share, not on what you do not know. Teaching is a natural next step after gaining some experience as a presenter, and the same principles apply. Teach what you know, concentrate on practical advice that people can use, and accept feedback as necessary for improving your own teaching skills.

Speaking on Children's Services: Where to Submit Proposals

American Association of School Librarians
  http://www.ala.org/ala/aasl/conferencesandevents/
  national/presenters/aaslnational.htm

Association for Library Service to Children
  http://www.ala.org/ala/alsc/boardcomm/alscforms/alscforms.htm

Public Library Association
  http://www.ala.org/ala/pla/plaevents/programproposal/
  programproposal.htm

Like speaking, teaching is something many of us practice in our everyday jobs. We teach library skills, Internet use, and research methods, and one might even view a preschool story-hour series as a course in preliteracy. Opportunities to teach in the field are not as common as presenting opportunities, but they are there. State libraries, library systems and consortia, and state library associations often present continuing education classes for working librarians. Many of these opportunities will require instructors to hold an MLS degree as proof of academic proficiency and background in the philosophical basis of librarianship.

If you wish to explore these opportunities, do a little homework first. Find the course schedules and see what types of classes are on the books. Look for what is offered that you might be able to teach, but also look for holes in the curriculum—classes that should be taught but are not. Find out how long the classes last and what level of expertise the students are expected to have. An advanced leadership academy for veteran, top-level librarians may not be the right venue for your first teaching experience. Find out how the classes are administered, and specifically who is in charge of scheduling and developing classes. Most state libraries have continuing education coordinators who are not only responsible for the classes taught through the state library, but are also likely to be aware of most of the other continuing education opportunities in the state. You can find a listing of state continuing education resources on the Colorado Virtual Library website at http://www.aclin.org/conted/contact.htm.

Talk to someone before you begin developing a class. There is no reason to waste energy preparing a class without an audience. Many established continuing education systems have already developed classes that are largely laid out with goals, objectives, texts, evaluation tools, and sometimes even outlines and notes. All that needs to be added is your experience and viewpoint. This is an excellent way to get experience teaching before you need to develop your own class.

When you do have to develop a class, keep in mind that the purpose is to impart useful information, not to present volumes of it. The only information that matters is what your students can absorb and apply. In a classroom setting you have the opportunity to illustrate, reinforce, and give students the opportunity to practice. You can assign reading and then, instead of presenting the same information, work with students to discuss, apply, and understand what they have read. Most of all, you can use the class to model good continuing education practices, giving them a basis for continued study on their own after the class.

You can create a local opportunity to practice your teaching skills by setting up a library academy. The idea is not new; the city of Orlando, Florida, came up with the idea of a citizen police academy in 1985. It was a set of classes that introduced citizens to the different aspects of police work so that they would understand what the police did, be more supportive of the police, and know how and when to help.[6] A library academy would help people understand how the library works, serve as a recruiting tool and a training ground for volunteers, and give staff members, including the children's librarian, a chance to practice valuable teaching skills. A children's library academy would give children's librarians a chance to interact directly with parents—instructing them on choosing books, engaging children in the type of literature-rich play that we model during story hours, and using library information resources to help their children with homework.

NOTES

1. Kathleen Dracup, "From Novice to Expert to Mentor: Shaping the Future," *American Journal of Critical Care*, November 2004, 450.

2. Sandra Bicksler, "New Colleagues: A Program for Mentoring School Library Media Specialists," *Knowledgequest*, September/October 2004, 28.

3. Ibid.

4. Dracup, "From Novice to Expert," 450.

5. Ibid.

6. City of Orlando, "The Orlando Police Citizen Police Academy," http://www.cityoforlando.net/police/Crime_Prevention/cp_cpa.htm.

Conclusion

If there is any single message contained in the preceding pages, it is that children's librarianship today is a complex field requiring broad expertise and the ability to work at many levels. It is no longer possible, if it ever was, for a children's librarian to just happily go about reading to children and helping them pick out books. We cannot be oblivious to all else happening in the library, the community, or the greater world, at least not if we want to provide excellent service. While most of us got into children's work because we love to serve children, a component of that dedication must be to make sure that children are well served.

The audience that children's librarians serve is large and diverse. The development of the idea of family literacy makes it clear that if we wish to truly impact children's lives, we must also serve the needs of parents and caregivers who spend more time with children than we ever will. The same reasoning leads us to the conclusion that we must support the work of our colleagues in the schools—both the teachers and the librarians—because they have so much more face time with children than we do.

Children's librarians cannot afford to wait on the sidelines while important decisions are being made in the library. If we wait for policies to be written and for priorities to be set, then we will find ourselves as low priorities, working within a system designed for and by adults. We must demonstrate an interest and a competency in administrative matters, and demand a place at the table. Once there, we must speak the language of administration if we want to be heard, understood, and taken seriously. We must advocate for children's specialists to move into administration in order to represent the needs of children at the highest levels of our organizations, whether those organizations are libraries or professional associations.

Children's librarians cannot simply do their jobs and expect the world to come to them, eager for what they have to offer. We must be active in promotion and public relations. People cannot appreciate our services if they do not know about them, and we cannot afford to assume that someone else will tell them. We must at times go beyond the walls of our libraries and beyond our regular audience, out into the world to meet those all-important potential customers. We have to go into our communities, into our schools, into cyberspace and the public airwaves. We need to go where the people are because too often they are not in our libraries.

Of course, all this is to support the actual work we do with children, which is exciting and challenging and frustrating and rewarding all at once. We serve children because we believe they are just as worthy of the best service as anyone else. We connect children with literature because we believe in the power of reading to change and enrich lives. Conversely, we believe that children who do not have reading in their lives face grave challenges in this world, and we are unwilling to see that happen. Finally, we believe in the right of free inquiry for all, that children's minds must be free to expand, to encompass the entire world.

We must not only defend these rights but also ensure that they offer the maximum benefit to children. What good is the freedom to read if nothing is available to read? What help is the power of reading if one does not know how to read? What good is equal service if no one is being well served? For these reasons, we study our craft and improve our skills. We build collections that will open doors to children. We program to promote a healthy interest in reading and all things that stimulate young minds. We design services to encourage and reward children's natural inquisitiveness, so that young people gain the tools they need to become independent in their reading and their thinking.

Being a children's librarian is a great and noble calling. See it for all that it is, and the rewards will be rich for you, and for the thousands you serve, who will one day inherit our world.

Competencies for Librarians Serving Children in Public Libraries

Effective library service for children entails a broad range of experience and professional skills. The librarian serving children is first of all fully knowledgeable in the theories, practices and emerging trends of librarianship but must also have specialized knowledge of the particular needs of child library users.

In developing both the original and this revised document, the committees preparing the *Competencies* looked at numerous sets of standards for children's services from state agencies, professional associations and individual libraries and systems. These competencies are broadly categorized into the following areas: knowledge of the client group; administrative and managerial skills; communications skills; materials and collection development; programming skills; advocacy, public relations and networking; and professionalism and professional development.

Although the *Competencies* seek to define the role of the librarian serving children, they will apply in varying degrees according to the professional responsibilities of each individual job situation. The assignment of responsibilities for planning, managing and delivering library services to children will vary in relation to the size and staffing pattern of the local public library. It is recognized that not all children's librarians in all positions will be involved in all of these activities, nor will they need all of these skills. Some libraries will have only one librarian responsible for providing all service to children, others will have more than one professional children's librarian sharing those responsibilities. In larger libraries with multiple outlets, there may be a coordinator or manager of children's services

Revised Edition, Association for Library Service to Children,
a division of the American Library Association

who oversees the planning, training, design and delivery of service by a number of building level service providers. Because the variety of situations and responsibilities differ so widely, these *Competencies* seek to be all-inclusive rather than to categorize minimum levels of activities and skills needed to serve children in the public library.

The philosophical underpinning for children's services in all public libraries is that children are entitled to full access to the full range of library materials and services available to any other library customer. Other documents that affirm this service philosophy include the American Library Association's (ALA) Library Bill of Rights, the Freedom to Read and Freedom to View statements of ALA.

It is the policy of this organization that a master's degree from a library/ information program from an ALA accredited graduate school is the appropriate professional degree for the librarian serving children in the public library.

The following *Competencies* make it clear that the children's librarian must do more than simply provide age-appropriate service. Children's librarians must also be advocates for their clientele both within the library and in the larger society, and they must also demonstrate the full range of professional and managerial skills demanded of any other librarians.

Each edition of the *Competencies* has been arranged in a systematic manner beginning with knowledge of the community and client group. This gives a solid foundation for planning and managing. Communication is always a vital skill to articulate goals and objectives. Collection development provides the resources for services and programs. Finally, the future of service to children depends on advocacy and professional development. As society changes, so does the public library, and so must the public librarian. Professional growth and development is a career-long process.

It is recommended that libraries developing their own competencies or standards for service to children use this document in conjunction with relevant state standards or guidelines.

I. Knowledge of Client Group

1. Understands theories of infant, child, and adolescent learning and development and their implications for library service.

2. Recognizes the effects of societal developments on the needs of children.

3. Assesses the community regularly and systematically to identify community needs, tastes, and resources.

4. Identifies clients with special needs as a basis for designing and implementing services, following American Disabilities Act (ADA) and state and local regulations where appropriate.

5. Recognizes the needs of an ethnically diverse community.

6. Understands and responds to the needs of parents, care givers, and other adults who use the resources of the children's department.

7. Creates an environment in the children's area, which provides for enjoyable and convenient use of library resources.

8. Maintains regular communication with other agencies, institutions, and organizations serving children in the community.

II. Administrative and Management Skills

1. Participates in all aspects of the library's planning process to represent and support children's services.

2. Sets long- and short-range goals, objectives, and priorities.

3. Analyzes the costs of library services to children in order to develop, justify, administer/manage, and evaluate a budget.

4. Writes job descriptions and interviews, trains, encourages continuing education, and evaluates staff who work with children, consulting with other library administrations as indicated in library personnel policy.

5. Demonstrates problem-solving, decision making, and mediation techniques.

6. Delegates responsibility appropriately and supervises staff constructively.

7. Documents and evaluates services.

8. Identifies outside sources of funding and writes effective grant applications.

III. Communication Skills

1. Defines and communicates the needs of children so that administrators, other library staff, and members of the larger community understand the basis for children's services.

2. Demonstrates interpersonal skills in meeting with children, parents, staff, and community.

3. Adjusts to the varying demands of writing planning documents, procedures, guidelines, press releases, memoranda, reports, grant applications, annotations, and reviews in all formats, including print and electronic.

4. Speaks effectively when addressing individuals, as well as small and large groups.

5. Applies active listening skills.

6. Conducts productive formal and informal reference interviews.

7. Communicates constructively with "problem patrons."

IV. Materials and Collection Development

   A. Knowledge of Materials

      1. Demonstrates a knowledge and appreciation of children's literature, periodicals, audiovisual materials, Websites and other electronic media, and other materials that constitute a diverse, current, and relevant children's collection.

      2. Keeps abreast of new materials and those for retrospective purchase by consulting a wide variety of reviewing sources and publishers' catalogs, including those of small presses; by attending professional meetings; and by reading, viewing, and listening.

      3. Is aware of adult reference materials and other library resources, which may serve the needs of children and their caregivers.

   B. Ability to Select Appropriate Materials and Develop a Children's Collection

      1. Evaluates and recommends collection development, selection and weeding policies for children's materials consistent with the mission and policies of the parent library and the ALA Library Bill of Rights, and applies these policies in acquiring and weeding materials for or management of the children's collection.

      2. Acquires materials that reflect the ethnic diversity of the community, as well as the need of children to become familiar with other ethnic groups and cultures.

3. Understands and applies criteria for evaluating the content and artistic merit of children's materials in all genres and formats.

4. Keeps abreast of current issues in children's materials collections and formulates a professional philosophy with regard to these issues.

5. Demonstrates a knowledge of technical services, cataloging and indexing procedures, and practices relating to children's materials.

C. Ability to Provide Customers with Appropriate Materials and Information

1. Connects children to the wealth of library resources, enabling them to use libraries effectively.

2. Matches children and their families with materials appropriate to their interest and abilities.

3. Provides help where needed, respects children's right to browse, and answers questions regardless of their nature or purpose.

4. Assists and instructs children in information gathering and research skills as appropriate.

5. Understands and applies search strategies to give children full and equitable access to information from the widest possible range of sources, such as children's and adult reference works, indexes, catalogs, electronic resources, information and referral files, and interlibrary loan networks.

6. Compiles and maintains information about community resources so that children and adults working with children can be referred to appropriate sources of assistance.

7. Works with library technical services to guarantee that the children's collection is organized and accessed for the easiest possible use.

8. Creates bibliographies, booktalks, displays, electronic documents, and other special tools to increase access to library resources and motivate their use.

V. Programming Skills

1. Designs, promotes, executes, and evaluates programs for children of all ages, based on their developmental needs and interests and the goals of the library.

2. Presents a variety of programs or brings in skilled resource people to present these programs, including storytelling, booktalking, book discussions, puppet programs, and other appropriate activities.

3. Provides outreach programs commensurate with community needs and library goals and objectives.

4. Establishes programs and services for parents, individuals and agencies providing child-care, and other professionals in the community who work with children.

VI. Advocacy, Public Relations, and Networking Skills

1. Promotes an awareness of and support for meeting children's library and information needs through all media.

2. Considers the opinions and requests of children in the development and evaluation of library services.

3. Ensures that children have full access to library materials, resources, and services as prescribed by the Library Bill of Rights.

4. Acts as liaison with other agencies in the community serving children, including other libraries and library systems.

5. Develops cooperative programs between the public library, schools, and other community agencies.

6. Extends library services to children and groups of children presently unserved.

7. Utilizes effective public relations techniques and media to publicize library activities.

8. Develops policies and procedures applying to children's services based on federal, state, and local law where appropriate.

9. Understands library governance and the political process and lobbies on behalf of children's services.

VII. Professionalism and Professional Development

    1. Acknowledges the legacy of children's librarianship, its place in the context of librarianship as a whole, and past contributions to the profession.

    2. Keeps abreast of current trends and emerging technologies, issues, and research in librarianship, child development, education, and allied fields.

    3. Practices self-evaluation.

    4. Conveys a nonjudgmental attitude toward patrons and their requests.

    5. Demonstrates an understanding of and respect for diversity in cultural and ethnic values.

    6. Knows and practices the American Library Association's Code of Ethics.

    7. Preserves confidentiality in interchanges with patrons.

    8. Works with library educators to meet needs of library school students and promote professional association scholarships.

    9. Participates in professional organizations to strengthen skills, interact with fellow professionals, and contribute to the profession.

    10. Understands that professional development and continuing education are activities to be pursued throughout one's career.

Last updated 4/27/99

Library Bill of Rights

The American Library Association affirms that all libraries are forums for information and ideas, and that the following basic policies should guide their services.

I. Books and other library resources should be provided for the interest, information, and enlightenment of all people of the community the library serves. Materials should not be excluded because of the origin, background, or views of those contributing to their creation.

II. Libraries should provide materials and information presenting all points of view on current and historical issues. Materials should not be proscribed or removed because of partisan or doctrinal disapproval.

III. Libraries should challenge censorship in the fulfillment of their responsibility to provide information and enlightenment.

IV. Libraries should cooperate with all persons and groups concerned with resisting abridgment of free expression and free access to ideas.

V. A person's right to use a library should not be denied or abridged because of origin, age, background, or views.

VI. Libraries which make exhibit spaces and meeting rooms available to the public they serve should make such facilities available on an equitable basis, regardless of the beliefs or affiliations of individuals or groups requesting their use.

Adopted June 18, 1948, amended February 2, 1961, and January 23, 1980, inclusion of "age" reaffirmed January 23, 1996, by the ALA Council.

Code of Ethics of the American Library Association

As members of the American Library Association, we recognize the importance of codifying and making known to the profession and to the general public the ethical principles that guide the work of librarians, other professionals providing information services, library trustees and library staffs.

Ethical dilemmas occur when values are in conflict. The American Library Association Code of Ethics states the values to which we are committed, and embodies the ethical responsibilities of the profession in this changing information environment.

We significantly influence or control the selection, organization, preservation, and dissemination of information. In a political system grounded in an informed citizenry, we are members of a profession explicitly committed to intellectual freedom and the freedom of access to information. We have a special obligation to ensure the free flow of information and ideas to present and future generations.

The principles of this Code are expressed in broad statements to guide ethical decision making. These statements provide a framework; they cannot and do not dictate conduct to cover particular situations.

  I. We provide the highest level of service to all library users through appropriate and usefully organized resources; equitable service policies; equitable access; and accurate, unbiased, and courteous responses to all requests.

  II. We uphold the principles of intellectual freedom and resist all efforts to censor library resources.

  III. We protect each library user's right to privacy and confidentiality with respect to information sought or received and resources consulted, borrowed, acquired or transmitted.

IV. We recognize and respect intellectual property rights.

V. We treat co-workers and other colleagues with respect, fairness and good faith, and advocate conditions of employment that safeguard the rights and welfare of all employees of our institutions.

VI. We do not advance private interests at the expense of library users, colleagues, or our employing institutions.

VII. We distinguish between our personal convictions and professional duties and do not allow our personal beliefs to interfere with fair representation of the aims of our institutions or the provision of access to their information resources.

VIII. We strive for excellence in the profession by maintaining and enhancing our own knowledge and skills, by encouraging the professional development of co-workers, and by fostering the aspirations of potential members of the profession.

Adopted by the ALA Council June 28, 1995

BIBLIOGRAPHY

Adams, Helen R. "Privacy and Confidentiality: Now More Than Ever, Youngsters Need to Keep Their Library Use under Wraps." *American Libraries*, November 2002, 44–48.

Alter, Jonathan. "It's 4:00 pm, Do You Know Where Your Children Are?" *Newsweek*, April 27, 1999, 28–33.

American Library Association. *Code of Ethics of the American Library Association*. Adopted by the ALA Council June 28, 1995. http://www.ala.org/ala/oif/statementspols/codeofethics/codeethics.htm.

——— . *Library Bill of Rights*. Adopted June 18, 1948, amended February 2, 1961, and January 23, 1980, inclusion of "age" reaffirmed January 23, 1996, by the ALA Council. http://www.ala.org/ala/oif/statementspols/statementsif/librarybillrights.htm.

Anthony, Robert S. "Shhh! And Cover Your Computer Screen." *Black Issues Book Review*, January–February 2004, 17.

Arnold, Renea. "Public Libraries and Early Literacy: Raising a Reader." *American Libraries*, September 2003, 48–51.

Baxter, Kathleen A., and Marcia Agness Kochel. *Gotcha! Nonfiction Booktalks to Get Kids Excited about Reading*. Englewood, CO: Libraries Unlimited, 1999.

Benne, Mae. *Principles of Children's Services in Public Libraries*. Chicago: American Library Association, 1991.

Bertot, John Carlo, Charles R. McClure, Devise M. Davis, and Joe Ryan. "Capture Usage with E-Metrics." *Library Journal*, May 1, 2004, 30–32.

Beslie, Laurent. "Ranks of Latchkey Kids Approach 7 Million." *Christian Science Monitor*, October 31, 2000, 3.

Bicksler, Sandra. "New Colleagues: A Program for Mentoring School Library Media Specialists." *Knowledgequest*, September/October 2004, 28–29.

Bielick, Stacey; Kathryn Chandler, and Stephen Broughman. *Homeschooling in the United States: 1999.* NCES Technical Report, 2001-033. Washington, DC: U.S. Department of Education, National Center for Education Statistics, 2001. http://nces.ed.gov/pubsearch/pubsinfo.asp?pubid=2001033.

Celano, Donna, and Susan B. Neuman. *The Role of Public Libraries in Children's Literacy Development.* Harrisburg: Pennsylvania Library Association, 2001.

Chan, Lois Mai. *Cataloging and Classification: An Introduction.* 2nd ed. New York: McGraw-Hill, 1994.

Dewey, Melvil. *Abridged Dewey Decimal Classification and Relative Index.* 14th ed. Albany, NY: Forest Press, 2004.

Diamant-Cohen, Betsy. "Mother Goose on the Loose: Applying Brain Research to Early Childhood Programs in the Public Library." *Public Libraries,* January/February 2004, 43.

Dracup, Kathleen. "From Novice to Expert to Mentor: Shaping the Future." *American Journal of Critical Care,* November 2004, 448–50.

Eberhart, George M. "Two State Bills Affect Minors' Reading Privacy." *American Libraries,* December 2003, 21.

Faurot, Kimberly. *Books in Bloom: Creative Patterns and Props That Bring Stories to Life.* Chicago: American Library Association, 2003.

Fiore, Carole D. *Running Summer Library Reading Programs: A How-to-Do-It Manual.* New York: Neal-Schuman, 1998.

Geisel, Theodor Seuss. *Horton Hears a Who!* New York: Random House, 1954.

Gillespie, John Thomas. *The Newbery Companion: Booktalk and Related Materials for Newbery Medal and Honor Books.* 2nd ed. Englewood, CO: Libraries Unlimited, 2001.

Gray, John. *Men Are from Mars, Women Are from Venus: A Practical Guide for Improving Communication and Getting What You Want in Your Relationships.* New York: HarperCollins, 1992.

Gurian, Michael and Patricia Henley, with Terry Trueman. *Boys and Girls Learn Differently! A Guide for Teachers and Parents.* San Francisco: Jossey-Bass, 2001.

Haycock, Ken. "Literacy, Learning and Libraries: Common Issues and Common Concerns." *Feliciter* 49, no. 1 (2003): 36–43.

Hennen, Thomas. *Hennen's Public Library Planner: A Manual and Interactive CD-ROM*. New York: Neal-Schuman, 2004.

Hernon, Peter. "Service Quality and Outcome Measures." *Journal of Academic Librarianship*, January 1997, 1–2.

———. "Service Quality in Libraries and Treating Users As Customers and Non-users As Lost or Never-Gained Customers." *Journal of Academic Librarianship*, May 1996, 171–72.

Himmel, Ethel, and William James Wilson. *Planning for Results: A Public Library Transformation Process*. Chicago: American Library Association, 1998.

Honig, Alice Sterling. "A Passion for Play." *Early Childhood Today*, November/December 2000, 32–33.

Illinois State Library. *Read Together, Grow Together: The Family Literacy Initiative*. Springfield: Illinois State Library Special Report Series, 1995.

Krashen, Stephen. *The Power of Reading: Insights from the Research*. Englewood, CO: Libraries Unlimited, 1993.

Kyrillidou, Martha. "From Input and Output Measures to Quality and Outcome Measures, or, From the User in the Life of the Library to the Library in the Life of the User." *Journal of Academic Librarianship*, January–March 2002, 42–46.

Langerman, Deborah. "Books and Boys: Gender Preferences and Book Selection." *School Library Journal* 36 (March 1990): 132–36.

Lima, Carolyn W. *A to Zoo: Subject Access to Children's Picture Books*. 6th ed. Westport, CT: Bowker-Greenwood, 2001.

Lynch, Mary Jo. "Reaching 65: Lots of Librarians Will Be There Soon." *American Libraries*, March 2002, 55–56.

MacDonald, Margaret Read. *Shake-It-Up Tales: Stories to Sing, Dance, Drum, and Act Out*. Little Rock, AK: August House, 2000.

———. *The Storyteller's Start-up Book: Finding, Learning, Performing and Using Folktales*. Little Rock, AK: August House, 1993.

Machet, Myrna, and Elizabeth J. Pretorius. "Family Literacy: A Project to Get Parents Involved." *South African Journal of Library and Information Science* 70, no. 1 (2004): 39–46.

Marino, Jane. "B Is for Baby, B Is for Books." *School Library Journal*, March 1997, 110–11.

Matthews, Virginia H. "Children Couldn't Wait Then Either, but Sometimes They Had To." *American Libraries,* June/July 2004, 76–80.

———. *Library Services for Children and Youth: Dollars and Sense.* New York: Neal-Schuman, 1994.

Maughan, Barbara, Richard Rowe, Rolf Loeber, and Magda Stouthamer-Loeber. "Reading Problems and Depressed Mood." *Journal of Abnormal Child Psychology,* April 2003, 219.

McClure, Charles R., Amy Owen, Douglas L. Zweizig, Mary Jo Lynch, and Nancy Van House. *Planning and Role Setting for Public Libraries: A Manual of Options and Procedures.* Chicago: American Library Association, 1987.

McConnell, S. R., and H. L. S. Rabe. "Home and Community Factors that Promote Early Literacy Development for Preschool-Aged Children." In *Just in Time Research: Children, Youth and Families,* edited by A. Smith et al. Minneapolis: University of Minnesota, Hubert H. Humphrey Institute of Public Affairs and CYFC, 1999. http://www.extension.umn.edu/distribution/familydevelopment/DE7286.html#05.

Mediavilla, Cindy. *Creating the Full-Service Homework Center in Your Library.* Chicago: American Library Association, 2001.

———. "Why Library Homework Centers Extend Society's Safety Net." *American Libraries,* December 2001, 40–42.

Millbower, Lenn. "Turn Up the Music: Rev Up Participants' Emotions through Song." *Training and Development,* March 2004, 19–20.

Minkel, Walter. "AK to Nix Kids' Privacy Rights." *School Library Journal* 50 (April 2004): 22.

———. "Summer Reading Season." *School Library Journal* 48 (August 2002): 33.

Moran, Barbara B. "Practitioners vs. LIS Educators: Time to Reconnect." *Library Journal,* November 1, 2001, 52–53.

Nelson, Sandra. *The New Planning for Results: A Streamlined Approach.* Chicago: American Library Association, 2001.

New Hampshire Library Association. *NHLA Intellectual Freedom Handbook.* Concord, NH: New Hampshire Library Association, 1998.

Nord, C. W., J. Lennon, B. Liu, and K. Chandler. *Home Literacy Activities and Signs of Children's Emerging Literacy: 1993 and 1999.* Washington, DC: U.S. Department of Education, 1999.

Poll, Roswitha. "Impact/Outcome Measures for Libraries." *Liber Quarterly* 13 (2003):329–42.

Price, Anne, and Juliette Yaakov, eds. *Children's Catalog,* 18th ed. New York: H. W. Wilson, 2001.

———. *Middle and Junior High Catalog,* 8th ed. New York: H. W. Wilson, 2000.

Putnam, Robert D. *Bowling Alone: The Collapse and Revival of American Community.* New York: Simon and Schuster, 2000.

Rettig, Michael A. "Guidelines for Beginning and Maintaining a Toy Lending Library." *Early Childhood Education Journal* 25, no. 4 (1998): 229–32.

Rydell, Katy. *A Beginner's Guide to Storytelling.* Jonesborough, TN: National Storytelling Press, 2003.

Sawyer, Ruth. *The Way of the Storyteller.* New York: Viking Press, 1942.

Schwartz, David M. "Ready, Set, Read—20 Minutes Is All You'll Need." *Smithsonian,* February 1995, 82–86.

Sears, Minnie Earl. *Sears List of Subject Headings.* 18th ed. New York: H. W. Wilson, 2004.

Segal, Joseph P. *The CREW Manual: A Unified System of Weeding, Inventory, and Collection-Building for Small and Medium-Sized Public Libraries.* Austin: Texas State Library, 1976.

———. *The CREW Method: Expanded Guidelines for Collection Evaluation and Weeding for Small and Medium-Sized Public Libraries.* Revised and updated by Belinda Boon. Austin: Texas State Library, 1995.

Shedlock, Marie L. *The Art of the Story-Teller.* New York: D. Appleton, 1915.

Staerkel, Kathleen, Mary Fellows, and Sue McCleaf Nespeca. *Youth Services Librarians As Managers.* Chicago: American Library Association, 1995.

Steele, Anitra T. *Bare Bones Children's Services: Tips for Public Library Generalists.* Chicago: American Library Association, 2001.

Sullivan, Michael. *Connecting Boys with Books: What Libraries Can Do* (Chicago: American Library Association, 2003).

———. "The Fragile Future of Public Libraries." *Public Libraries,* September/October 2003, 303–8.

Talab, R. S. *Commonsense Copyright: A Guide for Educators and Librarians.* 2nd ed. Jefferson, NC: McFarland, 1999.

Vaillancourt, Renée J. *Bare Bones Young Adult Services: Tips for Public Library Generalists.* Chicago: American Library Association, 2000.

Virginia State Library. *Up and Running: A Step-by-Step Guide to Managing Your Summer Reading Program.* Richmond, VA: Library of Virginia, 1997.

Vogel, S. "Gender Differences in Intelligence, Language, Visual-Motor Abilities, and Academic Achievement in Students with Learning Disabilities: A Review of the Literature." *Journal of Learning Disabilities* 23, no. 1 (1990): 44–52.

Walter, Virginia A. *Children and Libraries: Getting It Right.* Chicago: American Library Association, 2001.

———. *Output Measures for Public Library Service to Children: A Manual of Standardized Procedures.* Chicago: American Library Association, 1992.

"Where Does Music Fit into the Curriculum?" *Curriculum Review,* January 1999, 4.

Ziarnnik, Natalie Reif. *School and Public Libraries: Developing the Natural Alliance.* Chicago: American Library Association, 2003.

Zuiderveld, Sharon, ed. *Cataloging Correctly for Kids: An Introduction to the Tools.* Chicago: American Library Association, 1991.

Zweizig, Douglas, Debra Wilcox Johnson, and Jane Robbins, with Michele Besant. *The Tell It! Manual: The Complete Program for Evaluating Library Performance.* Chicago: American Library Association, 1996.

INDEX

Michael Sullivan (MLS, Simmons, 1999) is the author of *Connecting Boys with Books: What Libraries Can Do* (American Library Association, 2003) and speaks widely on the topic of boys and reading. He has been a children's librarian or library director in public libraries for more than fifteen years. Sullivan is currently director of the Weeks Public Library in Greenland, New Hampshire, as well as a traveling storyteller and a chess instructor. His chess program at the Parlin Memorial Library in Everett, Massachusetts, was honored with an Outstanding Achievement Award in the U.S. Conference of Mayors City Livability Award competition in 2001. He is a former president of the New Hampshire Library Association and was the 1998 New Hampshire Librarian of the Year. In 2005, he was named as one of *Library Journal's* "movers and shakers."